THE Limits OF Participation

THE Limits OF Participation

Members and Leaders in Canada's Reform Party

Faron Ellis

For Leanne

Published by the University of Calgary Press
2500 University Drive NW, Calgary, Alberta, Canada T2N 1N4
www.uofcpress.com

The University of Calgary Press acknowledges the financial support of the Government of Canada through the Book Publishing Industry Development Program (BPIDP) for our publishing activities. We acknowledge the support of the Canada Council for the Arts for our publishing program.

We acknowledge the financial support of the Alberta Lottery Fund -- Community Initiatives Program.

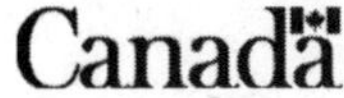

Canada Council for the Arts   Conseil des Arts du Canada

Library and Archives Canada Cataloguing in Publication

Ellis, Faron, 1962-
The limits of participation : members and leaders in Canada's Reform Party / Faron Ellis.

Includes bibliographical references and index.
ISBN 1-55238-156-0

1. Reform Party of Canada--History. 2. Canada--Politics and government--1984-1993. 3. Canada--Politics and government--1993- I. Title.

JL197.R34E44 2005   324.271'094   C2005-900973-X

Printed and bound in Canada by Houghton Boston

Cover design by Mieka West
Page design by Elizabeth Gusnoski

Contents

List of Tables

Preface

The analysis in this book represents a study of the Reform Party of Canada by way of focusing on the opinions, activities and influence of the party membership. The chapters that follow generally fall into two methodological types. Most chapters (1, 2, 4, 6 and 7) deal with the historical evolution of Reform from the perspective of the members as they engaged in the dynamic tension between exercising their power and following the guidance and vision of the party's leadership. Chapter 1 sets the stage for Reform's founding by providing an historical account of Canadian party politics with a particular emphasis on the western provinces and the prairie protest movements of the early twentieth century. Chapter 2 details Reform's founding in the mid-1980s while chapter 4 covers the party's expansion period as it organized beyond its western support base in the early 1990s. Chapter 6 examines Reform's dramatic 1993 parliamentary breakthrough, the often-chaotic parliamentary period that followed, and its 1997 federal election effort. Chapter 7 deals with the decommissioning of Reform as Manning persuaded members to form the Canadian Alliance but failed to convince them that he was the man to lead it into the 2000 federal election. An attempt has been made to write these chapters so as to make them accessible to the general reader, while still providing the more serious reader with an academically rigorous treatment of the events.

Chapters 3 and 5 focus on the attitudes, opinions and characteristics of activists as they struggled to make meaningful their participation in policy and strategic decisions. Chapter 3 focuses on the opinions of delegates attending the 1989 Reform Party Assembly, the first to be primarily composed of representatives elected at the constituency association level. Chapter 5 provides similar, but more extensive analysis of delegates attending the party's 1992 Assembly, the first to include representatives from constituency associations east of the Manitoba-Ontario provincial boundary. These chapters draw more heavily on statistical analysis of surveys of delegates, are better suited for an academic audience, but are written so as to also make them accessible to the more serious general reader.

The 1989 Assembly Study was conducted by distributing a questionnaire to all 636 delegates attending the 1989 Edmonton Assembly, of which 481 returned completed questionnaires for a completion rate of 75 per cent. Principal investigators were Faron Ellis and David Robb. The 1992 Assembly Study was sponsored by the University of Calgary Research Grants Committee and by the Social Science and Humanities Research Council (410-93-0400) and was conducted by mailing a questionnaire to all of the 1,290 delegates whose names appeared on party mailing lists; 893 delegates returned questionnaires for a completion rate of 69 per cent. Principal investigators were Keith Archer and Faron Ellis. Some additional demographic data has been garnered from a 1991 Reform Party Membership Study that was commissioned by the party and conducted via telephone interview during the summer of 1991. It consisted of a provincially stratified random sample of 1,786 Reform Party members. Principal investigator was Faron Ellis. Some use has also been made of the 1993 Reform Party Membership study which was funded through a National Science Foundation research grant (SES-931135) and consisted of a questionnaire mailed to a provincially stratified random sample of 4,000 party members in 1993. A total of 2,574 members returned questionnaires for a completion rate of 64.4 per cent. Principle investigators were Harold D. Clarke and Allan Kornberg.

Underpinning all of this analysis is the classic literature on the origins, organization and development of political parties and party systems. The prologue that follows represents an attempt at briefly summarizing the most germane parts of that literature and explaining its impact on the approach taken in this study. Readers desiring a more detailed review of this literature and its application to the Reform Party can consult my University of Calgary doctoral dissertation (1997), *A Genealogy of Dissent: Activism and Participation in Canada's Reform Party.*

Acknowledgments

In concluding a project that originated over a decade earlier, acknowledging all the individuals that have made contributions would constitute a Herculean task beyond the scope of what can be achieved here. To all those who are not mentioned by name I offer sincere gratitude.

There are a number of individuals and organizations, however, without whose contributions this work would not have been completed. They include: Keith Archer, Barry Cooper, Tom Flanagan and Roger Gibbins under whose guidance I completed my undergraduate and doctoral studies in the department of political science at the University of Calgary. My friends David Robb, Sean McKinsley, Jim Mahr and the late Senator Stan Waters were regular sources of information and inspiration. The many party staff and volunteer workers who helped administer the data collection process, at times hired me as a consultant, and often gave me unprecedented access to party documents and archives, deserved a great deal of credit even though for obvious reasons I cannot mention each by name. My wife, Leanne Wehlage-Ellis' continuous proofing and editing of multiple versions of chapters and manuscripts have made an invaluable contribution, as has her ongoing patience and encouragement.

Most importantly, my gratitude is extended to the thousands of Reform Party members, activists and leaders who participated in the many formal studies, informal interviews and casual conversations over the years. Without their participation, this work would not exist.

Prologue

In his landmark study *Political Parties: Organization and Power*, Angelo Panebianco contends that scientific research on political parties broke from the classical authors' focus on the organizational core of parties.[1] Instead of starting with the idea that parties are organizations, to be studied as organizations, as had the classical authors such as Weber, Michels, Duverger and Ostrogorski, recent scholars have shifted their focus towards party systems. Acknowledging that the understanding of political processes has benefited, Panebianco laments the lost organizational focus and advocates a serious return to the study of parties from the standpoint of their internal organizational dynamics. Only then, he argues, can we fully understand parties and their complex roles within the political system.[2] The approach used here follows Panebianco by providing an organizational perspective of the emergence of a new party.

Parties are modern institutions the appearance and development of which are bound up with the development of modern liberal-pluralist-democratic practices.[3] The diversification of political power and the existence of a plurality of organizations that are both independent and non-inclusive is an essential feature of modern liberal democracies. But pluralism is more than the recognition and articulation of diversity or differentiation. Pluralism is a normative as well as a descriptive term. It assumes a particular belief content that contains its own morally authoritative claim on legitimacy. Pluralism asserts that not only do differences exist, but also that difference itself is a moral good, "that difference and not likeness, dissent and not unanimity, change and not immutability, make for the good life."[4] In liberal-democratic pluralist polities, political parties are the voluntary institutions that are created as expressions of legitimate dissent, because pluralism assumes the moral legitimacy of dissent.

When a political consensus is produced, pluralistic consensus does not constitute a public single-mindedness or a populist common will. It assumes an endless process of adjusting and coordinating dissenting interests into and out of a continually changing coalition of reciprocal persuasion. Consensus does not exist naturally in a plurality but must be created through a process of organization and coordination of interests. Political parties can become the agents of dissent only when political stability has replaced factionalism and civil war as the outcome of disagreement. Thus, while pluralism provides the moral legitimacy for the existence of parties, it does not account for their development as a subsystem of the larger polity. For the most part, parties originated as organizational responses to the emergence of representative government, which had to be instituted before party systems could be established.[5]

Once the party system had been established, primarily by cadre parties made up of like-minded members of parliaments, near-universal enfranchisement facilitated the establishment of a new political phenomenon, externally created mass parties[6] (of which the Reform Party was an example). In attempting to represent and express the demands of a large, open membership, mass parties are subject to representational dilemmas not experienced by cadre parties. Mass parties organize in a manner that attempts to increase the degree of rank-and-file participation within the party's organizational structure. As mass parties developed, it was often assumed that increased channels for participation and internal democratic checks would naturally develop within their organizational structures. But when this did not always occur, or did not occur naturally, it quickly became understood that parties are first and foremost organizations, and organization entails structure, which in turn entails hierarchy. Not only do parties have members and supporters, but also leaders and professional administrators. In his landmark study of European socialist parties, Roberto Michels discovered that organization tends towards what he called an "iron law of oligarchy" and concluded that organization itself is antithetical to democracy.[7]

Michels argued that the oligarchic and bureaucratic tendencies of party organizations are matters of technical and practical necessity. "It is the inevitable product of the very principle of organization."[8] Yet Michels also recognized that democracy is inconceivable without organization, and therefore not only discovered an iron law but also a paradox.[9] In commenting on this problem, Seymour Martin Lipset observed that "modern man is faced with an irresolvable dilemma: he cannot have large institutions such as nation states, trade unions, political parties, or churches, without turning over effective power to the few who are at the summit of these institutions."[10]

This is a dilemma that Michels did not resolve. He observed that, given the leadership typically possesses the resources of superior political knowledge, access to information that is necessary to develop and secure their program, control over the formal means of communication with the membership, and a higher level of skill in "the art of politics," all large-scale organizations eventually give their officers a near monopoly of power, allowing for the concentration of power at the top. When faced with a challenge to their authority from within their own organization, Michels argued that leaders will not hesitate to undermine many democratic rights. They will attempt to legitimize their behaviour by arguing that the greater good of opposing established interests on behalf of its members justifies restrictions on the membership's input and influence. As we shall see below, Manning and the Reform leadership frequently conformed to this hypothesis.

Michels has been criticized, however, for being overly deterministic and seeing only the restrictive side of bureaucracy.[11] According to a strict interpretation of Michels' view, only direct democracy would constitute real democracy, a position shared by many Reformers. But under this unnecessarily restrictive view, any political system that delegates responsibility would be classified as inherently undemocratic. Democracy therefore would not be possible within any representative institution; including parties or in party systems.[12]

Robert McKenzie agrees that parties have a tendency toward oligarchy. However, like Panebianco, he points out that the origins of a party, the goals and principles of its founders, are important in explaining its initial organizational structure and, therefore, its relative impact on the party system and on democracy in general. While parties develop oligarchic structures, once in the electoral arena, that oligarchy may promote democracy to further its electoral appeal, as Reform did in the 1993 and 1997 federal elections. If intra-party democracy undermines the leadership's ability to present voters with clear, dissenting, policy options it may also undermine the possibility of that choice and therefore undermine the possibility for the very democratic reform its supporters desire. Thus, McKenzie argues that some limited form of oligarchy within parties can be conducive to promoting democracy in a party system.[13] Panebianco states that the debate over the application of Michels' iron law has not been conclusive.[14] Furthermore, he argues that focusing on whether or not evidence exists to support or refute Michels' "iron law of oligarchy" distracts us from the more important issue: an analysis of the relationship that existed between members and leaders within the Reform Party of Canada and the relative amount of influence members had by participating in various party activities.[15]

Duverger understood that in certain parties, leaders and representatives can be contaminated by the organization rather than controlling it. However, if a party originates because of demands for increased participation and democracy, as Reform did, the party's organization should reflect these origins and provide opportunities for members to influence their representatives and leaders.[16] Thomas Koelble accepts Duverger's point that organizational structure can be explained only by analyzing the party's origins. "On a superficial level Michels' iron law seems to be vindicated.... On a more complex level, however, it becomes clear that Michels' thesis is partially incorrect. Organizational structures do make a difference in the relationship between party leaders and the so-called masses."[17] As will become clearer in the chapters that follow, this analysis applies to Reform in its founding. Reform was founded upon the strategy of mobilizing a segment of the electorate that harboured growing expectations for more avenues of democratic participation. As such, Reform had to provide these potential recruits with more direct avenues for meaningful participation within its organization than the traditional Canadian parties were providing. Essentially, it had to outbid the existing parties in meeting the participatory demands of its potential recruits.

In analyzing the importance of the founding moment of institutions, Panebianco observed that the way in which the cards are dealt out and the outcomes of the different rounds played out in the formative phase of an organization continue in many ways to condition the life of the organization, even decades after its founding. The organization will certainly undergo modifications and even profound changes over time as it interacts with a continually changing environment. However, the crucial political choices made by its founders, the first struggles for organizational control, and the way in which the organization was formed, will leave an indelible mark. Few aspects of an organization's functioning and contemporary tensions appear comprehensible if not traced to its formative phase. Attention to the historical dimension becomes, in this way, an integral part of the organizational analysis of parties.[18]

To further this analysis, Panebianco suggest that we adopt a definition of organizational power that can account for the apparently contradictory demands of leadership manipulation and member influence. Power can be defined as a relation of exchange, and therefore reciprocal, but in the sense that the exchange is more favourable for one of the parties involved. It is a relation of force, in that one is advantaged over the other, but where the other cannot, however, be totally defenceless with respect to the advantaged one. He concludes with an understanding of power that is adopted here: power is relational and asymmetrical, but also reciprocal. It manifests itself in unbalanced negotiations in a relation of unequal exchange where one set of actors (the leaders) receives more than the other (the members). But power is never absolute. Its limits are implicit in the very nature of the interaction. In voluntary organizations, one can exercise power over others only by satisfying their needs and expectations. Leaders thereby paradoxically submit themselves to the latent power of the members.[19]

The power relation between Reform's leaders and members will henceforth be conceived as a reciprocal relation of unequal exchange. Reform's leaders definitely received more than did the members in this exchange. But the members nevertheless received something from the leaders in return. Furthermore, the outcomes of these relations depended on the degree of control that the leaders and members had over certain resources. As will be illustrated below, the Reform members controlled a considerable amount of financial and organizational resources at the local level, especially with respect to campaign resources, and particularly during the early, formative years.

Therefore, to understand Reform, and other new parties, one must understand the goals of all the founders: activists and members as well as leaders. We must also have a clear understanding of the ways in which these founding goals are reflected in a party's organizational structures and the early power struggles between the leadership (desiring to exercise near absolute control) and the membership (determined to have its input into the policy and strategic decision-making process). Only then can we determine what role activist members have in influencing the ongoing development of a party's policy and strategy.

Duverger examined a variety of parties and determined that the choice of an organizational structure was most often dictated by a series of factors including but not limited to the following: (1) whether the party was created from within an existing legislature or created externally (like Reform), with external creation typically leading to greater centralization; (2) membership recruitment and units of organization, with the amount of affiliation with pre-existing organizations key (Reform had no affiliation with any pre-existing organizations and constitutionally forbid such affiliation); (3) articulation and the type of vertical and horizontal links between various substructures of the organization (Reform exhibited almost complete vertical linkages with few intermediary substructures between the national party organization and the branch constituency associations); and (4) membership organization and recruitment, which has direct implications for financing of party activities, is typically based on either a cadre model of limited membership recruitment and input or on a mass basis where large numbers and regular membership input are sought (Reform was founded as a mass party designed to recruit as many new members to its ranks as was possible).[20]

Following Duverger, in their analysis of changing models of party organization, Katz and Mair distinguish between four types of party organization; cadre parties, mass parties, catch-all parties and cartel parties.[21] They contend, "the recent period has witnessed the emergence of a new model of party, the cartel party, in which colluding parties become agents of the state and employ the resources of the state (the party state) to ensure their own collective survival."[22] Cartel parties have in turn engendered a challenge to the cartel system that they created in that the collusion often leads to the creation of anti-political-establishment parties. Evidence is abundant that many features of this phenomenon could be found in the Canadian party system during the late 1980s and early 1990s.[23] Reform, as viewed from the perspective of its members, represented an opportunity to challenge the traditional parties' cartel monopoly of power. Reform's leadership, as well as it members, employed a form of anti-political establishment populist rhetoric as both a recruitment device and in justifying its policy agenda to the larger electorate. While all populist parties define themselves as friends of "the people" and in opposition to an established economic, political or imperial elite, anti-political-establishment parties declare war on the political class. Anti-political-establishment rhetoric extends populism by focusing its attack specifically on the political elite, something Reform did throughout its brief history as a party.[24]

Much of what we will observe in examining Reform's organizational structure will conform to what is expected of a mass-based party with extra-parliamentary origins in the late twentieth century. Reform was highly centralized and strongly articulated, exclusively through vertical links. Its primary organizational units were the national party and the local branch, both of which focused on mass membership recruitment and the development of candidates and leaders from within their own ranks. Its financial health was dependent on members' subscriptions and voluntary contributions. It was also dedicated to the training and education of its members and candidates. Under these organizational conditions, we would not have expected individual members of the party to carry much weight in policy and strategy decisions. That is, not only would we expect the leadership to have exhibited the tendencies towards oligarchy, as predicted by Michels and modified by Koelble and Mackenzie, but that the organizational structure would have allowed these tendencies to manifest in the leaderships' near absolute control of policy and strategy. This may have indeed become the case had it not been for the influence of the particular set of circumstance under with the party was founded.

An examination of Reform's origins and the resulting organizational structure will determine the extent to which the members were empowered constitutionally to affect policy and strategy. However, formal constitutional authority does not necessarily lead to practical influence and effective power. An examination of the party's development, from its 1987 inception through its 2000 decommissioning, will help in determining the actual power relationship between the membership and leadership. As the various rounds of competition were played out, the pushes of oligarchic tendencies and the pulls of membership influence set the membership and leadership on a collision course that led to Reform's decommissioning, the establishment of Canadian Alliance, and eventually the merged Conservative Party of Canada. While a great deal of scholarly attention has been paid to Manning's oligarchic tendencies, the focus here is on examining the memberships' opinion structure as a means to understanding its role in the reciprocal but unequal power relationship. In the final analysis, it will be argued that the membership's successes were contributing factors to Manning's decision to abandon Reform in favour of a more traditional, brokerage style party where he would have been less fettered by membership opinion in attempting to build an electoral coalition capable of winning government.

Introduction

Party Politics in Canada

The political history of western Canada is one of protest and dissent. After years, sometimes decades of attempting to achieve their political goals by participating in Canada's traditional national parties, westerners have demonstrated a habit of venturing out on their own, creating new, often radical, political vehicles capable of representing a political culture that many believe cannot be adequately represented within the larger, eastern-dominated Canadian parties. So significant have their exploits been, Canadian political scientists credit western political entrepreneurs with having twice transformed the Canadian party system. In 1921, aggrieved prairie farmers sent a wave of Progressive MPs to Ottawa to break the cozy two-party system that had been the norm since Confederation. Westerners continued their dissent by supporting Social Credit and the CCF during the 1930s and 40s. Only by electing prairie populist John Diefenbaker as their leader could the Progressive Conservatives break the pattern of protest party support in western Canada and usher in a new era. In 1993, westerners again embraced the politics of protest by sending fifty-two

Table 1.1 · Party Competition in Western Canada: Total Seats Won

	1st System (1867–1917)			2nd System (1921–1957)			3rd System (1958–1988)		
	Lib.	Cons.	Other	Lib.	PC	Other	Lib.	PC	Other
BC	17	53	0	54	63	48	49	118	106
Alberta	11	15	0	30	18	114	5	202	7
Saskatchewan	18	18	0	98	17	81	7	99	40
Manitoba	24	53	1	78	34	50	7	95	33

Table 1.2 · Seats Won in Western Canada During the Fourth Party System

	1993				1997				2000				2004		
	Lib.	PC	NDP	Reform	Lib.	PC	NDP	Reform	Lib.	PC	NDP	Alliance	Lib.	NDP	Cons.
BC	6	0	5	24	6	0	3	25	5	0	2	27	8	5	22[a]
AB	4	0	0	22	2	0	0	24	2	1	0	23	2	0	26
SK	5	0	5	4	4	0	5	8	2	0	2	10	1	0	13
MB	13	0	0	1	6	1	4	3	5	1	4	4	3	4	7

a. One independent, former Reform-Alliance MP Chuck Cadman in the BC riding of Surrey North is not included in the BC numbers. Including Cadman, there are a total of 36 BC MPs.

Reform MPs to Ottawa with the intention of reforming a political system they believed continued to conspire against their interests. This book is an exploration of the opinions, attitudes and ideas of those activists who built the Reform Party of Canada. Their efforts ensured that the twentieth century would close as it had began, with a political revolt from the West that would shatter the established Canadian party system.

Four Canadian Party Systems

Canada has had not one, but four distinct party systems since Confederation.[1] The first system lasted from 1867 until Robert Borden's Union Government, or about the 1917 election. Patronage politics, John A. Macdonald's National Policy, and the inclusion of the western provinces in the federation, albeit not on equal terms for the prairie provinces, characterized this system. Classic two-party competition between the Conservatives and Liberals was the norm. An agrarian protest movement transformed party competition after the 1921 election when Progressive candidates clobbered their opponents across the prairies and much of rural Ontario. They ushered in the second party system, which lasted until about 1957, was characterized by multiparty competition and regional brokerage politics, and ended when Diefenbaker eventually crushed the protest parties in the western provinces. As Table 1.1 demonstrates, it was during the second system when protest parties characterized party competition in the West by successfully competing with the traditional parties in all four western provinces.

The third system began with Lester Pearson's minority governments of the 1960s and was characterized by brokerage parties that relied heavily on party leaders' abilities to generate short-term electoral coalitions through a process of agenda building. But even when western representatives were fully included in the governing party during the Mulroney years of the 1980s, westerners again decided to express their regional dissent, break from the established pattern of partisanship, and bring a fourth system into being. When Reform Party of Canada candidates swept across the West in 1993, they were determined to represent a variety of perspectives that many westerners believed were not being adequately represented within the federal Liberal and Progressive Conservative parties, both of which appearing increasingly dependent on central Canadian votes for their electoral success.

The First System: Patronage Politics and Caucus Parties (1867–1917)[2]

Two parties dominated Canadian political life for the first half-century of Confederation. During this period Canada remained a mostly rural society with no established aristocracy, as in Britain, few large capitalists, as in the United States, and a weak and fragmented union movement. It did, however, contain a professional middle-class that sought from the party system, and government itself, their only avenue to exercising real power. As such, patronage dominated the system as a whole, partisanship pervaded the state administration, and party competition within the constituencies became contests for the control of government largesse.

The Conservative party emerged first as a result of John A. Macdonald's ability to establish the first governing coalition, and his subsequent use of patronage to build not only a loose party apparatus, but also a functioning state apparatus capable of implementing his National Policy. Party building, for Macdonald, was integral to state building. In exploiting the patronage prerogatives that came with power, Macdonald established a civil service that was dependent on the party for recruitment to its ranks. The interdependence of party and state was so pervasive that changes in the party in power produced large turnovers in civil service personnel.[3]

Party organizations in the first system were structured around the local constituency, the parliamentary caucus and its leader. There were few if any intermediary party structures. Long-term partisan attachments were channelled up through the local party associations, to the local MP (or defeated candidate) and his financial backers, to the party leader who assumed virtually all of the responsibilities for strategy, tactics and policy, as well as the management, organization and financing of the national party. Elections at the local level were prohibitively expensive and party leaders were forced to recruit candidates who had independent means of financing the contests, either through their personal resources or by way of access to other independent local sources. Government contracts were the expected reward for help in securing an electoral victory and the early parliaments contained a large number of "loose fish" whose vote the governing coalition could not necessarily count on if legislation adversely affected the local patronage relationship. At the same time, the massive scale of the National Policy dictated that the parties in general, and the Conservatives in particular, had to be closely aligned with Montreal and Toronto corporate and financial interests. The institutionalized reciprocal and multiple patronages, and corresponding large amounts of money, resulted in a scandal-plagued system that toppled Macdonald's government during the 1873 Pacific Scandal, the most famous but not the first or last of its kind.

With no intermediary party apparatus between the constituencies and the parliament, and the loose local organizations used mainly as vote-gathering machines, the parties were little more than coteries of political notables. For the most part, the parliamentary caucus was the party. Caucus was responsible for leadership selection with long-term party loyalty and service being viewed as prerequisites for ascending to leadership positions.[4] Control of the civil service and patronage at the local level gave the party in power a substantial advantage in maintaining its support base. Local ties to parties were enduring and consistent between the federal and provincial levels. National parties often used the resources of their provincial wings to vault them out of opposition and into power in Ottawa. With little to distinguish between federal and provincial local party organizations, party notables treated the system as one by moving freely between both levels as opportunities presented themselves or party needs dictated.

Party influence also pervaded the press and vice versa. Most newspapers were little more than partisan instruments, many published by the parties themselves. Journalism represented one of the most common routes into politics within a system where virtually all papers and journalists openly expressed their loyalties and gave editorial support in exchange for advertising and printing contracts. In the absence of formal party communications apparatuses, the close association between the parties and the press helped link partisans together, especially across constituencies, and gave the parties and their leaders reliable propaganda machines. The press could also present quasi-independent analysis in support of particular proposals while offering a continual source of criticism of a party's opponents. This symbiosis was evident in the actions of Macdonald when he helped establish Conservative papers in Toronto in an effort at stemming the influence of the Globe and its support for the Liberals.[5]

Overall, the first party system was stable and generally representative of the rural social order and emerging industrial economy that it helped bring into being. But a dynamically changing post-World War One society included civil service reform, and the political mobilization of immigrants, women and prairie farmers, meant that the old parties would also have to change or risk being swept aside by new parties that stood in opposition to many of the outcomes of the National Policy experiment. During the transition out of the old, first party system, a new federal protest party option emerged from the prairies in the form of the Progressives. They would be instrumental in transforming the established parties and the practice of partisan politics in Canada. Never again would Canadian federal politics revert back to a system of classic two-party competition. The West had arrived as a political region, and so to had a new type of politics.

The First Transition: Emergence of the Farmers' Parties (1917–1921)

Canadian society had changed dramatically in the first fifty years of Confederation. The National Policy had been largely successful in achieving its objectives.[6] Immigrants flooded into the prairies. Saskatchewan boasted Canada's third largest provincial population as a resource economy emerged in support of a productive agricultural sector. The industrial heartland was taking shape and the old north-south trade patterns had been supplanted by east-west routes along the railway and through the Great Lakes. Industrialization in the centre led to increased urbanization. Immigration and agricultural production led to prosperity and economic clout on the prairies. The former created a demand for reforms to the civil service and patronage politics. The latter demanded a fundamental rethinking of the National Policy, especially its tariff and transportation components. The traditional parties accommodated the demands from the centre but were much slower to recognize the demands from the periphery. As a result, the major impetus for reform of economic policy came from the prairie protest parties. By shattering the old, two-party system, the Progressives were instrumental in irrevocably altering partisan alignments on the prairies, creating competitive multiparty systems in each province. The fluidity in partisan alignments allowed for the entry of Social Credit and the Cooperative Commonwealth Federation after the Progressives were a spent force. As a result, multiparty competition continued at the federal level in all of the western provinces, in varying degrees, for the entire second party system.

The Progressive Party was a federal agrarian protest party that broke into the national party system by capturing sixty-five seats in the 1921 federal election. It supplanted the Conservatives as the second party in Parliament leaving it in a position to form the official opposition, a title the Progressives refused to accept because doing so would have implicated them within a system they were dedicated to abolishing.[7] During the

1921 federal election campaign, the Progressives campaigned by opposing the entire conceptual and practical framework of Canada's economic and political systems. W. L. Morton captures the frustration felt by many westerners:

> The concept of Canadian economic policy which the Progressives had formed and on which they acted was that of a metropolitan economy, designed by the control of tariffs, railways, and credit, to draw wealth from the hinterlands and the countryside into the commercial and industrial centres of central Canada.[8]

They viewed both the Liberals and Conservatives as instruments of central Canadian commercial, industrial, and financial interests, bent on implementing and maintaining a national policy that placed the western provinces in a colonial relationship with Ottawa. Because the prairie provinces had entered Confederation not as full partners but with limitations imposed on them for the "purposes of the Dominion," prairie voters understood their plight as subordinate communities, "subject to the land, fiscal and railway policies of the metropolitan provinces and the special interests of the French Canadians. They were, in short, colonies under the form of provinces.... The Progressive party was a full-blown expression of the West's resentment of its colonial status."[9]

Macdonald's National Policy was largely completed during the Laurier boom years of the late nineteenth and early twentieth centuries. Its success, however, engendered its own antithesis as the prairies emerged from the National Policy with considerable economic clout and a population large enough to mount a direct challenge to the metropolitan industrial and commercial centre. The result was a prairie populist revolt against the system that had brought the West into being. The Progressives demanded adjustments to National Policy that would loosen restrictions on international trade, specifically trade with the United States, or that Central Canada begin to pay its fair share of the costs of maintaining a protected internal market. Specifically, they advocated the restoration of the Crow's Nest Pass freight rates, the completion of the Hudson Bay Railway and corresponding branch lines, and a move away from increasingly nationalistic economic policies, including the ratcheting up of tariffs that was becoming the norm in many countries after World War One. The Progressives achieved only minimal success in these latter areas and won only minor concessions on freight rates. They had a much greater impact, however, in restructuring party competition in Canada.

Politically, the Progressives refused to be bound by the dictates of party discipline. They viewed the old discipline as the major inhibitor to representing their hinterland constituents' interests. They argued that strict party discipline, when combined with central Canadian dominance of the House of Commons, made each of the traditional parties indistinguishable proponents of the National Policy. Various factions within the Progressive party also went further in advocating specific structural changes to the party system. The Liberal-Progressive element, made up mostly of members who rallied around the party's early parliamentary leadership from Manitoba, advocated a realignment of parties along the lines of the liberal and conservative elements within the electorate.[10] They were countered by the Alberta Progressives who, more doctrinaire in their complete rejection of party government, proposed to completely eradicate parties in favour of group government.[11] The 1921 election demonstrated that many of these sentiments had deep roots throughout the prairies where the Progressives emerged as the dominant party in all three provinces. They captured 61 per cent of the vote and 15 seats in Saskatchewan, 57 per cent of the vote and 11 seats in Alberta, and 44 per cent of the vote and 12 seats in Manitoba. The party also made considerable inroads into Ontario where they polled 28 per cent support and elected 24 MPs. They rounded out their support base with two seats from BC and one from New Brunswick. However, their inability, or refusal to act as a coherent caucus in Parliament led to their swift repudiation as an effective voice for agrarian interests.

After the 1925 election, the Progressives' parliamentary representation was cut to 24 seats (9 from Alberta, 6 from Saskatchewan, 7 from Manitoba and only 2 from Ontario). Although continuing to win a majority of Alberta seats, and maintaining support levels above 30 per cent in that province through the 1930 election, the Progressives ceased to be a national force after the 1926 election.[12] By 1930, the party was in disarray. King had absorbed its more moderate members into the federal Liberal party, while its more radical elements splintered off in various smaller factions, some aligning themselves with Labour MPs to form the Ginger Group. While it did not survive as a party, the Progressive movement permanently changed the structure of party competition on the prairies. In doing so it helped engender a tradition of alienation within the western Canadian political culture that underpinned future generations of westerners' acceptance of new parties as legitimate sources of electoral protest.[13] But rather than withdrawing from the political system, as is most often the case with more general forms of political alienation, westerners continued to demand greater inclusion in the national institutions.

The Second System: Brokerage Politics and Ministerialist Parties (1921–57)

After the 1921 election, it became clear that the traditional parties would no longer be able to maintain the status quo. No longer could they expect the electorate to necessarily respond in predictable ways to the parties' definitions of the relevant social cleavages and the established structure of political debate. The war effort and the Union government experiment helped crystallize a modern, nationally self-conscious political culture in much of the country. At the same time, the conscription crisis shifted a significant plurality of Quebec voters into the Liberal camp, allowing it to dominate Quebec federal politics until 1984. While the Liberals were very successful in Quebec during Laurier's tenure in office, their percentage of the popular vote never exceeded 60 per cent. After 1917 the Liberals regularly received over 60 per cent of the popular vote in Quebec and in only two elections between 1917 and 1980 did they receive less than a majority of seats there.[14] Although an electoral realignment took place in Quebec during the second party system, it resulted in a long period of one-party dominance by a traditional party. The situation could not have been more different on the prairies. After 1921, nowhere on the prairies would party competition ever revert back to stable two-party competition between the two established parties. The effects of protest party competition would also be felt in British Columbia by the time of the 1935 election, so much so that for the next fifty years BC voters would witness extended periods of three-party, and sometimes four-party competition.

With the Quebec electoral situation stable, and with Quebec remaining under the cultural control of the Catholic Church, its impact on the national political culture during the second system was limited.[15] It was left to the Progressives and the Unionists to represent the new forces of change and achieve reform of the party system. The war's modernizing and nationalizing effects on the political culture were represented in the Unionists' campaign of 1917. Borden recognized the changing circumstances and developed a platform that, among other things, promised to reform the civil service and stop the institutionalized politics of patronage.[16] The old pattern of local-elite dominated parties, which was already being threatened by industrialization and urbanization in the central provinces and by immigration and agrarian agitation in the western provinces, gave way to the second system where national and regional elites, as well as newly organized interest groups, dominated the campaigns and strategies of the traditional parties.

The first significant changes were electoral reform and the adoption of democratic electoral institutions. Gerrymandering of constituency boundaries was for the most part stopped[17] and a near-universal franchise was adopted. The traditional parties began adopting regional brokerage strategies that changed the focus of party organization from constituency to region. Powerful regional elites organized electoral competition for their parties in the regions and, when in power, ministers were responsible for promoting regional interests upward into a national consensus. The party leaders were responsible for coordinating and defending the integrity of the brokerage process, something at which King proved more adept than the Conservative leader, R. B. Bennett. Multiparty competition in the western provinces, and the Liberals' ability to broker regional interests, defined the second party system. By absorbing much of the Progressive parliamentary caucus, King added a western support base to his secure Quebec component, thereby establishing a cross-regional electoral coalition and making the Liberal party the only truly national party, at least in the sense of being the only party regularly capable of forming a governing coalition.[18] By the time Bennett defeated King in the 1930 election, the Progressives were no longer competitive anywhere except Alberta. But their 1921 breakthrough had demonstrated the electoral viability of a regional campaign strategy. Although they faded from the electoral scene, their constituency and its interests remained. When Bennett's Conservatives proved incapable of successfully executing a regional brokerage strategy, King's Liberals were returned with another majority government in the 1935 election. But rather than returning to the traditional parties, much of the Progressives' constituency embraced Social Credit and the CCF. Not only had prairie discontent failed to abate, it had spread to British Columbia where 45 per cent of the electorate cast ballots for parties other than the Liberals or Conservatives.

In Alberta, Social Credit picked up where the Progressives and the United Farmers of Alberta left off. The party swept Alberta in 1935, both provincially and federally.[19] Social Credit championed Albertans' discontent with the National Policy and its agents, the central-Canadian-dominated federal parties. With control of the government in Alberta, Social Credit premier William Aberhart could go further than the Progressives in challenging Ottawa on the fundamentals of the federal political order.[20] Aberhart echoed and then accelerated the Progressives' alienation-driven demands for reform. Although the transfer of natural resource rights to the prairie provinces in 1930 marked the formal end of colonial status for these provinces, many Social Credit supporters still believed that political and economic imperialism continued. The Great Depression only served to punctuate the inequalities and inefficiencies of the federal system. With the federal government unwilling or unable to address the problem of "poverty in the midst of plenty," the battle for reform would now be carried primarily by the Alberta government.[21] But the federal Social Credit party also would remain a force, arguing throughout its existence that the western provinces had been left out of the Liberal's regional brokerage accommodation package.

Social Credit's dominance of Alberta was in part due to the effects of an electoral system that distorted its voter support into a disproportionately large number of seats while under-representing the competitive position of the federal Liberals. Although the Liberals regularly came within a few percentage points of Social Credit in popular support, Social Credit garner a majority of Alberta seats in every federal election until the Diefenbaker sweep of 1958. Social Credit support came primarily at the expense of the federal Conservatives. When Social Credit burst onto the scene in Alberta in 1935 by capturing nearly half of the popular vote (48 per cent), the Conservatives received only 17 per cent of the vote and would not recover in Alberta until the Diefenbaker transition. This left the Liberals as the only serious threat to Social Credit in Alberta. After hitting a low of 21 per cent in 1935, an election in which the CCF captured 18 per cent of the Alberta vote, the Liberals maintained a base of between 20 per cent and 35 per cent support throughout the second party system. However, by consistently winning a majority of Alberta's seats, Social Credit continued what the Progressives had achieved in the previous four elections. At no time in the second party system did a traditional party win a majority of Alberta seats, federally or provincially. It was during this period when the Alberta electorate established a tradition of supporting a party option until it had run its course, then shifting swiftly to another alternative, routinely decimating the previously entrenched party in the process. This pattern would repeat itself during the Diefenbaker transition, and again with Reform's 1993 victories.

The Co-operative Commonwealth Federation represented another challenge to the old system with its complete rejection of the principle of brokerage politics. The CCF campaigned on an ideologically socialist platform in an effort at redefining Canadian party politics and the national political agenda.[22] Nationally, the party hovered below 10 per cent support during the 1930s, but its limited national success was countered by its clusters of victories on the prairies and in BC. By 1945 the CCF broke through a significant electoral threshold in Saskatchewan, and to a lesser extent Manitoba and BC. It polled 16 per cent of the national popular vote and elected 28 MPs, moving past Social Credit for third place in the House of Commons. However, its seat base remained regional and even though the electoral system rewarded the CCF with over 20 seats in 1953 and 1957, the party was in general decline after 1945. For the most part, it could not withstand the Liberal brokerage strategy of co-opting popular CCF positions on welfare and government intervention in the economy.

The Liberals dominated Saskatchewan and Manitoba from the 1935 election onward, capturing 41 per cent of the vote in each province with the Conservatives managing only 19 per cent and 27 per cent respectively. The CCF made inroads, typically at the Tories' expense, by capturing 19 per cent of the Manitoba vote and 21 per cent in Saskatchewan. Social Credit never emerged as a competitive party in Manitoba, and after capturing 16 per cent of the vote and two Saskatchewan seats in 1935, it quickly faded from serious contention in that province. Throughout the second system the Liberals dominated federal elections in Manitoba with the CCF and Conservatives each regularly capturing approximately one-quarter of the popular vote. In Saskatchewan, a competitive two-plus party system developed with both the CCF and the Liberals capable of winning a majority of seats, something the CCF managed to accomplish in three of the six elections between 1935 and 1957. The Conservatives were henceforth reduced to minor party status in Saskatchewan for most of the second period.

British Columbia developed the most competitive system with the CCF capturing 34 per cent of the popular vote in 1935 and maintaining a support base of between a quarter and one-third of the electorate in every contest during the second system, sufficient to elect BC CCF members in every election after 1935. The Conservatives and the Liberals maintained similar support levels until 1953, when four-party competition emerged with the arrival of Social Credit. The federal Social Credit party would remain competitive in BC well into the 1960s, long after it had ceased to be competitive elsewhere.

Nationally, the Liberals dominated the second period, winning six majorities and forming two minority governments in nine elections. The second party system was characterized by a proliferation of protest party alternatives in the western provinces, first with the Progressive sweep of the prairies in 1921, and then with the emergence of Social Credit in Alberta and the CCF in the other provinces. At least one protest party maintained competitive support levels from 1921 to 1957 in every western province. Further, a non-traditional competition structure emerged in each of the western provinces, often providing voters with three- and sometimes four-party competition. The Conservatives, while maintaining a significant percentage of the popular vote in all western provinces, faired so poorly at electing MPs that they were never the most significant party in any western province during the second party system. That situation changed dramatically in the late 1950s when Diefenbaker ascended to the Conservative leadership.

The Diefenbaker Transition (1957–1962)

Under the leadership of John Diefenbaker, the Progressive Conservatives won the 1958 election with the largest majority government in Canadian history. Diefenbaker ushered in an electoral realignment that fundamentally restructured party competition throughout western Canada.[23] The Progressive Conservative resurgence on the prairies was so complete that in only two elections for the next thirty years would the Conservatives not win the largest plurality, or an outright majority of votes in every prairie province.[24] Diefenbaker's success came at the expense of the protest parties. In Alberta, Social Credit was reduced to 22 per cent of the popular vote in 1958 and would never again present a serious electoral challenge to the Conservatives.[25] The Conservatives would win close to half the Alberta popular vote until 1968 when they captured an outright majority, an accomplishment they would repeat for five elections afterwards.[26] The electoral system rewarded the Conservatives handsomely. In only 12 of the 214 contests for Alberta House of Commons seats between 1958 and 1988 were non-Progressive Conservative candidates elected.

Saskatchewan voters did not immediately warm to their native son with the Conservatives managing to capture only 23 per cent of the popular vote and three seats in 1957. By 1958, however, over 50 per cent of Saskatchewan voters cast ballots for the Conservatives. Diefenbaker's success in his home province came at the expense of both the Liberals and the CCF. The damage inflicted upon the CCF, in its most supportive province up to this time, led to the demise of the party. It eventually forged links with organized labour under the new banner of the New Democratic Party.[27] The CCF/NDP share of the popular vote would drop in Saskatchewan throughout the Diefenbaker period, to a low of 18 per cent in 1963, but rose after the Progressive Conservatives changed leaders, and by 1968 the NDP began to again elect MPs from Saskatchewan. A similar situation developed in Manitoba. Because of the structure of party competition there, the NDP regularly elected more MPs in that province than did the Liberals, despite being out-polled in popular support until 1979. British Columbia proved to be the most fertile ground for the NDP during Diefenbaker's tenure where the new links with organized labour immediately moved the NDP to the top of BC's complex four-party competition structure. During the early part of the third system the NDP consistently polled about one-third of the votes in BC, allowing it to win constituency contests with some regularity, first at the expense of the Conservatives, as Social Credit continued to split the right-of-centre vote, then at the expense of the Liberals once Social Credit faded.

The Third System: Leaders and Short-term Agenda Brokering (1963–1988)

Canada's third party system opened with the Progressive Conservatives in disarray over Diefenbaker's leadership and the Liberals returning to dominance again on the national scene.[28] Despite the Liberals' national successes, westerners remained loyal to the Conservatives. Once Trudeau assumed the Liberal leadership, his inability to adequately accommodate western interests within his governing coalition furthered the Liberals' demise to the point where elected western representation was all but completely brokered out of his governments. The Liberals' dismal record in western Canada during the third period is as important to the rise of the Reform Party as was Conservative dominance. Once the Conservatives came to power under Mulroney, and failed the test of adequately representing western interest within his governing coalition, most westerners did not view the Liberals as a viable alternative.

Under Trudeau, Liberal electoral support on the prairies, and later in BC, went into a tailspin. In Saskatchewan, the once powerful Liberal party elected only seven MPs during the entire third system. In six of the eleven elections between 1963 and 1988 no Liberals were elected from Saskatchewan. The situation was worse in Alberta where only five Liberal MPs were elected during the entire third period. In nine of eleven elections during this period, no Liberals were elected from Alberta. The Liberal party fared slightly better in BC and Manitoba where the multiparty competition structures allowed it to elect members throughout the third system, but in very modest numbers. By the late 1970s the Liberals were reduced to one or two seats in each province.[29] But they continued to form governments by forging enduring electoral coalitions that excluded the West. This was exemplified in 1980, Trudeau's last electoral victory, when only two Liberals were elected in all of western Canada.

During this period the brokerage process became leader-dominated by way of the electronic mobilization of information. Diefenbaker was the first to campaign effectively using the new communications opportunities presented by television, and all future leaders' effectiveness would be judged, at least partially, by their ability to communicate through that medium. Further developments included advances in polling techniques that allowed for a systematic upward flow of information to the party leadership. There was less need for powerful regional lieutenants and party members were relegated to subordinate status when compared to professional pollsters and advertisers. At the same time, provincial governments were quickly establishing themselves as the principal regional spokesmen, allowing the national parties to shift their focus from region to nation, and to direct their policy appeals to individual citizens in a process of short-term agenda building. As a consequence, dramatic changes took place in the organization of the two major parties. In one sense, the parties became the organizational extension of their leaders; machines designed to deliver votes in favour of the leaders' policies. The personalization of the parties' organizations stimulated the growth of national factions within each party and tended to transform policy disputes into leadership conflicts. This process became so pronounced that a leader's ability to manage factions would not only determine his tenure as leader, but as with the Conservatives, could characterize the public image of the entire party and seriously imperil its perceived ability to govern.

Under pressure to provide more participatory channels for their members, both the Liberals and the Conservatives attempted to strengthen and institutionalize their extra-parliamentary organizations. Activists would now meet regularly in convention to debate issues of policy, organization and, most importantly, leadership. However, with the exception of the leadership convention, these meetings had little impact on the national strategies and policy platforms of either the Liberals or Conservatives. Policy and strategy decisions were still tightly controlled by the leadership, which was not formally bound by the decisions delegates reached while meeting in convention. Leadership contests tended to be the most important avenue for ordinary members to fulfill meaningful roles in the party and, as such, leadership politics dominated party activists' attention. This situation hurt the Conservatives, who continued to air leadership divisions publicly, but benefited the Liberals who remained unified under Pearson's and then Trudeau's leadership.

Divisions over Diefenbaker's leadership left the Conservatives fractionalized. Internal party divisions were regularly fought out in public and dominated the party's agenda at the expense of policy and strategy priorities. Neither Stanfield nor Clark could effectively mend divisions, leaving the Liberals as the only party capable of building a governing coalition. In the process, however, national party competition was realigned along regional lines. Western voters abandoned the Liberals in favour of the Conservatives, and to a lesser extent the NDP, in multiparty contests that led to few Liberal victories. Quebec remained a Liberal fortress where Conservative victories were as infrequent as were Liberal wins in the western provinces. Under these conditions, none of the parties could legitimately claim to be a truly national party, at least not in the sense of geographical competitiveness.

As the major parties increasingly focused their attention on the large number of votes in Central Canada, when Ontario-Quebec interests conflicted with those of the West, as they frequently did during the 1970s and 1980s, the Liberals made a series of strategic choices that were viewed by many westerners as deliberate attempts to not only exclude western concerns from within the governing coalition, but to blatantly exploit western concerns as a wedge to shore up Liberal support in Central Canada. The Liberals used this strategy effectively during the 1970s and 1980s in developing a nationalist commercial policy that regularly rebuilt their electoral support in Ontario, but further alienated the bulk of western voters. As Johnston and his colleagues observed:

> Liberal nationalism advanced on two fronts: an increased commitment to protection for secondary industry and an attack on the primary sector... pitting energy producers against energy consumers. This culminated in the National Energy Program (NEP) of 1980, which sought to reduce foreign ownership in the oil and gas sector and to increase the federal government's share of energy rents.[30]

Interpreted as a direct attack on their economies, and as a means of stemming the flow of power to the West, the NEP demonstrated more than had any other federal government policy since Macdonald's National Policy the continuing colonial status of the western provinces. Westerners' inability to stop the NEP, and the fact that a national federal political party was openly exploiting the situation for its own electoral gain, only served to deepen the West's hostility towards the Liberal party, and the federal government more generally. As argued by Wiseman:

> The Liberals rejected the West, as much as it rejected them, by devising an electoral strategy that built on a Quebec base and played to the swing seats of metropolitan southern Ontario... During the Pearson and Trudeau years, therefore, the West's frustrations were doubly exacerbated: although it repeatedly rejected the Liberals, they kept winning office and consequently had too few western MPs for the Cabinet.[31]

The West's response to the NEP, and a host of other Liberal programs such as bilingualism, criminal justice reforms and expanded social welfare, combined with the structure of party competition to broker the Liberals out of competitive status in most western ridings, leaving the Conservatives as the dominant party, especially in Alberta where near complete single-party dominance prevailed.

The Political Climate in Western Canada in the Late 1980s

For many western Canadians the 1984 Progressive Conservative victory represented a watershed. After decades of witnessing the majority of their federal representatives relegated to opposition status, most westerners believed they would finally see their concerns seriously addressed by a federal government within which they now had substantial representation. The prevailing view was that western MPs, sitting in cabinet and the government caucus, would now have the power to redress the large number of regional grievances resulting from successive Liberal governments preoccupied with central Canadian concerns in general, and Quebec concerns in particular. By changing the players, it was thought, the current party and electoral system would finally work to the advantage of western Canadians. This attitude, while prevalent across the West, was centred in Alberta and dominated the political culture of that province. Thus, it was in Alberta where levels of western alienation were highest and where expectations of redress were strongest. While it will remain a matter of speculation as to whether any federal government could have ever lived up to Albertans' expectations, the Conservatives' electoral strategy, and consequently their parliamentary strategy, led to a series of policy initiatives that fell far short of what many Albertans had in mind.

Mulroney built a successful electoral coalition by adding the Québécois nationalist vote to the Conservatives' traditional western support base.[32] However, the magnitude of the Conservative victory, large in popular support and even larger in parliamentary representation, became problematic early in the government's first mandate. It surfaced as regional conflict within the policy process.[33] Although western MPs held more seats in the first Mulroney cabinet than westerners had ever held before, and many were senior cabinet portfolios, almost immediately, western interests again seemed to take a back seat to Central interests.

Regional cleavages opened wider as a result of the ongoing constitutional debate during both the Meech Lake and Charlottetown negotiations. Westerners who felt shut out of the process by both their provincial governments and the federal Conservatives were left with no traditional party option. When both the federal Liberals and NDP scrambled to support Meech Lake and then the Charlottetown accord in a continuing effort at winning votes in Quebec, many westerners again were left with no representation within a process that was designed to fundamentally alter the very institutions they had been protesting against for three generations.[34] Westerners seemingly watched from the sidelines again as the Conservatives were slow in dismantling the National Energy Program and made little headway in reducing government spending and the federal deficit.[35] Meanwhile, the Conservatives moved to position themselves within the issue space of the former Liberal government by continuing to accommodate the demands of many left-of-centre interest groups, by promoting bilingualism, and making no recognizable progress on criminal justice reform. The government also embarked on a monetary policy directed at cooling the overheated central Canadian economy while the West headed deeper into recession. A flashpoint occurred in the fall of 1986 when the federal cabinet decided to award Montreal's Canadair with a substantial military contract to maintain Canada's CF-18 fleet despite a technically and financially superior bid from Winnipeg's Bristol Aerospace.[36] It was at this time, only two years into the first Mulroney mandate, that a small group of westerners began organizing another formal political protest against the established parties.[37]

Conclusion

Although single-member-plurality electoral systems such as Canada's tend to produce long periods of stable two-party competition,[38] Canadian electoral history demonstrates that it is possible to build a successful new party by capturing a significant plurality of votes in an estranged region.[39] Furthermore, when new parties emerge, they often do so not in areas where there is complex multi-party structure at play. More often, new parties appear under conditions of what Maurice Pinard called one-party dominance: a system in which the traditional opposition parties cannot be considered a serious challenger, and therefore a new, third-party option becomes viable.[40] This situation existed in Alberta and most of western Canada in the late 1980s.

Graham White reinforces Pinard's analysis by arguing that voters' perceptions of the established opposition parties' ability to replace the incumbent party are an important factor in determining a new party's likelihood of success.[41] Without a third-party alternative, incumbent parties can maintain their electoral coalitions for extended periods of time, leading to long periods of stability, but also sudden shifts to third parties.[42] When a third party makes its electoral breakthrough, it will typically do so by siphoning votes away from the dominant party in areas where the dominant party was most solidly entrenched.[43] In Alberta during the late 1980s, the federal Conservatives were entrenched as the dominant party while the Liberals and NDP were discredited contenders. These dynamics presented Reform with the opportunity to emerge as a viable alternative once voters began to seek change.[44]

Having again participated within the governing coalition of one of Canada's traditional parties, and having again found the results of that participation lacking, many western voters appeared ready to embrace yet another round of organized dissent. When Preston Manning, son of former Alberta Social Credit premier Ernest Manning, emerged as a champion for the cause,[45] the Reform Party of Canada was born and the stage was set for another western-initiated transformation of the established Canadian party system.

2

The Founding – 1987 to 1989

The political dynamics of the 1980s presented western Canadians with another opportunity to express their dissent by launching an attack on the established political order. As had their prairie predecessors in the 1920s and 1930s, they built a political organization capable of routing one major party from the region and reducing the governing party to subordinate status in three of the four western provinces. In launching the Reform Party of Canada, westerners again transformed the Canadian party system by capitalizing on themes similar to those expressed by prairie populists of the past, including a perception that Canada's political elites and institutions were not capable of adequately representing the unique demands of the western electorate. But Reform was not an agrarian party, primarily because the West was no longer an agrarian hinterland. The new West of the 1980s, although still alienated from Ottawa, possibly more so than ever, was urban, capitalist and much more socially progressive than it had been fifty years earlier. But the West still contained a significant socially conservative element that the young party courted. Reform attempted to unite these diverse interests under the populist cause of promoting more democratic participation by westerners in the larger political system. The legitimacy of the embryonic organization would be judged by its ability to actualize those principles within the party's organization. Participation, in the form of direct membership input, would become one of Reform's unifying founding principles. Thus it is here, in their participatory roles as stewards of the founding ethos, where we witness the members' most important contributions to the Reform movement.

THE FIRST GATHERING – MAY 1987

The Reform Party of Canada was the outcome of a non-partisan assembly held in Vancouver in the spring of 1987.[1] The principal organizers were Preston Manning, Stan Roberts,[2] Robert Muir,[3] and a five-member steering committee. Francis Winspear[4] and The Canada West Foundation[5] provided additional financial and organizational support. The assembly was promoted and publicized by the Byfield family through their weekly *Western Report* publications.[6] In determining who would be eligible to attend, assembly organizers developed a screening process designed to recruit delegates of all political stripes from each of the four western provinces. Initially they set targets of sixty delegates from each province and sixty more to be chosen at large. A steering committee was established to appoint delegate selection committees in each province. The selection committees were responsible for choosing delegates from persons nominated by the general public. Qualifications included requirements that delegates be knowledgeable in at least one of the subjects to be dealt with,[7] demonstrate commitment to seeking fundamental change in the Canadian political system, and that they possess an open mind with respect to their choice of political vehicles. The latter qualification limited the number of sitting MPs, MLAs and established-party organizers in attendance. Committees were also charged with selecting at least one delegate from each federal electoral constituency in western Canada. Any resident of western Canada was entitled to nominate a delegate.[8] On the surface, the assembly was billed as a strictly non-partisan affair, advocating no specific plan for direct political action. Founding a new party would be considered as one possible outcome, but so to would collaboration with existing parties. The primary task faced by delegates was to draft an agenda for constitutional, political and economic change. If a new party were to be founded, it would be based on that agenda.

The assembly agenda proclaimed three objectives: to receive and review proposed solutions to the key economic, social, constitutional, governmental, and political problems confronting the West; to decide on a short list of fundamental reforms that western Canadians would like to see implemented by the Canadian parliament – a Reform Agenda; and to receive and review proposals concerning the most appropriate political vehicle for advancing the Reform Agenda in the next federal election, including a proposal for founding a new national political party. Topping the issue agenda was a Triple-E Senate amendment to the Meech Lake constitutional accord, the entrenchment of property rights in the Canadian Charter of Rights and Freedoms, and a number of non-constitutional issues such as provincial resource rights, deficit reduction, free trade, economic diversification, welfare reform, and regional fairness in federal procurements. Also included was a discussion of western separation. The separation issue, potentially the most contentious, was never considered a serious option by the organizers or most delegates. Manning demonstrated this early. In commenting on the brief appearance and disappearance of recent separatist groups he made it clearly understood that he would have no part in leading a separatist party. "We want to tell the rest of the country not that the West is leaving, but that it is arriving."[9] He went on to argue that the test will be whether or not "the West is shrewd enough and mature enough to put together something that sticks."[10] He also made it clear that, despite the pretense to non-partisanship, the organizational effort resulting from the policy session would include the founding of a new federal party. Prime Minister Mulroney recognized this and declined to send a federal Progressive Conservative delegation. In writing to the Reform Association Mulroney stated:

> The topic for your main dinner event on Saturday evening is a presentation on the concept of a new federal political party, and it is clear that is the principal reason you are convening the meeting. It seems to me that another regional party risks fracturing and reducing the influence of western Canadians on national policy. That would be contrary to Canadian interests and contrary to Western Canada's interests, so you will understand that I would not want to designate a representative to such a conference.[11]

Mulroney's position reflected what would become the most common Progressive Conservative response to Reform in its early years and would help in stunting Reform's momentum at least until after the 1988 federal election. However, as Reform gained support, Progressive Conservative rhetoric grew in harshness and volume. When it included attacks on Reform's supporters, Conservative disdain often did more to entrench the appearance of a centralist bias in the Mulroney Conservatives than blunt Reform's momentum. Calgary South West MP Barbara Sparrow's response was representative of the Conservatives' strategy and would allow Reform to capitalize on what it portrayed as the Tories' contempt for the West. "Any attempt to form a new party would be very foolish... The West's power would be diluted to no purpose," mused the Alberta MP. [12] Continuing, she turned her attention to the Alberta voters:

> I'm getting mad at Albertans for not realizing how good this government has been to them in the past three years. No one could have given them more – the country is broke. An appalling amount of money was confiscated from the West by the Trudeau Liberals. But we have to say 'the hell with it' because the money is gone. We can't return even a part of it.... its a delusion to believe that any better deal could be offered to Westerners by a new splinter party.[13]

Despite the lack of a federal Progressive Conservative endorsement, about three hundred delegates registered for the assembly, mostly from Alberta, but including representatives from all the western provinces.[14] Delegates attended workshops, debated policy resolutions and, most importantly, decided to form a new party. On the Saturday afternoon of the assembly they gathered to listen to Manning advocate that political option. In what has been described as a speech that "deserves to become known as one of the great political speeches of Canadian history," [15] Manning presented his vision of an ideologically balanced, western-based, non-separatist, national political party dedicated to addressing the regional grievances being voiced at the assembly. He regularly demonstrated ideological and partisan balance by arguing that the new party must be attractive to Liberals and New Democrats from the West, as well as disaffected Conservatives. He opened his address with what would become a familiar refrain. His vision would place the new party within the non-partisan reform tradition of the West and of Canada. In distinguishing his plan from those of the strange and extreme, he invoked a tradition that included reformers from Howe, Baldwin and Lafontaine, through Brown, Macdonald and Cartier, and the great reformers of the West, Riel, Haultain, Woodsworth, Wise Wood, Douglas and Aberhart. In advocating the revival of a reform tradition older than Confederation itself, he assured delegates that they were heirs to a noble tradition of nation building rather than a radical splinter group that would precipitate the breakup of the country.[16]

Manning outlined four reasons why a new political party was required at this time. Each built upon the twin themes of economic and political alienation combined with the structural inability or unwillingness of the three traditional parties to address western grievances. He argued that while the West was in deep economic trouble, no federal party was willing to make western interests its top priority. He claimed that the Conservatives' decline across the West was creating a dangerous political vacuum that the Liberals and NDP, as presently constituted, could not adequately fill. He concluded by arguing that the current cluster of Canadian parties required an influx of fresh, bold, new ideas that only a new party could provide.[17] Manning then provided three options for the delegates to consider: (1) to continue to attempt to work within the existing party structure; (2) to pursue some extreme option such as to threaten secession; or (3) to form a new federalist party. Manning advocated the third alternative by addressing several hypothetical objections that could be marshalled against the idea. After dismissing each in turn he supplied what he called "a broad and yet very clear" set of directions and specifications for the architects of a new party. Initially, he advocated a positive orientation and vision. The new party should offer a positive alternative rather than simply promoting a litany of complaints and grievances. It should have standards of performance, policy and people that exceed those of the existing parties. It should be ideologically balanced and draw supporters from across the political spectrum. It should be staunchly anti-separatist and channel the energy of the separatists towards the federal reform alternative by rallying around the slogan, *The West Wants In*. Finally, he advocated a new federal party that would have "room to grow" into a truly national party by eventually expanding across the country.

The speech achieved two key objectives. It established Manning as the early favourite to become leader of the party and indicated the direction he would steer Reform upon assuming that role. His insistence on ideological moderation indicated his desire to build a mass-based party, with as diverse a membership as possible, allowing for geographical growth that may otherwise be muted if the party was too right wing. In emphasizing the western origins of the movement, however, he secured the adoption of a regional electoral strategy designed to capitalize on western discontent. One component of contemporary western alienation was an inherent distrust of federal government management of the national economy. This distrust of Ottawa often led to a more general distrust of all interventionist government policies, an ideological position shared by many on the right. And although the West's political culture is not universally right wing, those who are most alienated from Ottawa tend to be more right of centre than those who are less alienated. By initially directing the party's mobilization efforts at an alienated, western support base, the party would recruit activists who would be much more right-wing than Manning's rhetoric advised, or his own preferences may have allowed.[18]

On the final day of the assembly, delegates were presented with a ballot that included several options. They ranged from supporting and reforming an existing federal party, to creating a new pressure group, creating a new broadly based federal party, or pursuing some other alternative to be suggested by the delegates. An original draft of the ballot included the separatist option but this was dropped from the final version. Delegates voted 76 per cent in favour of forming a new party and immediately drafted a party constitution and statement of principles. They then established a steering committee to draft platform proposals.[19] All of these would be presented to delegates attending a founding assembly to be held in Winnipeg later that same year.

Delegates also passed policy resolutions supporting a Triple-E Senate, entrenchment of economic rights in the constitution, the creation of a western Canadian free-trade zone, support for provincial government economic policies that would not interfere with free markets, and a general endorsement of less government. Most observers correctly concluded that the platform would appeal mainly to those on the right of the political spectrum. In these areas it was a platform Manning supported. However, ideological differences began to emerge during the social issue workshops. Manning felt compelled to intervene by lecturing delegates on the need to form a broadly based party free of the extreme proposals emanating from some of the workshops.[20] While the principles that emerged were moderate in comparison to some of the extremism being advocated by a minority of delegates, many early activists would continue to pursue an eclectic range of socially conservative proposals during the party's early policy development processes.

Table 2.1 · Attendance at the Founding Convention: Winnipeg, 1987

	Maximum Allowed	Minimum Desired	Regi-stered	Total Present	% of Total Present
BC	256	128	90	76	29%
Alberta	208	104	140	129	49%
Saskatchewan	112	66	10	6	2%
Manitoba	112	66	65	51	19%
Territories	16	8	0	0	0%
Totals	**704**	**372**	**305**	**262**	

Source: Reform Association of Canada Memorandum: "Result of the Convention," 5 November 1987.

The Founding Assembly - October 1987[21]

Delegate selection for the founding assembly presented the Reform Association with its first organizational challenge as a party: the establishment of branches capable of electing qualified delegates from within their own ranks. A set of formal delegate selection guidelines was established and included many provisions that would set precedent for future branch practices. Anyone who was at least eighteen years of age and a member of the Reform Association could seek delegate status from the riding within which they lived.[22] Local advertising of an open public meeting had to take place at least one week in advance, and all ridings were eligible to elect eight delegates. The interim executive recommended that at least one delegate be under the age of thirty, but it imposed no formal quota. It also attempted to ensure that each constituency was represented by at least four delegates and, if need be, make appointments as necessary.[23] The interim executive chose sixteen people as honorary delegates who were entitled to speak at the assembly but not vote. The executive council and the founding convention committee members also qualified for ex officio delegate status. Most delegates were, however, nominated and seconded from the floor by persons eligible to vote at local meetings. Under these criteria, the assembly had the potential to attract over seven hundred delegates. Less than two-fifths that number attended. As Table 2.1 indicates, attendance at the founding assembly revealed that Albertans were clearly the most receptive to Reform's early mobilization efforts. This was in no small part due to Manning's organizational efforts and his leadership bid, both of which were concentrated in that province.

The Alberta character of the earliest recruits would be instrumental in consolidating the participatory and western alienation orientations of the young party. It would also further Reform's right-of-centre ideology and set a pattern for the recruitment of members who shared these attitudes and opinions. Flanagan described the situation at the time of Reform's founding:

> The populist assault on party discipline was especially plausible in the West because western MPs had gone along with their national parties on regionally unpopular issues such as the National Energy Program and the CF-18 maintenance contract. And while public opinion in the West is not monolithically conservative, it certainly contains a large conservative element that a regional party must regard. This is especially true in Alberta, and at this stage the Reform Party was for all practical purposes an Alberta party. The headquarters were in Alberta, most of the key activists were Albertans, and the Manning name resonated in that province far more than it did elsewhere.[24]

Delegates accomplished three tasks at the founding assembly. They chose Manning as leader, albeit by acclamation, they adopted Manning's twenty-point Statement of Principles, and they voted on twenty-nine policy resolutions that constituted the foundation upon which the party would mobilize activists.

Rather than actively campaigning for the leadership, Manning simply acted as though he had already assumed the mantle and spent the months between the two 1987 Assemblies speaking across the prairies about the need for a new party under his direction, and according to his vision. Ted Byfield, an early protagonist for a new western-based political party and an early favourite to lead the party, declined to enter the race, deciding instead to support the party in principle through his editorial commentary.[25] Stan Roberts officially entered the race in mid-October; only a few weeks prior to the Winnipeg assembly and after most of the delegates were already supporting Manning. Roberts' support came mainly from BC, was dominated by former Liberals, and represented one of the two primary groups of initial organizers.[26] The two contenders presented delegates with very contrasting campaign styles. Roberts took a traditional approach that was supported by ample campaign paraphernalia, news releases and a hospitality suite. The approach failed to inspire delegates. Manning's campaign was modest by any standard and certainly in comparison to Roberts'.[27]

Almost immediately, acrimony erupted on a scale similar to that which regularly tarnished traditional party leadership contests, much of it initiated by the Roberts camp as they waited for more of their delegates to be bussed to the meeting. The two candidates attempted to keep the situation from boiling over by meeting with the steering committee to resolve these and a number of other organizational disputes. The steering committee eventually presented delegates with a proposal to forego the leadership vote at this assembly and hold a special leadership convention. Manning argued against the resolution and when delegates agreed, and decided to hold the leadership vote, Roberts withdrew his candidacy and Manning was acclaimed leader.

The leadership contest established two significant precedents in the early life of the party, one symbolic, and the other substantive. Symbolically, it enshrined within the party Manning's leadership style; a leadership guided by policy as opposed to glitz, or, in the language of Reformers, "substance over personality." This campaign style would be further institutionalized in the party once it developed formal procedures for nominating its election candidates. It also established a precedent whereby contests for leadership positions, including local candidate nominations, would deviate from traditional-party practices of stacking selection meetings with instant delegates recruited for the sole purpose of electing a candidate. From this point on, and throughout the party's organization, entitlement to vote would require membership subscription and registration by some predetermined date well in advance of the meeting. The procedural wrangling also established a precedent ensuring that future disputes amongst the leadership would be settled by votes of the assembly or by other plebiscitary mechanisms such as party-wide referenda.

A further outcome of the brief leadership contest occurred when Roberts withdrew from the inner circle of organizers. Without the BC Liberal influence on the executive council, and within Manning's circle of advisors, the party was left without a left-of-centre voice within its founding leadership core. Although Manning urged moderation, he supported policy positions that were by most standards right of centre. While publicly rejecting the political debate defined in the narrow terminology of the left, right, and centre, he did little to discourage the adoption of policies that were substantially right wing. But without a cadre of genuine moderates in leadership positions, Manning was left as one of the most moderate influences in what was becoming an increasingly right-of-centre party.

Further, his own Statement of Principles that was adopted by the party, while including several ambiguous declarations about "personal and collective responsibility," was for the most part a declaration of fiscal and social conservatism.[28] When the Statement of Principles became the foundational document upon which most members would be recruited, it was no accident that most early members would be correctly characterized as right wing. When ideology played a role in internal party conflict, it was most often the membership that demonstrated a more consistent right-wing orientation than did Manning. As a result, Manning's efforts increasingly were directed towards expanding the ideological base of the party rather than ensuring it remained consistently right of centre. From this point on, Manning's leadership would tend to moderate and blur the ideological consistency of the party rather than make it more ideologically pure.

In its infancy, Reform was essentially a plebiscitarian movement where the membership acted primarily to ratify the leadership's vision rather than substantially contribute to policy and strategy. As a new party with extra-parliamentary origins and built by way of a push from a central group of political entrepreneurs, it is understandable that Manning's vision dominated the founding.[29] Early recruits were mobilized into the party because it provided leadership organized around a founding vision they supported, and for the most part, they simply ratified its implementation. This situation would continue for the first two years of the party's existence until it had successfully organized enough branches whose activists could begin to use the procedural mechanism allowed them, at assembly and through the party's communications apparatus, to increase their influence on policy and strategic decisions. The most highly involved early activists would eventually form caucuses within their branches and play significant roles in proposing policy resolutions that would keep the party positioned on the right. Over time, as the leadership attempted to maintain its control over policy development and strategy at the expense of significant input from a growing membership, the formal mechanisms of membership control were strengthened within the party's constitution and in the practical functioning of the party. But for the most part, early activists were content to act as a plebiscitarian check on a leadership they genuinely supported.

The Party Constitution

The most important clause in the original Reform Party Constitution was the provision that the party not run candidates in federal electoral districts outside of the western and northern constituencies, at least until such time as two-thirds of the membership voted to do so.[30] Membership was open to Canadian citizens who were eighteen years of age or older and who supported the principles of the party.[31] There was no provision for indirect membership based on an association with another group or subgroup within the party. As such, the party's membership base could expand only as the party successfully established branch constituency associations, first exclusively in western Canada, and later in Ontario and the Maritimes. The party explicitly forbade membership by, or party affiliation with any pre-existing organization including corporations and trade unions.[32] There were no provincial organizations or interest groups such as women's, youth, or aboriginal wings that were accorded special status within the organization. Each recruit was automatically made a member of the national party and the local branch within which the member resided. Subscription fees of $10 per year were collected and split equally between the local branch and the national party. The national party office maintained a national membership registry that allowed for direct contact with every party member and an extremely efficient means of renewing subscriptions and soliciting financial contributions. Throughout its history, Reform would depend more heavily on its members and supporters to finance the party than would the traditional parties. As Table 2.2 demonstrates, contributions by businesses were extremely sparse in the early years and never exceeded a quarter of total revenue.

A two-tiered structure was implemented throughout the party's organization whereby there were no intermediary organizations or sub-units between the national party and the local branches.[33] With no pre-existing organizational structure to imitate, the leadership was free to experiment with whatever sub-unit structures it deemed necessary. That a high degree of centralization existed was not a surprise.[34] What was novel about Reform was that the membership had any real influence at all. But Reform was founded at a time when many westerners were openly hostile to the strict party discipline being displayed by the traditional parties. Voters' lack of control over their MPs led some – those most susceptible to Reform's mobilization strategy – to question the legitimacy of the entire party system. In order to capitalize, the party would have to do more than simply state that it would act differently than the traditional parties. It would have to incorporate the representational mechanisms it advocated for the larger system into its own party structure. It attempted this in several ways.

TABLE 2.2 · Financial Contributions to Reform Party, 1989–1999 (thousands of dollars)

	'89	'90	'91	'92	'93	'94	'95	'96	'97	'98	'99
Individuals ($)	1,206	2,076	4,737	5,633	5,077	3,407	3,407	4,935	5,538	4,423	4,295
(%)	(89.3)	(93.8)	(90.6)	(90.2)	(71.8)	(71.4)	(78.6)	(68.9)	(62.9)	(76.6)	(68.3)
Business ($)	141	138	491	613	1,022	570	816	908	1,911	1,291	1,505
(%)	(10.4)	(6.2)	(9.4)	(9.8)	(14.5)	(11.9)	(18.8)	(12.7)	(21.7)	(22.4)	(23.9)
Other ($)[a]	4	0	0	0	973	798	115	1,320	1,350	57	484
(%)	(0.3)	(0.0)	(0.0)	(0.0)	(13.8)	(16.7)	(2.7)	(18.4)	(15.3)	(1.0)	(7.7)
Total ($)	1,351	2,214	5,228	6,246	7,072	4,775	4,337	7,162	8,800	5,772	6,284

a. Most of the other funds were contributed to the national party by the western constituency associations.

Source: Elections Canada.

The original Reform constitution allowed members to initiate referenda of the general membership by submitting a petition signed by 15 per cent of the members.[35] That this provision was never used suggests that the party never faced a membership revolt severe enough to necessitate the initiation of the referendum clause. This is not to imply that the party was free of conflict or significant skirmishes between the members and the leadership. It was not. However, when disagreements surfaced, one of several things typically occurred to solve the problems without the membership using its powers of last resort. In most cases, when the general membership was unhappy with certain leadership-sponsored policy proposals, the members used the party assembly and the executive council-sponsored referenda to bring the leadership back in line. In some cases, dissenting members protested by leaving the party. At other times, when individual members where deemed to be damaging Reform's public image, the leadership would simply expel them. In a few extraordinary cases that will be elaborated upon below, the leadership reverted to plebiscitary techniques to expelled dissidents. In most cases, however, membership dissent took the form of scuttling the leadership's carefully crafted plans when they reached the party's Assemblies.

The Reform constitution formally recognized its membership, meeting in assembly, as "the highest authority and supreme governing body of the Party."[36] This in itself was not unique amongst Canadian parties. In describing the structures of the three traditional parties, Pelletier observes that the party convention was the supreme governing body of all the parties.[37] But the parties were distinguished by their actual operations. Despite formally recognizing their memberships as supreme, neither the Liberals nor the Conservatives actualized those goals in that their leaders were not bound by policy decisions reached at conventions. Until Reform emerged, only the NDP dictated that all party authorities, including the leader, had to comply with resolutions adopted at their party's conventions. And although the NDP paid official homage to active membership participation, its organizational structure was based on a federation of semi-autonomous provincial parties that limited member influence within a national organization that barely existed between elections.

The Reform constitution dictated that the policies and objectives of the party were those set forth in the Reform Party of Canada Statement of Principles and Policies (Blue Book) and could only be amended by a majority vote of an assembly or by way of internal party referenda.[38] The leader, in consultation with the party's executive council, could determine interim policy between Assemblies, with the qualification that interim policies could not be inconsistent with policies and principles established at previous Assemblies, and all interim policies and objectives had to be placed before the next assembly for ratification.[39]

Although the leadership was always formally bound by the members' decisions, the practical influence of the membership took time to develop. With no intermediary sub-party units available to challenge the leadership's active role in policy development and strategic planning, activists used the assembly delegate-selection process and local policy development initiatives to channel their demands upwards and further their influence. In this way, Reform's Assemblies became the focal point for articulating members' demands and for exercising some control over the leadership. The Reform assembly became closer in practice to what all parties proclaimed formally, the supreme governing body of the party. This in no way implies that Manning and the leadership were without significant influence within the party. They were not. Nor that the membership made most of the important decisions. They did not. Ample evidence does exist, however, that Reform members did have the final say in determining whether or not the party would adhere to Manning's objectives or those of the membership, if and when the two conflicted.

Formally, the party constitution stated that Reform would have a leader and an executive council.[40] The leader was elected by the general membership. Members were eligible to vote in leadership contests only if they were party members on the date on which the leadership vote was announced by the executive council. This procedure was meant to avoid the cumbersome, and often troublesome, practices associated with holding delegate selection meetings. It also substantiated Reform's populism by allowing each member a direct say in determining who would be party leader. The drawback was that the party would not have been able to use a leadership contest as a means for membership expansion. At each assembly, delegates were provided a ballot asking if they believed a leadership vote should be called. Ballots were cast in secret and the results were announced to the assembly on the same day as the vote. A fifty per cent vote in favour of a leadership contest would have triggered a leadership contest within six months.[41]

The Executive Council was made up of the party leader, three councillors from each province and one councillor residing in each territory so long as those provinces and territories qualified for maximum representation on the council. One further member of the executive council was the chief executive officer of the Reform Fund Canada, the party's financial arm.[42]

While having fewer formal, constitutional powers than the members, the leadership wielded a great deal of practical power, especially in Reform's early, developmental years. These powers were exercised both in the day-to-day operations of the party and in policy and strategic development. The party constitution provided for an active role by the national leadership in organizing the local branches, in membership recruitment, candidate training and recruitment, and in the education of party members. The party provided a generic "constituency constitution" as part of its general constitution that was designed to instruct branch activists on how to organize themselves. Centrally featured were the extensive procedures for candidate nomination contests that allowed for national party input into recruitment, training and education.[43] This is an expected function of a new mass-based political party and, overall, the national party was successful in developing the procedures used by the branches and in directing their relatively uniform branch structures.[44] In spite of Reform's populist tendencies, the national party's influence in directing the organization of branches was genuinely welcomed by most early branch activists. For the most part, branch activists were novices with little previous formal political involvement and usually in need of national party support and direction. Despite some highly publicized incidents involving dissidents, the national party procedures were readily accepted and executed by most branch activists as they struggled to establish functioning local riding associations capable of carrying on party business.

The party constitution gave the leadership authority to reject branch nominees who sought to contest elections as Reform candidates, paralleling a similar provision in the Canada Elections Act. It also provided the leadership with the authority to implement the policies and objectives of the party, including the authority to strike task forces and establish committees as it saw fit.[45] Policy task forces were established as committees of the executive council and consisted of ordinary party members, although the chairman had to be a member of the executive council. The task forces reported to the party and the membership by publishing their reports and presenting them to delegates gathered at assembly. The executive council could request polls and referenda of the party membership, but these were not always binding on the leadership. The executive council also enjoyed the authority, by way of its own internal policy committees, to research and develop policy recommendations for presentation to assemblies and for consideration by the leader and executive council between assemblies. Conflicts about the use of these powers became the focal point of early jurisdictional and power sharing disputes.

In most cases where disputes about shared power or unwanted influence by executive council occurred, they were driven by branches attempting to exercise their formal powers at the expense of executive council's practical power. Initially, the early activists sought out and adhered to the leadership's procedural advice and policy directions within the centralized party structure. Once the branches were established, activists initiated attempts at exercising their formal powers by demanding more practical influence over policy and greater autonomy in their local activities. With the leadership intent on continuing to direct the party from the centre, the activists set out to use their constitutional powers at assemblies to adjust both the formal and practical power distribution in their favour.

The 1988 Federal Election

Having adopted a constitution and founding principles, Reform ended 1987 with three thousand members and the goal of electing a block of western MPs in the next federal election. The primary organizational tasks were establishing branches in at least fifty ridings across the western provinces and in building an effective communications network. Manning assumed the responsibilities for planning the overall strategy, developing and defining the "Agenda for Change" platform, and presenting his vision of the new party to early branch activists who were charged with the task of mobilizing recruits into their fledgling constituency associations.[46] In selling his message, Manning focused on opposition to the Meech Lake constitutional accord and the government's preoccupation with the Quebec agenda at the expense of western concerns. More specific attacks were directed against the Conservative record on government procurement and the CF-18 maintenance contract, the Official Languages Act and Senate reform. Early promotional activities included a series of Western Workshops on Reforming the Senate of Canada that were organized in conjunction with the Committee for a Triple-E Senate and the Canada West Foundation.[47] At the same time, the national office and executive council worked closely with the local activists to quickly establish their branch organizations and prepare for candidate nomination meetings.

The party prepared a Constituency Organization Handbook with specific instructions on how to build a branch political organization from the bottom up. Included were sections on assembling the required resources and registering their nominated candidates with Elections Canada and the national party. Other sections included procedures for establishing viable organizations through the adoption of a formal constitution, undertaking communications activities, setting up public meetings and conducting literature drops. Each branch was asked to recruit at least three hundred members before the election and organizing fundraising activities to raise $5,000 for operating expenses and a $10,000 election war chest.[48] The need to secure subscriptions and other donations meant that membership recruitment dominated early branch activities. The need to nominate and register at least fifty candidates to run in the upcoming federal election presented the national party with its most formidable task.[49] National organizers developed a set of guidelines for developing a candidate profile, conducting a search, and recruiting and nominating a candidate. In most cases these elaborate procedures were well beyond the new, and still small, branches' abilities. Although Manning traveled tirelessly in promoting the party throughout the first half of 1988, by June only eleven Reform candidates had been nominated. When Manning announced that he would challenge former Prime Minister Joe Clark for his Yellowhead, Alberta seat he began to draw larger crowds and by August the party was ready to hold its pre-election policy assembly in Calgary.[50]

About 250 delegates attended the 1988 Calgary Assembly. Many were selected at the constituency level, but given that most branches could not fill their allotted number of positions, attendance was essentially open to anyone willing to participate. Some policy resolutions were submitted from the constituency associations but the assembly's primary focus was the proposed election platform drafted by chief policy advisor Stephen Harper. Although not part of the original Reform Association, Harper attended the 1987 Vancouver Assembly as an observer and came armed with a paper entitled "Political Reform and the Taxpayer" that he had written with fellow student John Weissenberger. In it, they denounced the "liberal-socialist philosophy" of the Canadian political establishment and called for a genuinely conservative Taxpayers Party. The paper so impressed Manning that he invited Harper to address the 1987 founding assembly in Winnipeg where Harper won rave reviews from delegates and organizers alike. Manning immediately appointed Harper Reform's chief policy officer. Delegates debated and modified over thirty-five policy resolutions contained in four planks. Included were five constitutional-reform resolutions with extended discussion of Meech Lake and a draft constitutional amendment to reform the Senate. Six resolutions advocated political reform while twelve concentrated on social reform. Delegates also debated twelve economic reform resolutions. Key amongst these was support for deficit reduction, tax reform, regional economic fairness tests and free trade.[51] The 1988 election platform was published as the party's first Blue Book.[52] The adoption and publication of the Blue Book and the party's *Reformer* newsletter would come to represent the core of its communications strategy up to, and for some time after, the 1988 federal election. The Blue Book's formal role in party life expanded to the point where amendments to it quickly became the focus of constituency association activity once the branches began to use their assembly powers to exercise greater influence in the policy process. Nevertheless, at this stage of its development, and as the Calgary policy assembly indicated, Reform was all but completely dominated by the executive council, Manning, and his close circle of advisors.

The party's first internal jurisdictional dispute erupted just prior to the 1988 election. Manning had been carefully nurturing the party's image as a moderate alternative to the three traditional parties and free of extremists.[53] In fact, much of the early national office support to the branches was directed towards establishing organizations that could not be infiltrated by fringe groups advocating extreme causes. Despite those efforts, in October 1988 the members of the Capilano-Howe Sound constituency association nominated *North Shore News* columnist Douglas Collins as their candidate for the federal election. Collins was known for his inflammatory and racist comments, as well as being openly critical of the party and its leadership. Upon learning that Collins would be uncontested, Manning attempted to dissuade him from running by promising to cover his campaign expenses to date and to not run a Reform candidate in the riding if Collins decided to run as an independent. Collins refused and Manning responded by declaring he would only accept the nomination if the constituency association passed a resolution rejecting racial discrimination and Collins endorsed that resolution. Collins was unrepentant and at a nomination meeting attended by over 990 people, but with only 178 registered voting members, his candidacy was solidly endorsed. The meeting overwhelmingly passed a resolution condemning Manning's actions and Collins was declared the Reform candidate. Manning stood his ground and refused to recognize the nomination. Realizing that he would not be running under the Reform banner in the election, Collins retreated, leaving the party and taking many of his supporters with him.[54] A replacement was nominated one week later and the issue appeared to have been resolved. However, the incident had lingering effects on the party's early development. Importantly, it indicated the lengths to which Manning would go in keeping the party free from radical elements. In that sense, it lent credibility to his pronouncement that he would not lead a party of the "strange and extreme." It also demonstrated that he was willing to endure short-term procedural disputes within the party to keep it as free of extremists as was possible. But the effects of the dispute were not as short-lived as Manning may have hoped. Many of the local Capilano-Howe Sound activists who did not leave with Collins remained unsatisfied with the leadership's handling of the situation and would make their dissatisfaction known at the 1989 Assembly. They would be instrumental in leading a movement to disrupt the leadership's careful management of the convention and derail the executive council's proposed amendments to the party constitution. In doing so they demonstrated to all branch activists the latent power at their disposal within the organization.

By the time of the November 1988 federal election, Reform had been in existence for only a year. When the election was called on October 1, the party had nominated only twenty-eight candidates, far short of the fifty needed to qualify for official party status with Elections Canada. By the time nominations closed three weeks later, the party had managed to organize branches and nominate candidates in seventy-two western ridings. But it was still organizationally weak at the national party level leaving the 1988 Reform campaign to consist of seventy-two almost independent, local campaigns with the national party simply supplying the policy platform.[55] Most of the local campaign work itself was left to local activists with limited direction from the national executive council members. As Manning described the campaign:

> Each [branch] would run a 'guerrilla' campaign under the control of a local constituency association and campaign team. These campaigns would be linked together by some common literature and advertising, a common platform, access to the services of our head office in Edmonton, and public appearances by myself as leader. Otherwise, every constituency was virtually on its own.[56]

The timing of the election and resulting organizational activities affected the party's early development in two important ways. First, the national party did not have time to develop an elaborate organization structure of its own before it had to expend virtually all its limited resources on branch development and candidate nominations. While establishing local branches is typically the first activity of new parties, Reform's need to establish organizations capable of successfully nominating candidates and contesting elections within the first year of operation spread the national party's resources extremely thin. Even though the party began with a centralized organizational structure, endogenous environmental factors led to the branches being the first level of the party structure to be developed in earnest.

Secondly, the limited national party resources combined with the early focus on branch organization to provide the early local activists, many having no previous formal political experience, with a great amount of autonomy in designing and executing their own campaigns. Although all of the campaigns would use generic Reform publications as promotional material, and would be bound by the party's platform and principles, early activists expanded upon and interpreted that platform in a wide variety of ways. This was to be expected from activists drawn to a party that promoted local issue representation as one of its founding principles. Almost immediately, strongly entrenched caucuses developed at the local level that remained in control of most branches at least until the next round of candidate nominations in 1992. These early activists, perceiving themselves to have built their own organizations and executed their own campaigns with little interference or support from the national party, would jealously guard their autonomy in the years following the 1988 election. Thus, while the party was founded because of an impetus from the centre, and formally exhibited a democratically centralized organizational structure, its early development was extremely decentralized. This pattern solidified a strong sense of local autonomy amongst the early activists who regularly opposed future national party objectives that they perceived to encroach upon their autonomy.

As expected, western alienation was centrally featured in the 1988 Reform campaign. Manning promoted Reform as the only party able to adequately represent western constitutional issues by focusing on the party's Triple-E Senate proposal. But when the constitution and Meech Lake failed to materialize as salient campaign issues, Reform had to retreat to its economic agenda.[57] Unfortunately for Reform, its economic agenda did not significantly distinguish it from the governing Conservatives. Reform supported free trade with the US and when the election turned into a single-issue campaign, Reform competed with the Conservatives for the same votes on an issue that was extremely ideologically charged. Most potential Reform voters seemed willing to again vote Conservative for the greater good of finally actualizing the long-standing western goal of free trade with the Americans. On the surface, the final results did not appear encouraging for the long-term prospects of the party. While Reform garnered over 250,000 votes, it failed to elect any members to Canada's thirty-fourth Parliament. The party captured 15.5 per cent of the Alberta vote, but only 5.1 per cent of British Colombians, 3.9 per cent of Manitobans, and 2.9 per cent of Saskatchewan voters supported it. Beneath the surface, however, there did appear to be prospects for growth. While no Reform members were elected, nine Reform candidates finished second in Alberta ridings while five placed third. In the Yellowhead riding, Manning reduced Joe Clark's margin of victory to under seven thousand votes from over thirty thousand in 1984. Support levels fluctuated between constituencies across the West, but in 1988 and the years immediately following it was clearly concentrated in Alberta and greatest in rural and southern Alberta constituencies. The results indicated that where the party was well organized, Reform could mount a serious challenge to the Conservatives.

The First Electoral Victories

Having elected no MPs in the 1988 federal election, Reform would continue to develop primarily as an extra-parliamentary organization until after the 1993 election. Nevertheless, 1989 presented the party with two opportunities to further develop its electoral machinery and enhance its profile in Alberta. The first opportunity arose when a Conservative candidate elected in 1988 from the rural riding of Beaver River died before being sworn into the new parliament. After considering his options, Manning declined to seek the party's nomination for the subsequent by-election. He reasoned that his talents could be much better utilized building the party from outside of Parliament rather than spending the bulk of his time in Ottawa as a caucus of one. Reform's commitment to local constituency representation also presented a problem. The party was carefully nurturing its image as something different from the traditional parties and parachuting the leader into a by-election could be interpreted as a politics-as-usual approach by many of the alienated voters Reform was attempting to recruit.

Deborah Grey, the party's candidate in Beaver River for the 1988 general election was nominated to again represent Reform in the by-election. After finishing a distant fourth in the general election less than six months earlier, Grey nearly tripled her vote and won a riding that had voted Conservative since the Diefenbaker sweep of 1958. The Conservative vote was halved, as was the Liberal vote. The NDP vote dropped to less than one-third of its 1988 total. Reform interpreted the Beaver River by-election victory as an indication that, with the free trade issue out of the way, continued hostility towards the Conservatives presented the new party with significant opportunities to gain ground in Alberta.

The party's other important 1989 electoral victory came when Stan Waters won the Alberta Senatorial Selection Election held in conjunction with Alberta's municipal elections that fall.[58] The Senate election campaign presented the party with an opportunity to expand its electoral machinery by contesting a campaign on a scale much larger than it had in any single federal constituency. In coordinating the Alberta-wide campaign, the national party office also had the opportunity to expand its administrative and professional staff. Because the Senate election was a provincial affair, Reform would have to establish a provincial wing in Alberta to contest the election. The executive council struck a Senate Election Committee and canvassed the twenty-six Alberta branches of the federal party for direction on whether it should enter the provincial fray and on how to proceed if it should. Members responded by encouraging Reform to participate, but under the understanding that it would only engage in the Senate election and not contest provincial elections. A nomination meeting was scheduled for late August at Red Deer. Each Alberta branch was entitled to send ten voting delegates to the meeting and to suggest candidates. A measure of Reform's growing organizational strength in Alberta came when all but a handful of constituency associations sent the maximum number of delegates allowed. In a fiery nomination speech, Waters, a former commander in the Canadian military, delivered a galvanizing critique of federal spending. When he announced that his goal would be to "carve into the hearts of every Ottawa politician the words Cut Spending," many of the delegates could be seen already marking their ballots even though all the other candidates had not yet spoken. Waters handily won the nomination on the first ballot.[59]

Table 2.3 · Results of the 1989 Alberta Senate Election (% of vote)

	Calgary	Edmonton	Other Urban	Rural	Totals
Stan Waters (Reform)	47	31	42	53	41.5
Bill Code (Liberal)	20	34	28	19	22.5
Bert Brown (PC)	19	14	30	28	20.5

Other candidates captured 14% in Calgary, 21% in Edmonton and 15.5% of the total vote.

Reform was the first to nominate a candidate and was at least as active in its campaign efforts as were the other parties. The party's budget exceeded $250,000, with over $80,000 earmarked for television advertising. A strategic planning committee consisting of executive council chairman Diane Ablonczy, Jim Denis and Manning met regularly to guide the overall direction of the campaign. Manning also campaigned actively for Waters but typically not in the same place at the same time so as to maximize exposure. Waters' tour revolved around the all-candidate forums that were held throughout the province. Party volunteers distributed over a 250,000 pieces of literature that presented the party as the only legitimate western alternative to the Conservatives.

Unlike the 1988 general election, increasing voter unrest over Meech Lake and the proposed Goods and Services Tax provided Reform with ample opportunity to distinguish itself from the other parties. Despite a rather lacklustre start, the Senate election campaign picked up momentum and by the time the election was held, over 40 per cent of Albertans cast ballots. Waters won the election with over 250,000 votes. He collected more than half of all rural votes and close to half of the Calgary vote. He also won all but two other urban centres and finished a close second to the Liberal candidate in Edmonton. The party's strength in Calgary and other urban areas represented the most significant gains for the party over the 1988 federal election results and demonstrated that the party's strength was more broadly based, and less rural than most pundits had anticipated.

The Senate Selection Election victory established Reform as a significant player in Alberta electoral politics. Often disregarded altogether or dismissed as a mere footnote to history, the Senate Election victory did more to lend credibility to the young party than any event prior to the

1993 federal election. The party not only proved that its organization was capable of contesting elections on a scale comparable to the established parties, but that it could also deliver the votes. From this point onward, Reform became the voice of dissenting right-of-centre opinion in Alberta. Public recognition of its new role in Alberta politics helped raise the party's profile throughout western Canada. Membership exploded with as many as a thousand members a month being recruited into the fledgling organization. Party coffers swelled at both the branch and national levels. The media began to take a much greater interest, as did the traditional parties, especially the federal Conservatives, whose attacks on Reform grew in frequency and ferocity. Clearly, by the end of 1989, Reform had begun to change the partisan landscape in Alberta, and was setting its sights on the rest of western Canada.

Conclusion

The early history of Reform indicates that its founding was a response to the specific set of cultural and political circumstances that existed in western Canada during the late 1980s, but also have deep roots within the Canadian prairie political culture. Its founding principles and early electoral strategies embodied these values and continued to anchor the party's policies and rhetoric for most of its existence. Although its constitution formally acknowledged the membership, meeting in assembly, as the supreme governing body in the party, there is little doubt that Manning and his vision dominated the early stages of Reform's development. As an extra-parliamentary, mass-based, populist political party, Reform's organizational structure was highly centralized. Yet the electoral contests of 1988 proved to be turning points in the young party's development. Before the central organization could be fully established, intense branch activity forged a sense of autonomy amongst local activists, leaving them with the expectation that they would be fully integrated into the party's decision-making process. Immediately after the senate election victory, Reformers would meet in Edmonton for the party's 1989 policy assembly. The Edmonton gathering was the first to include full participation by delegates elected almost exclusively from the branches. The constituency associations also participated in the policy process for the first time by submitting, reviewing and amending resolutions prior to the assembly. This convention represented the first stage in a gradual process whereby members began to exercise their practical influence in the party, often at the expense of the leadership's influence or in opposition to the leadership's desired outcomes. From this point on, Reform would no longer be solely a party made in its leader's image and according to his vision. Manning and his closest advisors would continue to play leading roles in policy development and strategic expansion, but they would never again be able to do so at will or without the eventual approval from party members.

3

The Maturing Membership – The 1989 Assembly

Reform couched its anti-political-establishment message in populist rhetoric. Portraying itself as a party that would represent the interests of average voters, it pitted *the people* against an unrepresentative political elite, and itself against the traditional parties staffed with Ottawa insiders and political professionals. Throughout 1989 and 1990 it cast itself as an outsider, chastising the traditional parties over Meech Lake and singling out the Conservatives for abandoning the West by adopting the Liberals' centralist agenda. It argued that the solutions to the constitutional impasse could be found in greater citizen participation in a decentralized, less interventionist federal government. It assured its newly mobilized activists that not only would the party advocate increased citizen participation in the larger political system, but that it would also provide its members with greater opportunities to participate in the governing processes of their own party.[1] Nevertheless, as is typically the case with new parties that are created from outside of legislatures, the leadership controlled the agenda and the organization. As electoral opportunities quickly presented themselves, however, Reform was forced to rely heavily on its newly created branches to carry a large burden of the responsibilities prior to the party fully establishing its organization at the centre. Branch activists gained a sense of autonomy that they insisted on maintaining once the 1988 election had passed and the leadership began to reassert its control over the policy and strategic agendas. Further complicating the situation were the opinions and attitudes of the activists who comprised the executive caucuses of the branch organizations. Most believed the party's populist rhetoric and expected the party to actualize it internally. The leadership quickly learned that Reform had mobilized individuals who were adamant that their participation would extend beyond merely having a plebiscitary check on the leadership. Moreover, having gained considerable experience in establishing and running their own local organizations, branch activists were ready and willing to explore the limits of their constitutional powers within the larger party organization. In a sense, they were intent on testing their own party's ability to live up to its rhetoric. The party's assemblies would become the arena in which these battles were most often fought.

The 1989 Reform Party Assembly held in Edmonton just after the Alberta senate election presented party activists with their first opportunity to directly impact the party's strategic and policy agendas. Prior to 1989, branch activists confined their participation largely to local endeavours, mostly due to their small numbers and limited resources. By 1989, however, all of the Alberta branches and most in BC were fully functioning political organizations with established local caucuses ready to expand their participation into policy development and strategic planning. For the most part, they succeeded. Although the leadership would continue to dominate both areas for some time to come, the Edmonton Assembly delegates demonstrated that Manning would now have to secure approval from the members prior to implementing major policy or organizational initiatives. He learned of these new developments in dramatic fashion when delegates rejected his entire package of amendments to the party constitution and regularly challenged his carefully crafted policy and strategic plans.

PROFILES OF CANADIAN POLITICAL PARTIES AT CONVENTION

Each of Canada's federal parties took a different approach in awarding convention delegate credentials in the period of Reform's founding. Although constituency associations remained the essential building blocks of convention representation, most parties adjusted the proportion of constituency representatives to provide greater representation from other socio-demographic groups. For example, both the Liberal and Conservative parties awarded delegate credentials equally across all constituencies in the country, regardless of the strength of the branch organization. Both parties also made provision for the representation of women and youth groups, as well as allowing for large numbers of ex officio delegates such as members of parliamentary caucuses, provincial party officials, and others.[2] As a result of these provisions, delegates from constituency associations comprised only 54 per cent of the 1983 and 73 per cent of 1993 Conservative convention delegates, and 55 per cent of the 1984 and 68 per cent of the 1990 Liberal convention delegates.[3]

The New Democratic Party shared some features with the Liberals and Conservatives, but also differed in several important respects. NDP conventions tended to attract their largest number of delegates from constituency associations (72.0 per cent in 1981, 64.7 per cent in 1987 and 68.6 per cent in 1989),[4] but the NDP awarded delegates to constituencies based on the number of registered members in each branch.[5] Consequently, a strong regional imbalance existed at NDP conventions with disproportionately large numbers of delegates from Ontario and the West (particularly Saskatchewan and British Columbia), and correspondingly small numbers from Quebec and the Atlantic provinces.[6] The NDP also provided delegate status to affiliated union organizations on the basis of one delegate for each thousand members. In addition, some central labour organizations received delegate credentials. In total, union delegates typically comprised about one-fifth to one-quarter of all delegates.[7] The remaining categories of NDP delegates (federal council, caucus and youth) usually comprised between 8 per cent and 12 per cent of the total.

Reform's allocation of delegate credentials reflected its anti-special interest orientation. Having only three categories of voting delegates at the 1989 Reform Assembly – delegates elected at the branch level, sitting members of the House of Commons, and executive councillors – by far the largest number came from delegates elected from the branch constituency associations.[8] The party allocated one delegate for each forty members in a recognized constituency association up to a total of 240 members, and one delegate for each additional hundred members or major fraction thereof. In 1989, delegates had to be party members for not less than forty-five days prior to the announcement of the assembly. Executive Council members and sitting party members of the House of

Commons were each allocated one position. The party had no provision for increasing the representation of women, youth or other identifiable groups through ancillary organizations, campus clubs or quotas at the branch level.[9]

Historically, political elites have come disproportionately from high socio-economic status groups, with higher than average levels of income and education, from relatively prestigious occupational groups, and were more likely to be middle-aged and male.[10] Studies from the 1980s and 1990s indicated that while some of these patterns persisted, there were also important changes within the parties as they tried to ensure that activists, and other key party representatives, had characteristics that more accurately reflected those whom they purported to represent. The Liberals, Conservatives and New Democrats all attempted to increase the representation of women at their conventions. The Conservatives and Liberals each required that women comprise at least one-third of the constituency delegates attending their 1983 and 1984 leadership conventions. By 1990, the Liberal party required gender equality among delegates from constituency associations and youth clubs. As a result, the percentage of women attending Liberal conventions increased from 18 per cent in 1968, to 40 per cent in 1984, and 45 per cent in 1990. Similarly, the percentage of female delegates at Conservative conventions increased from 19 per cent in 1967, to 37 per cent in 1983, and 34 per cent in 1993.[11]

Perhaps surprisingly, the NDP did not move toward gender equality any more rapidly than the Conservatives, and lagged behind the Liberals. Although the NDP required gender equality in a number of key party positions, such as between the party president and associate president, among the eight vice-presidents, and among the members of federal council chosen by convention,[12] it did not require gender equality among either the constituency delegates or the union delegates until its 1995 convention. Although there had been some effort to increase the number of women chosen by constituency associations, that progress was not matched by union delegates where men continued to outnumber women by a ratio of 85 per cent to 15 per cent.[13] The overall percentage of women at NDP conventions increased from 26.1 per cent in 1971, to 30.9 per cent in 1983, and 36.8 per cent in 1989.[14] In contrast, Reform made no formal efforts to balance gender representation. As the data in Table 3.1 indicate, men outnumbered women at its 1989 convention, but only marginally more so than at NDP or Conservative conventions during the same period.

Table 3.1 · Selected Socio-demographic Characteristics of Convention Delegates

	NDP (1989)	Liberal (1990)	PC (1993)	Reform (1989)
Gender				
Male	63.4	55.0	66.0	68.3
Female	36.6	45.0	34.0	31.7
Age				
21 and under	3.5			1.6
22–29	9.9	35.0[a]	32.0[a]	4.0
30–39	31.4	15.0	14.0	12.6
40–49	23.6	20.0	24.0	17.1
50–59	12.9	16.0	19.0	23.3
60 and over	18.6	14.0	12.0	41.5
Education				
Secondary or less	20.1	27.3	22.8	26.1
Some post-secondary	27.1	30.9	26.7	21.9
Complete post-secondary	52.9	41.8	50.5	52.0

a. Youth delegates = under 30 years of age.

Sources: Archer and Whitehorn, *Political Activists*; Perlin, "Attitudes of Liberal Convention Delegates"; and Courtney, *Do Conventions Matter?*

Party activists also tended to be disproportionately middle-aged.[15] The Liberals and Conservatives moved to counteract this trend in the 1980s by greatly expanding the opportunities for young people to participate through campus clubs and youth organizations. As a result, the percentage of delegates under thirty years of age increased at Conservative conventions from 20 per cent in 1967 to 40 per cent in 1983 and 32 per cent in 1993. At Liberal conventions, the percentage of delegates younger than thirty increased from 20 per cent in 1968 to 36 per cent in 1990.[16] Such overrepresentation of youth activists led George Perlin to consider whether or not the traditional parties were in danger of coming under the dominance of their youth wings. Neither the New Democrats nor Reform faced such a dilemma.

Given the tendency of activists to be somewhat unrepresentative of the population at large, and Reform's unwillingness to alter this pattern by

Table 3.2[17] · Selected Socio-demographic Characteristics of Reform Party Assemblies & the General Membership (1989–1993)

	1989 Assembly	1991 Membership	1992 Assembly	1993 Membership
Gender				
Male	68.3	66.9	71.1	70.3
Female	31.7	33.1	28.9	29.7
Age				
21 and under	1.6		1.2	
22–29	4.0	6.9 *(<35)*	3.6	5.0 *(<30)*
30–39	12.6		12.8	12.1
40–49	17.1	27.7 *(35–49)*	21.5	17.7
50–59	23.3	31.8 *(50–64)*	23.3	18.4
60 and over	41.5	33.6 *(>65)*	37.8	46.8
Education				
Grade School	7.1	21.3	2.0	21.6
High School	19.0	30.1	25.4	20.5
Some post-secondary	21.9	17.6	29.0	16.1
College Graduate	12.1		9.2	20.3
University Graduate	19.5	31.0 *(All Univ.)*	18.6	21.6 *(All Univ.)*
Multiple Degrees	20.4		15.8	
Income				
$10–$20,000	9.4	-	3.5	13.6
$20–$30,000	11.7	-	8.3	31.6 *(20–39)*
$30–$40,000	18.3	-	10.2	
$40–$50,000	18.3	-	12.5	27.0 *(40–59)*
$50–$80,000	24.8	-	31.0	13.6 *(60–80)*
$80,000 or more	17.5	-	34.5	14.1

way of quotas or special delegate status, we would expect its assembly delegates' demographic profile to also be unrepresentative of the electorate. However, because Reform recruited all but a handful of delegates from its branches, we would also expect its delegate profile to more closely reflect the party membership's demographic base. The data in Table 3.2 indicate that this was indeed the case. In 1989, Reform drew the majority of its delegates from the middle-aged and senior groups with close to two-thirds (64.8 per cent) being fifty years of age or older. This compares to 65.4 per cent for the larger membership (1991). Two in five delegates were sixty years of age or older. There was also no significant gender gap between those attending assemblies and the general membership.

Approximately one-third (31.7 per cent) of the delegates to the 1989 Assembly were women while women accounted for 33.1 per cent of the general members in 1991. Female representation dropped slightly at the 1992 Assembly to 28.9 per cent but was matched by a corresponding drop in 1993 female general member representation (29.7 per cent). Nor were there significant age differences between delegates and members. For example, 12.6 per cent of the delegates attending the 1989 Assembly were between the ages of thirty and thirty-nine years old while that age group comprised 12.8 per cent of the 1992 Assembly delegates and 12.1 per cent of the 1993 membership. Delegates were somewhat better educated than the average member and had a slightly higher average income. Both of these slight differences were to be expected given that education and income are positively correlated and delegates had to pay all costs associated with attending assemblies, including a $200 to $300 registration fee. Overall, the evidence indicates that Reform Assemblies were highly representative of the party's general membership, if not the electorate at large.

1989 Reform Party Assembly

The policy development and delegate selection processes for Reform's first full-fledged policy convention began in early 1989 when the party's executive council set the assembly date and requested input from members, branches, and the party's task forces. The Reform national office supplied background papers and memos on the "primary subjects of discussion" while staff compiled and resubmitted all resolutions back to the branches and delegates who had pre-registered for the assembly. Each branch then had the opportunity to hold a meeting to review the draft resolutions and vote on them prior to sending their delegates to Edmonton.

Table 3.3 · Registration at the 1989 Reform Assembly

Province	Observers	Delegates at Large[18]	Voting Delegates	Other Delegates	Totals	%
BC	47	41	141	2	231	25.7
Alberta	184	146	239	3	572	63.6
Saskatchewan	11	6	16		33	3.7
Manitoba	9	3	43		55	6.1
Outside West	7	1			8	0.9
Totals	**258**	**197**	**439**	**5**	**899**	

Source: Reform Party of Canada.[19]

Table 3.4 · 1989 Assembly Breakdown of Delegates and Respondents by Province

Province	Total Delegates[20]	Percentage	# of Respondents	Percentage
BC	184	28.7	111	23.1
Alberta	388	60.5	303	63.0
Saskatchewan	22	3.4	17	3.5
Manitoba	46	7.2	30	6.2
Not Identified	1	0.2	20	4.2
Totals	641		481	

Assembly registration reflected the areas in which the party was best organized after its first two years of operation. As Table 3.3 indicates, Albertans dominated the assembly, accounting for nearly two-thirds (63.6 per cent) of the total. British Columbia accounted for one-quarter of all delegates (25.7 per cent) while the prairies east of Alberta accounted for most of the remainder. The data in Table 3.4 demonstrate that the sample of delegates who returned questionnaires accurately reflected the breakdown of delegate registration by province of residence, and as was demonstrated above, was demographically representative of the party's social base at that time.

Activists were predominantly older, well-educated males employed in a wide variety of occupations. The most numerous group were professionals, accounting for almost one-third of all delegates (31.7 per cent). Close to a quarter (23.1 per cent) of all delegates indicated they were retired, while 11.9 per cent stated they worked in white-collar jobs. Agriculture accounted for only 9 per cent of delegate employment and 5.1 per cent stated they were homemakers. Only 2 per cent stated they were students. Education levels were consistent with the high levels measured in other parties. Over half of the delegates had completed at least one post-secondary program. A further 21.9 per cent had attended a post-secondary institution and 19 per cent had completed high school but not attended post-secondary studies.

When asked about their previous political activities, close to two-thirds (63.5 per cent) stated they had been members of another federal political party prior to joining Reform.[21] Of these, 78.1 per cent had been members of the federal Progressive Conservative party with less than 5 per cent coming from any other party. Two in five delegates were members of a provincial party with most of those Progressive Conservatives or Social Credit members (51 per cent and 25 per cent respectively).

Attitudinally, delegates demonstrated opinions that were consistent with the party's founding principles. They also indicated strong support for Manning, although they tended to be more ideologically charged than his admonishments indicated he would have preferred. Manning frequently lectured members and supporters that the old left-wing and right-wing labels no longer applied to the reality of Canadian politics and that they should therefore not attach them to the party or themselves.[22] Nevertheless, when asked to use a seven-point ideological continuum[23] to rank themselves, their party and other parties,[24] the vast majority of respondents (96 per cent) made use of the scales. As demonstrated in Table 3.5, delegates

Table 3.6 · 1989 Assembly: Ideology by Province

	British Columbia		Alberta		Saskatchewan/ Manitoba	
	Mean	Standard Deviation	Mean	Standard Deviation	Mean	Standard Deviation
Self	5.09	0.89	5.10	0.96	4.91	0.92
Reform Party	5.03	0.78	5.12	0.75	5.07	0.80
People in Province**	4.12	1.17	4.61	0.93	3.72	1.28
Provincial PC[a]	5.09	1.04	4.21	1.14	4.53	1.08
Most Canadians**	3.93	0.89	3.63	0.90	3.95	1.12
Federal PC*	3.63	1.43	3.43	1.29	4.05	1.52
Provincial Liberals	3.22	1.22	3.24	1.06	3.44	0.85
Federal Liberals	2.77	1.09	2.57	1.11	2.63	1.22
Provincial NDP**	2.34	1.36	1.85	0.91	1.95	0.99
Federal NDP*	2.06	1.05	1.77	0.94	1.79	1.30

Range = 1 (left) to 7 (right).
* $p < .05$
** $p < .01$
a. Provincial Social Credit Party in BC.

Table 3.7 · 1989 Assembly: Influence Hierarchy

	Mean	Standard Deviation
Federal Cabinet	5.9	1.36
Media	5.1	1.31
Banks	4.6	1.43
Lobby Groups	4.6	1.34
Unions	4.1	1.26
Leader of the Opposition	2.6	1.31
Senate	2.2	1.43
Opposition MPs	2.1	1.17
Other Opposition Parties	2.1	1.18
Government Backbenchers	1.9	1.22
Average Canadian Voter	1.7	1.07
Average Western Voter	1.3	0.71

Range = 1 (very little influence) to 7 (a great amount of influence).

assigned themselves and their party scores of 5.08 and 5.09 respectively, indicating a right-of-centre ideological bent, but not excessively right wing. They placed the people in their provinces and most Canadians near the centre of the continuum with their provincial electorates slightly to the right of centre, and most Canadians slightly to the left. They placed all three established federal parties, including the governing Conservatives, on the left of the continuum and to the left of the average Canadian. The placement of the federal Conservatives is most interesting and indicates that delegates supported the proposition that the Conservatives had moved into the Liberals' centrist, or in Reformers minds, centre-left issue space. Consistent with commonly held beliefs about party ideology, they placed the NDP furthest to the left, with the Liberals closer to the centre but still clearly on the left. They viewed the Conservatives as ideologically closest to the average Canadian, but Reform and themselves closest to the people in their province.

Provincial breakdowns contained in Table 3.6 indicate that there was considerable ideological consistency among delegates from the different western provinces and few differences in their perceptions of themselves or Reform. Where differences occurred, they were slight and predictable. Albertans viewed the people in their province as the furthest to the right (4.61) while BC delegates viewed people in their province as close to the ideological centre (4.12), but still slightly right of the average Canadian. Albertans were the only delegates to view their provincial Conservative party to the left of the average citizen in their province, and generally ranked the federal parties further to the left than did delegates from outside Alberta.[25] Thus, despite being cautioned against using right-left ideological labels by a leader delegates genuinely supported, the vast majority of 1989 Reform Assembly delegates were willing to make use of the scales and placed themselves and others in an expected order.

One of the enduring features of Reform's anti-political-establishment populism was the belief amongst its members that the average citizen had little or no influence on policy matters once a majority federal government was elected. This sentiment was embodied in Reform's statement of principles and developed further in many of its proposals for referenda, MP accountability and citizen initiative.[26] At the conceptual level, these attitudes compromised an overall anti-elitism that manifested itself in a belief that average citizens, the voters, were at the bottom of the political power hierarchy, while politicians and organized special interests were closer to

TABLE 3.8 · 1989 Assembly: Issue Positioning

	Strongly Agree	Agree	Disagree	Strongly Disagree
ECONOMY				
Gov't intervention in economy increasingly a major problem	76.6	19.6	1.3	2.5
Interest rate policy designed to benefit centre	70.9	23.4	3.6	2.1
GST justified	3.0	5.3	19.8	71.9
SOCIAL POLICY				
Abandon universality	41.0	43.0	9.2	6.8
Increase multiculturalism	2.8	5.2	23.6	68.5
Assimilate immigrants	60.6	34.4	3.9	1.1
Get tough with polluters	68.8	30.1	0.9	0.2
Ensure environment even at expense of living standard	42.0	47.0	9.3	1.7
FEDERALISM				
Provinces maintain control over natural resources	44.3	46.1	8.4	1.1
Federal government responsible for social program standards	8.9	55.6	26.3	9.2
Reform should contest provincial elections	9.1	13.4	36.6	40.9

the top. Table 3.7 indicates where 1989 Assembly delegates placed a number of groups when asked to rank their influence over government policy.

As expected, delegates correctly placed the federal cabinet alone at the top of the influence hierarchy (5.9) and a considerable distance from the next most influential groups. A second level of the influence hierarchy included the media (5.1) and other organized, extra-parliamentary groups such as the banks (4.6), lobby groups (4.6) and unions (4.1). A third level of the hierarchy formed a considerable distance from the previous level and included formal groups within parliament. The leader of the opposition led this group at 2.6, noticeably lower than any of the extra-parliamentary groups. The Senate, government backbenchers, opposition MPs and parties all hovered around the 2 range, very low on the scale. Delegates felt that the average Canadian voter (1.7) had very little influence and that western voters (1.3) had the least influence of all. This perceived influence hierarchy clearly indicated delegates' anti-political-establishment sentiments and their support for Reform's early populist rhetoric.

Delegates were also asked a series of questions relating to Reform's key policy positions. The data in Table 3.8 indicate that the vast majority of delegates supported the party's western, right-of-centre, anti-political-establishment agenda. Reform activists were almost universally united in their agreement (96.2 per cent) that government intervention in the economy through high levels of spending and regulation is increasingly a major problem. Similarly, 94.3 per cent believed that the federal government's interest rate policy was designed to benefit the central Canadian economy without regard for the economic interests of other regions. A similar proportion (91.7 per cent) disagreed with the proposed 9 per cent Goods and Services Tax.[27] They opposed proposals for furthering multiculturalism (92.1 per cent) and the vast majority agreed that immigrants should assimilate into the Canadian mainstream (95 per cent). Interestingly, delegates also overwhelmingly supported a tougher stand against environmental polluters (98.9 per cent), even if that meant a lower standard of living (89 per cent), positions not normally associated with the right.

When asked about the future direction of their party, over three-quarters disagreed with entering provincial politics (77.5 per cent). Interestingly, despite supporting decentralization in some areas, 1989 Reform delegates did not envision a complete gutting of the federal government. Nearly two-thirds agreed (64.5 per cent) that the federal government has the responsibility to ensure national standards for some social programs even if that means infringing on provincial autonomy. But they also demonstrated where they would draw the line. More than 90 per cent stated that the provinces must maintain control over natural resources even if that conflicted with national interests as defined by the federal government. Delegates were also united in their opposition to federal language policy[28] and the Meech Lake constitutional accord (Table 3.9).[29] The vast majority of delegates (83.4 per cent) agreed that Meech should be completely rejected. None of the delegates thought that the accord should be ratified in its present form while 5.4 per cent would have accepted it with certain amendments. A further 11.1 per cent would have accepted it if the accord contained a parallel Triple-E Senate amendment. Delegates demonstrated similar hostility to federal language policy with 82.7 per cent believing the federal government should abandon its bilingualism policies

Table 3.9 · 1989 Assembly: Opinion of Selected Policy Options

	Percentage Agreeing
Federal government language policy should:	
Be accelerated	0.0
Continue in its present form	0.2
Be limited to federal government services only	17.1
Be abandoned	82.7
The Meech Lake constitutional accord should be:	
Ratified as is	0.0
Ratified with amendments	5.4
Ratified only with parallel Triple-E-Senate amendment	11.1
Completely rejected	83.4
Should Quebec:	
Be granted special status within Confederation	0.5
Receive some constitutional recognition of uniqueness	13.0
Accept the 1982 constitution	58.0
Leave Confederation	28.5
Preferential treatment for immigrants:	
Accept only those who can make strong contribution	34.2
Some preferential treatment	39.1
Limited preferential treatment	20.9
Accept all equally without qualifications	5.8
Responsibility for immigration policy should reside with:	
The federal Government alone	31.2
Primarily federal with some provincial input	55.8
Primarily provincial with some federal input	11.2
The provincial governments alone	1.8
Responsibility for environmental policy:	
The federal government alone	2.7
Primarily federal with some provincial input	52.9
Primarily provincial with some federal input	41.9
The provincial governments alone	2.5
Federal economic policy should be designed to:	
Attract as much foreign investment as possible	12.4
Have some procedure for screening foreign investment	53.6
Restrict foreign investment in key sectors	27.3
Place strict limitations on foreign investment	6.7

altogether and another 17.1 per cent believing bilingualism should be limited to federal government services.

Their opinions were less united on some constitutional issues, but still consistent with Reform's policy positions. Very few delegates were willing to grant Quebec special status within Confederation but 13 per cent thought Quebec should get some form of constitutional recognition of its differences. The majority of delegates (58 per cent) thought that Quebec should accept the 1982 Constitution. Over one-quarter (28.5 per cent) stated that Quebec should simply leave Confederation. These opinions, when combined with the near universal opposition to Meech Lake, indicated how Reform would position itself in the continuing constitutional debates and from which sector of the electorate the party would draw much of its support, at least until after the 1992 Charlottetown referendum. This tactic was instrumental in helping Reform solidify support amongst those with the greatest animosity to Quebec and in establishing the party as a representative vehicle for western interests. The policy outcomes, however, resulted in the party quickly being labelled as hostile to Quebec, an image that would hamper Reform later as it attempted to transform itself into a national party. Be that as it may, any attempt at softening the party's Quebec position, as was demonstrated later during the Charlottetown referendum, would be met with strong resistance from rank-and-file members.

Delegates' opinions were also consistent with their party's immigration policy. At the time, Reform policy linked immigration to overall economic policy. It stated that "immigration should be essentially economic in nature" and "genuine refugees should be welcomed" but that "immigration policy should not be used to solve the crisis of the welfare state" and "immigration policy must be more sensitive to public opinion."[30] Most delegates adhered to some interpretation of those policies with one-third (34.2 per cent) stating that Canada should accept only those immigrants who can make a strong contribution to the country. Close to two in five (39.1 per cent) stated that some preferential treatment should be given while another 20.9 per cent thought there should be only limited preferential treatment. Only 5.8 per cent stated that they thought Canada should accept all immigrants equally without qualifications. Delegates also wanted the federal government to continue to play the leading role in Canada's immigration policy. Close to one-third (31.2 per cent) thought that the federal government should have complete control over immigration policy. The majority (55.8 per cent) thought that the federal government should take the lead

Table 3.10 · 1989 Assembly: Policy Options to Reduce the Federal Deficit

	Mean	Standard Deviation
Reduce size of government administration	1.7	1.1
Reduce special interest grants	2.6	1.3
Privatize crown corporations	3.3	1.4
Reduce spending on social programs	4.0	1.8
Contract out services	4.8	1.4
Increase corporate taxes	5.5	1.8
Other/Specific	6.0	2.7
Increase personal taxes	7.0	1.4
The GST	7.6	1.7

Range = 1 (most important) to 9 (least important).

on immigration, but allow for some provincial government input. These data further reinforce the proposition that Reformers envisioned a continuing role for the federal government in certain areas of national public policy. Only 11.2 per cent thought that the provinces should be primarily responsible for immigration and even fewer still (1.8 per cent) thought that immigration should be exclusively a provincial responsibility.

Results were mixed when delegates were asked about environmental policy jurisdiction. The vast majority of delegates wanted both levels of government involved, with 52.9 per cent stating that the federal government should take the lead and 41.9 per cent believing the provinces should have primary control. A majority of delegates (53.6 per cent) wanted the federal government to have some procedure for screening foreign investment and a further 27.3 per cent wanted restrictions in key economic sectors.

Delegates were also asked to rank order their preferences for reducing the federal deficit. The data in Table 3.10 indicate that early Reform activists believed reductions in the size and scope of government activities was the best way to reduce the federal deficit. They would have started by paring the size of the federal bureaucracy, moved on to privatizing crown corporations, and then to cutting social programs. Delegates' anti-elitism was observed when they singled out grants to special interest groups as the second most important area in which to cut. Many Reform activists perceived these programs not only as costly and inefficient, but also as symbols of government-sponsored special interests that furthered a deepening citizen-elite cleavage. Delegates were least willing to see their individual tax burdens increase through higher personal taxes or the GST. They were so opposed to higher taxes that they offered a host of their own suggestions as preferable to tax increases.

Overall, responses indicated that Reform activists had been recruited primarily away from the federal Conservatives, tended to be middle class, predominantly male, and older. They considered themselves to be right of centre and demonstrated attitudes hostile to Quebec's constitutional agenda. They tended to support less government, provincial resource autonomy, and parliamentary reform, but also envisioned a role for the federal government in many areas of national concern. Delegates brought these and other opinions them as they began considering how to amend and expand the party's policy Blue Book and its constitution.

Revising the Party Constitution

Delegates debated over 150 resolutions at the 1989 Assembly, including strategic resolutions on expanding the party nationally and the possibility of entering provincial politics. The provincial drive came mainly from some Alberta members. Buoyed by their recent Senate election success and disenchanted with their provincial Progressive Conservative government under the leadership of Premier Don Getty, some reasoned that a new provincial Reform party could supplant the Alberta Conservatives in the same manner the federal party planned to displace the national Conservatives. However, many Alberta members were also provincial Conservatives and opposed Reform's foray onto their turf. They argued that the Alberta Conservatives could be revitalized with a leadership change and that there was less need for a new party in this arena. Reform's leadership, including Manning, continued to publicly state that they would not help build, finance or lead a new provincial party in Alberta or anywhere else. They argued that a new provincial role for Reform would unnecessarily tax the limited resources of the young federal party and that the party faithful ought to first concentrate their efforts on building a successful national party.[31] Delegates voted on a range of proposals including defeating a no-expansion resolution and passing several others that called for an ongoing review of all expansion proposals. While not explicitly rejecting provincial involvement for all time, delegates sent the matter to committee for further study and to be debated again at a future assembly.

They established a permanent committee to deal with all expansion issues under the mandate of Reform becoming a national party.[32]

After temporarily settling the expansion debate, delegates began testing the limits of their formal powers by derailing a major leadership-sponsored reworking of the party constitution. Led primarily by BC delegates, many still upset over the Collins affair and subsequent executive council decisions, delegates appeared determined to carefully scrutinize all the proposed constitutional changes and keep as much power as possible in the hands of activists at the branch level. A rift between the national office and some prominent BC branch directors had been simmering since Manning rejected Collins's nomination, and was growing wider as time passed. As membership grew and party activities expanded, tension also built up between many early branch activists, who were determined to remain in control of the organizations they built, and the leadership that was equally determined to present a cohesive and moderate public image. A key component of the tension centred on how the executive council, determined to keep dissidents from embarrassing the party, would exercise its discretionary power to expel or silence troublemakers.[33]

The leadership presented delegates with a redrafted party constitution that sought to address both the national party's concerns while still providing constituency associations with an appeal procedure if the leader rejected a duly nominated local candidate. While many of the amendments were of a housekeeping nature, debate focused on those that would have allowed executive council interference in what delegates perceived to be exclusive constituency association matters. Led by the dissident BC group who presented the assembly with their own version of an alternative constitution, delegates defeated a leadership-sponsored proposal to give the executive council "absolute discretion" to intervene in any nomination and nullify the nomination of any candidate if it felt doing so would be in the "best interests of the party." However, delegates also defeated a proposal that would have given the branches complete control over candidate nominations. Instead they opted for a balanced approach that allowed for branch predominance but also for some executive council input in extreme circumstances. Delegates continued to test the limits of their powers by rejecting all of the leadership-sponsored methods for settling nomination disputes and sent that issue to committee for further study. They then focused their attention on defeating a series of amendments to Section 3 of the party constitution that they perceived would have further limited the authority of branch executives to manage their own affairs.

Section 3 of the Reform constitution established constituency associations and defined their responsibilities and relationship with the national party. The leadership proposed to add several sections, the most controversial dealt with what its task force on Grass-Roots/Leadership Relations called alleged irregularities at branch meetings that may lead to the adoption of radical policy proposals or unacceptable nominations for electoral candidates. The proposed amendment would have allowed executive council "in its discretion where it feels the overall best interests of the Party are involved, to intervene with respect to any decision and to nullify such decisions."[34] Allegations of irregularities could come from the executive council, from a group of at least twenty-five members in good standing from the branch, or from a majority of members of the executive committee of a neighbouring constituency association. Infractions would consist of "procedural irregularities or the take-over of a meeting by radical elements or non-Reform Party participants."[35] After arguing that these were unnecessary and overly intrusive restrictions on local autonomy, and that it centralized power unnecessarily in the hands of the party's leadership, the BC delegates were joined at the floor microphones by delegates from other provinces with similar concerns.

It quickly became evident that the leadership was in for a much tougher fight than it had anticipated and that it would have trouble garnering the two-thirds majority needed to pass its constitutional package. After lengthy discussion as to the admissibility of the BC delegate-sponsored alternative constitution, a motion was made to debate both drafts but make no final decision at this assembly because of possible irregularities in accepting or rejecting either. This motion was defeated and debate resumed. A second motion was proposed that would have limited debate to only the leadership-sponsored constitutional amendments. This led to another round of objections from the floor and no vote was recorded before the Chair decided to break for lunch and attempt to sort matters out before resuming for the afternoon session. Returning from consultations with organizers and the leadership, the Chair reconvened the meeting by presenting delegates with two options. They could proceed to consider, and pass or reject, the constitutional amendments as recommended by the leadership's constitutional committee, or leave the constitution as it was but review it and reconsider amendments at a later assembly. Debate on these options continued until a motion was made to proceed to pass or reject the leadership's proposed amendments. Further discussion ensued and before a vote could be called on that motion, another motion was allowed. It proposed that all internal constitutional matters be tabled and dealt with later. This motion was carried and the standoff ended with no changes being made to the party constitution.

Establishing Policy Precedents

With the constitutional wrangling out of the way, delegates set their sights on policy. Two precedent-setting policy resolutions were passed at the 1989 Assembly: the Abortion Resolution and the Quebec Resolution.[36] Delegates also debated and passed a series of other policy resolutions, but because of time limitations caused by the protracted constitutional debate, they were presented to the Chief Policy Officer and the party Policy Committee as general guidance rather than an official party policy. The Abortion Resolution and the Quebec Resolution, however, were singled out for special consideration. Each was debated and made part of the official policy platform.

The Abortion Resolution represented Reform's first formal attempt at providing a working definition of how its MPs would actualize Principles 13 and 14 of the party's 1987 founding Statement of Principles. The Abortion resolution followed the precedent established by Reform's only sitting parliamentarian, Alberta MP Deborah Grey, and would apply similarly to other moral issues that MPs would be asked to vote on once they arrived in Ottawa. The process would begin with the Reform candidate stating "clearly and publicly, her/his own personal views and moral beliefs on the issue," typically during the election campaign or while seeking the Reform nomination.[37] Once the issue came before Parliament, Reform MPs would invite public debate and seek a consensus within the constituency.[38] If a constituency consensus could be determined, the MP was obliged to faithfully vote that consensus. If no consensus existed, or was unclear, the MP could vote in accordance with his or her own publicly recorded position on the issue.[39]

The Abortion Resolution formed the foundation for Reform policy development, or more importantly, the lack of policy development on specific moral issues such as abortion, capital punishment and euthanasia. The approach allowed Manning to direct debate on these matters in two important ways. He could control radical elements within the party by arguing that any attempts to develop firm policy stances on these issues would be contrary to the spirit of the Abortion Resolution and would hamper MPs in their ability to faithfully represent their constituents, one of Reform's key populist planks. At the same time he could adhere to the principles of the resolution and declare his personal opinion on these issues. In doing so, his pronouncements were often interpreted as more than the opinions of just another candidate for office or individual MP. As party leader, his personal pronouncements were often interpreted to be party policy, as they most likely would have been if the leader of another federal party had made them. The strategy served Manning and the party well during its extra-parliamentary period and as a vote-gathering instrument in the West. It had less utility and appeal when applied in a parliamentary caucus setting after the party's 1993 breakthrough.

For most delegates the highlight of the 1989 Assembly undoubtedly was Manning's keynote address, "Leadership For Changing Times." Manning stuck with familiar themes in delivering the first half of his address (fiscal reform, democratic reform and populism) before unveiling what was to become the party's Quebec Resolution. The speech was startling in its candour and in Manning's ability to reasonably challenge Meech Lake era orthodoxy. In rejecting official biculturalism and effectively arguing, "the Pearson-Trudeau-Mulroney approach to constitutional development has produced a house divided against itself," he positioned Reform as the only federal party willing to openly oppose not only Meech Lake, but the entire Quebec-centred constitutional process. And he went further. Manning rejected as inherently flawed the conception of Canada as a federation built out of two founding races. On behalf of western Canadians he declared:

> First, we do not want to live, nor do we want our children to live, in a house divided against itself, particularly one divided along racial and linguistic lines. Second, we do not want nor do we intend to leave this house ourselves.... We will, however, insist that it cease to be divided. Third, either all Canadians, including the people of Quebec, make a clear commitment to Canada as one nation, or Quebec and the rest of Canada should explore whether there exists a better but more separate relationship between the two.[40]

He then said what had previously been unspeakable for a mainstream politician outside of Quebec. "In short, we say that living in one Canada united on certain principles, or living with a greater constitutional separation between Quebec and the rest of Canada, is preferable to living in a house divided."[41] Delegates later overwhelmingly endorsed Manning's hard-line approach and ushered in the first phase of the party's attempted transition from a regional party of western Canadians to a national party for all of English Canada.[42]

The dissent encountered during the protracted party constitution fight had been soothed by Manning's speech and the Quebec Resolution. Once again, he left delegates secure in the knowledge that they were not alone in their unorthodox opinions about the future of the country and that he and Reform would not shirk from their stated goals of representing that dissenting opinion.

Conclusion

Although the leadership of the Reform Party continued to play a prominent role in shaping and defining policy and strategic decisions, the 1989 Assembly demonstrated that activists would not be held without influence. Many analysts have correctly observed that Manning and the leadership often held and exercised considerable power within the party. But these interpretations often overlook the role of the membership in modifying the leadership's proposals and goals. Within Reform, there existed a healthy tension between the centralizing forces of leadership control and the decentralizing forces of branch activism and autonomy.

Opinion data from the 1989 Reform Assembly demonstrated that activists were opposed to the thrust of the Conservative government's economic and constitutional agendas, especially those that made concessions to the province of Quebec. They identified themselves as ideologically right of centre and ideologically distinct from the traditional parties, and much of the Canadian electorate. They supported increased democratic participation based on their perceptions of a citizen-elite cleavage within Canadian politics, and demonstrated that they would use their powers at assembly to fulfill their roles as representatives of the membership. For the first time they demonstrated to their own leadership that they expected their party to adhere to its populist principles while managing itself internally. Delegates also made it clear that they would continue to demand practical input into policy and strategy decisions as the party began its formal expansion outside the West.

4

Expanding Beyond the West – 1990 to 1992

Reform membership continued to grow throughout the Meech Lake period.[1] By mid-1990 the party was capitalizing on its strategy of filling the anti-Meech representational vacuum that was created when all three traditional parties scrambled to support the accord in Parliament. Reform's hard line against Quebec's distinct-society demands was paying huge dividends in the West with the party boasting over forty thousand members, although still concentrated primarily in Alberta and BC. Ready to embark on a national expansion plan that would require a fully functioning party administration at the centre and continued development of its policy platform, Reform had to also juggle the difficult provincial politics issue. These matters would dominate debate at the 1991 Assembly and prepare the ground for the first national test of the organization during the 1992 Charlottetown constitutional referendum. They would also test the limits of the membership's powers in relation to a leadership that was intent on increasing its authority in conjunction with its expansion drive.

Expansion: Setting the Stage

In early 1990, the party launched its task force on the Reform of Provincial Politics in Alberta.[2] Manning, while continuing to argue against entering provincial politics, used the task force's twelve-city Town Hall Meeting tour and a further six-week tour with Stan Waters to apply pressure to the Alberta government over its continued support of Meech Lake. They argued that the Alberta government's support for Meech betrayed Albertans' constitutional ambitions and pointed to the federal government's refusal to appoint Waters to the Senate as evidence.[3] The process garnered some media attention for the party in Alberta and would eventually result in sufficiently ambiguous feedback to allow Manning and the task force considerable latitude in drafting a policy position on provincial involvement. More importantly, because of the growing unrest in Alberta over the provincial government's record of fiscal management, Manning had the opportunity to promote and further develop Reform's fiscal policy.

Later that spring, Manning embarked on his first official tour outside the West. While in Ontario he maintained his unyielding opposition to the developing "crisis negotiations" by the first ministers as they tried to salvage Meech.[4] Bolstered by Reform's membership growth, he frequently exercised his authority to set interim policy. While not substantive in nature, many of the seemingly spontaneous policy pronouncements were aimed at drawing increasingly disgruntled central Canadian voters away from the other parties. They also indicated his intention to more forcefully pursue his vision of a more ideologically balanced party. In doing so, he angered many early Alberta and BC activists. Not only did it appear that the leadership was expanding the party into Ontario prior to officially being authorized to do so, an affront to the populist impulses of the members and a reversal of the gains members thought they had made at the Edmonton Assembly, but in preparation for expansion Manning had sent a letter to members advocating his desired change in Reform's ideological makeup. As we have seen, activists defined themselves as consistently right of centre and had demonstrated that they believed in the party's populist rhetoric. Manning's actions appeared to disregard both and repercussions would be felt at the next assembly. Nevertheless, the failure of the Meech Lake Accord, the nine-month delay in appointing Waters to the Senate,[5] and the continuing GST controversy provided Reform with ample opportunities to promote its founding policy positions. By October, membership had topped the fifty thousand mark and was growing at a rate of three thousand per month. The party began to register in national public opinion polls and by late 1990 it was capturing 8 per cent nationally, with 24 per cent support on the prairies and 20 per cent in BC.[6] Further, the party organized its first interim constituency associations in Ontario in preparation for the expansion debate to be held at the party's 1991 Saskatoon Assembly.[7]

The 1991 Reform Party Assembly

Delegates attending the 1991 Assembly addressed over sixty policy resolutions, debated and voted on party expansion, and addressed the internal constitutional issues tabled from the 1989 Assembly. Manning and Harper chaired most of the policy debate and intervened often when they felt delegates were straying too far from core principles. Harper opened the policy session with an articulate speech outlining the resolution-review process and the need for moderation and consistency in policy adoption.[8] The resolution-development process was similar to that which was first developed for the 1989 Assembly. The Policy Resolution Committee compiled all resolutions submitted by the party's policy committee, the branches, and individual members. At considerable risk to the reputation of the young party, the Policy Committee then sent unfiltered copies of the resolution packages to each constituency association for a final, often public, review.

The first policy resolution exposure draft contained nearly 166 resolutions. About one-third that number would make it to the Assembly floor. The policy committee worked diligently to point out that some of the early resolutions were poorly worded or completely inappropriate, especially several concerning immigration and multiculturalism. For example, the Lethbridge, Alberta branch submitted close to a dozen resolutions, one of which proposed that any immigrant charged with a criminal offence be deported, prior to having been convicted of the offence. When the resolution was initially proposed, several party members attending the Lethbridge meeting raised objections, but the meeting decided to submit all its resolutions and leave it up to the policy committee, and other branches, to weed out those they found inappropriate. However, the policy committee did not cull this resolution or any others that were submitted by any of the branches. Rather, it re-submitted all branch resolutions, and many of its own, back to the constituency associations in an exposure draft. Having received the immigration resolution in their exposure packages, along with the policy committee's unsupportive comments, the Lethbridge members voted against having their own resolution appear in the final package. Similar situations occurred in other constituencies and, in many instances, branches voluntarily withdrew their own resolutions. On the other hand, the policy committee warmly received another Lethbridge resolution dealing with popular ratification of constitutional changes. The resolution read as follows: "Resolved that the Constitution Act 1982 be amended to provide for the popular ratification of constitutional change. In addition to approval by the legislature, each province supporting a constitutional amendment would have to secure approval from its electorate by way of achieving a simple majority of votes cast during a popular and democratic referendum." The Policy committee's remarks stated: "The Lethbridge resolution is very well thought out and clears up an ambiguity in current Party Policy. Although the draft legal text provided may have minor deficiencies, this work is excellent." This resolution, with minor amendments from the assembly floor, was passed and incorporated into the Blue Book as official policy. Approximately two thousand party members in fifty-four branches participated in the ten-month policy development process[9] resulting in approximately one-half of the policy resolutions originating from, or being substantially formed by the constituency associations.

Given the extreme nature of some of the exposure draft resolutions, the 1991 Assembly opened with repeated, early appeals for moderation from party leaders who were backed up by delegates at the floor microphones. After some often heated debate, delegates tended to adopt the moderate course recommended by Harper as he skilfully chaired many early policy sessions. During an extended Saturday afternoon session, delegates voted to uphold Reform's opposition to comprehensive bilingualism and its opposition to most language laws at any level of government. They reaffirmed the party's existing policy opposing government financial support for multiculturalism and accepted a Manning-sponsored resolution supporting unconditional funding to the provinces for health care. The party's immigration policy was clarified with delegates supporting immigration based on Canada's economic needs without regard to race, creed or national origin. Further refinements to Reform's fiscal and economic policy were made with resolutions opposing tax concessions to private corporations and demanding that changes in the GST rate be subject to referenda. Delegates also passed resolutions calling for a national debt retirement fund, opposition to government subsidization of business, and support for increased competition. They called for the realignment of Canada's domestic economic policies, endorsed resolutions supporting environmental conservation and greater harmonization of federal and provincial environment regulatory powers. Resolutions on gun control were debated but tabled for future assemblies. Delegates placed the party on record as opposing government subsidization of energy mega-projects and discriminatory taxes and ownership regulations in the energy sector. Overall, the leadership and most delegates were pleased with the results of the policy sessions. However, the leadership's focus on moderation often left many policy resolutions without substance. As Manning later commented: "while the principles were sound, more work was obviously required on the details."[10]

One policy area that received detailed consideration was the tension between populist representation of constituents' interests and the political practicality of functioning as a party in a parliamentary system of government. With Manning acting as chair, delegates eventually passed resolutions that altered party policy on a future Reform caucus' use of free votes in Parliament. While maintaining support for the principle of general free votes in the House, until such votes became the norm, a Reform caucus would allow MPs a free and publicly recorded vote in caucus, but once a caucus decision was reached, in most instances all MPs would vote as a block. The only qualification to this position would be if MPs could clearly demonstrate that their constituents were opposed to a particular caucus position, in which case they would be allowed to vote in a manner that was consistent with the preferences of their constituents.[11]

Expansion and the Party Constitution

Undoubtedly, the most important decisions reached at the 1991 Assembly concerned expansion, both nationally and provincially, and the incorporation of these decisions into the party constitution. Delegates first addressed the provincial expansion issue by rejecting Manning's carefully drafted, moderate proposal. The resolution would have allowed provincial involvement under very controlled conditions. Manning, while still maintaining that he had no interest in establishing provincial parties, had prepared a complex formula whereby delegates could choose between several options. They could choose to have the party receive applications from provincial or territorial Reform parties to use the name, logo and platform of the party, or they could choose to not become involved in provincial politics but not openly oppose any group attempting to register a provincial Reform party. The first option would have allowed Manning and the leadership to carefully manage and control all provincial applications.[12] The second would have allowed expansion without either the leadership or membership's influence. Alternatively, they could reject provincial involvement and use all legal means available to protect the Reform name, logo and trademarks from unauthorized use by other groups. They chose the third option but not before strengthening the final resolution to include using all legal means to also protect the federal party's membership lists from unauthorized use, and to protect Reform from any group claiming to have an association with it. This decision was significant in that it again demonstrated that delegates would use their own judgment and not necessarily fall in line with even the leadership's most carefully crafted proposals. While future examples would arise where Manning would be able to manipulate his party's plebiscitary mechanisms, in this instance the delegates rejected Manning's attempt at gaining complete control over provincial expansion.

Delegates did, however, overwhelmingly endorse the national expansion resolution, including several regional safeguard mechanisms. They ratified, by a 94 per cent vote, a resolution calling on the party to petition its western members, by way of a binding referendum, to expand Reform's federal operations east of Manitoba.[13] Party members later ratified the expansion proposal with 92 per cent voting in favour. Delegates were also adamant about finishing the work begun at the 1989 Assembly where delegates approved studying the expansion option based on the condition that a system of checks and balances be included with any expansion strategy. The 1991 delegates concurred by insisting that provincial equality conditions be written into the party constitution once expansion occurred. To that end, they voted to entrench the party's founding principles in the constitution and include as the new first principle support for a Triple-E Senate. By incorporating the Statement of Principles into the formal constitution delegates ensured that future amendments to the principles would now require two-thirds majority support. And they went further in their attempts at ensuring the young party's western character would not be radically altered by the anticipated influx of easterners. All future amendments to the party's policy Blue Book would not only have to pass a majority vote at an assembly, but would now also have to pass by a majority of votes in a majority of provinces. Constitutional amendments would continue to require a two-thirds majority vote but would now also require a majority vote in a majority of provinces to pass.[14] These safeguards had several practical implications. Because delegate representation at Reform assemblies was based on membership levels in the individual branches, there was considerable concern that Ontario's large number of branches could someday constitute a statistical majority. By including the provincial majority provisions, future Ontario delegates could not unilaterally alter policies, the party constitution, or the Statement of Principles.

Delegates then turned their guns on Manning. Reacting to the fallout from their leader's inaugural eastern tour, delegates reaffirmed their commitment to have, at the very least, a plebiscitary veto over interim policy. Many disagreed with the latitude Manning had been taking in interpreting core policy, especially his plans to broaden Reform's ideological base. Delegates ratified a constitutional amendment that had originated from the branches and was designed to formally solidify the role of the assembly as a plebiscitary check on the leadership. Although continuing to enjoy the authority of establishing interim policy, in the future Manning and the leadership would now do so with the knowledge that not only would all interim pronouncements and strategic objectives have to meet the test of remaining consistent with established Blue Book policies, but that they would also have to be ratified by a future assembly. Given the scope of issues addressed in the Blue Book, and the fact that many of the policies were not yet fully developed, the leadership would still enjoy substantial interpretive latitude. But delegates ensured that all policy pronouncements resulting from those interpretations would have to be approved by future delegates or be dropped from the interim policy list.[15]

The leadership, however, was not without its victories. Delegates agreed to changes in the organization of constituency associations, including provisions for increased party (executive council) monitoring of deviations from the established norms. Examples of the former included provisions that all assembly delegates and alternates would have to be elected at the branch level rather than simply being appointed, as was still occurring.[16] Further provisions allowed for increased executive council scrutiny of branch constitutions, including any amendments to the standardized procedures, any undue changes in officers or directors, and the election of all positions at the branch level. The branches achieved their goal of being recognized as having the exclusive right to nominate election candidates and the leadership lost the right to conduct independent assessments of the potential candidates. The leadership did, however, retain the authority to arrange and conduct candidate training and development programs. The leadership also obtained the right to intervene with respect to any nomination and to nullify the nomination of any candidate where it determined the best interest of the party were involved.[17]

Overall, the constitutional changes strengthened the local autonomy of the existing branches, while formalizing the role of the leadership in directing and establishing new branches in Ontario and the Maritimes. As in the past, the national organization would play a major role in educating new branch activists and in candidate training. The western branches, however, achieved their sought-after formal autonomy and were instrumental in institutionalizing a number of formal plebiscitarian checks on the leadership. In the end, many of the established practices within the party's organizational structure were finally codified after the aborted attempts of 1989. The organizational structure would formally remain two-tiered with the leadership dominating the expansion and interim policy development processes. The membership, through the branches, would recruit and nominate candidates for office from amongst their own ranks while preparing to do the lion's share of financing and promoting the party and its candidates during electoral contests.

Backed by the national expansion vote, Manning used his keynote address to outline his vision of what he called the New Canada.[18] More importantly, Manning was for the first time addressing a national audience as leader of a national party, albeit one that would concentrate on recruiting supporters in English Canada. Carried live on national television, his speech was directed at that national audience as much as it was at the assembled delegates. After reiterating the "old Canada" theme of a "house divided," Manning embarked upon a comprehensive articulation of both the problems and solutions to the country's constitutional, economic and cultural conditions, past, present and future. He argued that it had "been attempts to more tightly integrate the institutions, languages, and cultures of the English and the French by political and constitutional means which has been the greatest single cause of political disunity in the northern half of the North American continent over the past two-hundred years."[19] Continuing, he reasoned that in each instance where these attempts have failed to unite Canadians, they have precipitated a crisis that has been solved, "not by pursuing an even more intimate relationship, but by establishing a more separate political relationship between the two within a broader political framework."[20] Citing examples from 1763 to the present, he maintained that the current constitutional crisis was derived directly from the revival of the false concept of Canada as an equal partnership between two founding races, languages, and cultures.

In response to the Old Canada, Manning offered a new, forty-two-word definition of his vision of the New Canada. "New Canada should be a balanced, democratic federation of provinces, distinguished by the conservation of its magnificent environment, the viability of its economy, the acceptance of its social responsibilities, and recognition of the equality and uniqueness of all its provinces and citizens."[21] The speech, somewhat subdued in its content and delivery, especially when compared with the Edmonton Assembly address, was nevertheless appropriate for the occasion and achieved several public relations goals. It established Reform as the only national party to be officially opposed to continued constitutional concessions to Quebec, thus positioning Reform as the only alternative for English-speaking Canadians interested in expressing their dissent about the protracted constitutional wrangling. However, as had happened in 1988, if the constitution failed to materialize as a significant election issue, Reform would have to distinguish itself on other issues. To prepare that ground, Manning used his 1991 Assembly speech to introduce potential Ontario supporters to what he described as a moderate, reasoned alternative for Canadians interested in political and fiscal reform.

Eastern Expansion and National Office Reorganization

While the party formally organized in Ontario and the Atlantic provinces, it expanded and reorganized its Calgary national office and began its candidate recruitment and nomination process in the western constituencies. The party hired University of Calgary political scientist Tom Flanagan as director of policy, strategy and communications. It assigned outgoing executive council chairman Diane Ablonczy as special assistant to the leader and sent Gordon Shaw to the Maritimes to organize branches east of Quebec. Incoming executive council chairman Cliff Fryers was appointed chief operating officer and numerous professional administrators were moved into positions previously held by volunteers.[22] By mid-summer the party was boasting over 60,000 members and reported its 1990 annual revenue to be $2.1 million. Manning's spring tour of Ontario made stops in eight cities drawing total crowds of over 11,000 and raising over $100,000. The following week, Ontario party organizers conducted up to twenty-five constituency information meetings a night. Ontario membership climbed to over 12,000, from less than 6,000 at the time of the Saskatoon Assembly just two months earlier. Reform began to register in Ontario public-opinion polls and by the end of the spring, Environics measured Reform support at 24 per cent of decided voters. Ontario organization proceeded more smoothly than it had three years earlier in the West. The national party office had conducted extensive Ontario preparations prior to the 1991 Assembly, building a preliminary infrastructure with most of the local organizers hand-picked by the national party rather than being originally elected by their embryonic branches. The party began the summer having formally established 74 of 99 Ontario branches. By summer's end Reform boasted 84,000 members in 180 branches across the country.

The remainder of 1991 and early 1992 saw the party implement its expansion strategy with more muted results. Growing pains were evident as the party failed to meet overly ambitious fundraising objectives, purged some remaining high-profile agitators from within its membership ranks, and experienced considerable national office turmoil as the party grew beyond Manning and his close circle of advisors' ability to oversee all operations. In an effort at financing its expansion, the party launched a major funding drive in mid-1991 called the Save Canada Fund. It ambitiously aimed to raise $12 million in less than six months. The campaign, conceived by executive council and sprung on an unsuspecting membership, would have seen three thousand volunteers each hold face-to-face meetings with ten specifically chosen people and ask each person to make a financial contribution based on perceptions about that individual's financial capabilities and their level of commitment to the party. The membership did not respond as expected and less than $3 million was raised by the time the project concluded eighteen months later. Through the Save Canada Fund, the party's executive council learned what survey results would later indicate; party members, while generally willing to make financial contributions themselves, were much less willing to solicit donations from others.[23] It also demonstrated that the leadership circle's internal cohesiveness in support of Manning's vision did not always radiate uniformly throughout the membership.

Executive council also moved to complete its purge of high profile party dissidents who, because of increasing media interest in Reform, were now being provided with regular opportunities to embarrass the party. The council disbanded all remaining area councils,[24] removed a prominent Manitoba dissident from the executive council, revoked the membership of another in BC, and demanded that a branch activist in Ontario resign from his official position on the local executive after it was revealed that he had taken part in the Brockville flag-stomping incident two years earlier while he was a member of the federal Progressive Conservatives.[25] The Manitoba dissident situation proved the most important test of the party's ability to govern itself internally. The dispute had erupted into a bitter battle between four branches and the national office when dissident branch activists accused the national office of being out of touch with the party's grassroots. In response, the Reform leadership claimed that those in control of the dissident branches were incompetent and intentionally stalling membership recruitment and organizational efforts. Manning delayed dealing effectively with the situation until the dispute reached a critical point, a management style he would often employ when dealing with disputes in his parliamentary caucus. When the dissidents began establishing an independent Manitoba wing, an organizational level not allowed under the party constitution, Manning sent a letter to individual members within those branches urging them to practice what he called internal democracy and deal with the situation before the executive council was forced to act. Manning threatened that if the members decided not to take care of matters themselves, he would not punish individual dissidents but would use his position as leader to punish the entire branch by boycotting their activities and refusing to campaign on their behalf. In the end, the membership sided with Manning and the dissidents were quashed. But the fallout from the dispute cost the party in terms of membership recruitment and its ability to effectively organize in the province, resulting in only one Reform victory in Manitoba in the 1993 federal election.

The Manitoba situation was exemplary of the problems brought on by the rapid pace of membership growth and the members' expectations concerning the appropriate levels of internal democracy. As was evident with the 1991 Assembly resolution process, Reform's culture of grassroots participation allowed activists in some often weakly organized branches to pursue extreme policy proposals and garner negative media attention. When the national office moved to quell that attention, cries of anti-democratic tendencies by the leadership were made, which in turn attracted more negative media attention. Some academic analysts were less critical. As Allan Tupper commented:

> Some flexibility has to exist even in a very populist party or its leader faces paralysis... A party can still be populist even when the

> leadership takes positions that offend substantial portions of the membership. The party need not give up its claims to populism unless there was some fundamental issue over which most members were at odds with the leader. If your norm is the Liberals, Conservatives and even the NDP, all of whom make little pretense to internal democracy, the Reform party has a long way to go before it must surrender its claim to populism.[26]

Or, as Barry Cooper offered:

> The current round of dissension is evidence the Reform party is maintaining true to its populist roots. The day the loose cannons are muzzled is when you know party central has clamped down and the party has become the captive of the "great minds" at head office.[27]

The leadership would learn more about how far they could extend their authority before the membership stopped following them later in 1992 during the Charlottetown referendum. At the same time, the early activists were discovering the limits within which the party's central leadership was prepared to tolerate obscure and radical ideas emanating from their ranks. They were also discovering that active challenges to the leadership's authority from within the party would be met with considerable force. More importantly, they were about to discover that their tenure as the sole organizers and opinion leaders within their own branches was coming to an end.

Candidate Recruitment

With the national party preparing the ground in Ontario, western constituencies embarked upon their most comprehensive candidate recruitment process yet. At the Saskatoon Assembly the party adopted a code of conduct for Reform MPs and a strict set of guidelines and procedures for candidate recruitment. Included in the candidate recruitment package was a candidate information sheet designed to "enable the potential candidate, and his or her spouse, to assess whether he or she should seek a Reform Party nomination," and "to enable Reform Party Constituency Nominating Committees to assess the qualifications of each candidate and to conduct necessary background checks."[28] The information sheet consisted of two parts. The first was a personal résumé while the second contained a comprehensive list of questions that potential candidates could expect to be asked during the course of their candidacy. The second section asked candidates to inform the nominating committee of any potential conflicts of interest that may affect their candidacy. The package also included a section designed to alert the nominee and his or her family about the implications for personal relationships when individuals become public figures.

Potential candidates were requested to write a formal letter of intent to the chairman of the branch nominating committee and complete the information sheet. Upon review, committees would conduct personal interviews with each candidate and make a recommendation. Recommendations ranged from advice that a candidate not continue to seek the Reform nomination, that the candidate should gain further experience before seeking a nomination, or that the candidate should proceed to seek the nomination. All recommendations were advisory and no member-in-good-standing could be barred from contesting a Reform nomination, regardless of the potential candidate's willingness to complete the information sheet or the recommendations of the nomination committee. Except for a few isolated incidents that shall be expanded upon below, the candidate recruitment process worked well in achieving the goals of providing quality candidates for office, informing potential candidates about the demands upon MPs and their families, and keeping fringe candidates and extremists to a minimum.

By the spring of 1992 the western candidate contests helped membership balloon to over one hundred thousand. By way of example, membership in the southern Alberta riding of Lethbridge expanded from 1,500 to over 5,500. Almost 3,200 members cast ballots at a nomination meeting attended by over four thousand people. Other Alberta meetings regularly drew large crowds with over 1,300 members casting ballots in Medicine Hat, 1,000 in St. Albert, 1,400 in Ponoka, and 1,500 in Red Deer. Reform's momentum did not go unchallenged by the federal Conservatives. After test-marketing a negative advertising campaign in two Ontario ridings, the Conservatives aimed to discredit Reform in its southern Alberta stronghold. Beginning in Calgary, a series of billboard advertisements, radio ads and over three hundred thousand flyers were delivered as part of a concerted effort by Conservative organizers to "give Calgarians second and third thoughts about Reform policies."[29] The campaign included several unsuccessful publicity stunts more reminiscent of an opposition party than a party in power. The strategy also had the unintended effect of demonstrating to many westerners that Reform was a major player in federal politics, a role Reform would successfully fulfill in the upcoming Charlottetown constitutional referendum.

The Referendum Test of the Organization

The Charlottetown Constitutional Accord referendum allowed Reform to test its electoral readiness and organizational strength on a scale not yet attempted: in a national campaign. It also represented the most dramatic example of the membership's ability to force the leadership to remain true to declared policy and platform positions, despite the leadership's preoccupation with short-term strategic concerns. Manning, increasingly reliant on the advice of strategist Rick Anderson,[30] demonstrated little enthusiasm for the constitutional debate. In his extensive spring speaking tours, Manning advocated a moratorium on all constitutional talks and concentrated his efforts on promoting Reform's criminal justice policy.[31] After Unity Minister Joe Clark and the nine premiers outside of Quebec negotiated the Pearson Accord (the forerunner to the Charlottetown Accord), Manning found enough in the agreement, particularly the Senate clauses, to grudgingly support the deal in an effort at achieving constitutional peace.[32] However, the Senate reform provisions were a pale shadow of what Reform had been advocating since 1987 and had just one year earlier enshrined as the party's first principle. Arguing that Reform could make a significant parliamentary breakthrough in a partially reformed Senate, demonstrate its effectiveness over time, and achieve further reforms later, Manning abandoned his previous Triple-E rigidity for a more immediate short-term agenda. Reluctant to campaign strongly against what initially appeared to be a popular constitutional deal, he reasoned that downplaying Reform's opposition could potentially spare it the moniker of being the only party to have opposed "the deal that saved Canada." Furthermore, Manning attempted to sit on both sides of the short-term fence. At the same time he retreated from established party policy on Quebec and the Triple-E Senate for the sake of short-term electoral gain, he readied to publicly blame the Prime Minister for any future breakdown in a process that Manning now supported. Whatever his thinking, Manning had finally extended his role in interpreting interim policy and objectives to the point where he was in direct conflict with Reform's founding principles, which were still strongly supported by the membership. Thus, as Tom Flanagan observed, "the stage was set for a collision between Manning and the party."[33]

Manning began the Charlottetown referendum campaign by sending a letter to the Reform membership in which he proposed three options: the party could oppose the package, reluctantly support it, or run an information campaign only.[34] He made it clear to party officials that he preferred the third option. His position did not sit well with many key strategists and one, Stephen Harper, publicly stated that he would oppose the deal no matter what the rest of the leadership decided.[35] After sending out the membership letter, Manning immediately went on holidays leaving the national office staff, most of whom were convinced that the membership would give them no choice but to campaign on the No side, to set up a communications program, solicit public and membership opinion, and organize Reform's response. Upon Manning's return, momentum for establishing a No campaign had become unstoppable and the party began establishing an official No committee.

Even while an Angus Reid-Southam News survey was showing 61 per cent of English Canadians and 49 per cent of Quebecers were initially supporting the accord, the Reform constitutional hotline recorded overwhelming opposition to the deal. Of the five hundred calls that came in during the first thirty-six hours, even before the party publicized the hotline's existence, 61 per cent were from members of whom 93 per cent rejected the package. Similarly, 83 per cent of non-members who called were opposed. Candidates and branch officials were equally opposed, as was the Reform membership. After tabulating 28,826 of the over 130,000 questionnaires the party mailed to members to solicit opinion on Manning's three-options, Reform officials announced that 69 per cent supported a No campaign, only 2 per cent supported the Yes side while 29 per cent favoured Manning's preference for a neutral information campaign.[36] On all communications fronts, the party was being told by its supporters, members and activists that it had no choice but to oppose the Charlottetown Accord.[37]

Having been reigned in by the members, Manning announced Reform's intention to campaign for the No forces, but his enthusiasm remained muted leading to several questionable strategic decisions that would eventually cost the party organizational talent when many of those opposed to the decisions either voluntarily left their positions or were fired.[38] Nevertheless, Reform developed a six-point plan that included registering a Reform Party Referendum Committee on the No side, development of the "KNOW MORE" campaign theme and issuing a challenge to the Yes side to defend the accord in public debates. Reform sought to establish, through its hotline and by setting up a 1-900 number, that a No vote was a vote by a "proud citizen of Canada which includes Quebec."[39] One important question remained: could Reform get its message out?

Understanding that the No forces could not match the Yes forces dollar-for-dollar in the referendum campaign any more than Reform could match the three traditional parties dollar-for-dollar in a federal election campaign, the Charlottetown referendum campaign allowed Reform to test the grassroots organization it would have to rely on in the next election. Not being able to afford a high profile national advertising blitz, Reform opted for a word-of-mouth No campaign that fit both its populist image and its budget. It also afforded the party the opportunity to test the ability of its members, volunteers and constituency organizations to win public support without a major media push from the centre. In these areas the campaign was wildly successful. The party produced a thoughtful and well-designed broadsheet flyer that calculated thirty-four areas where additional political agreements would have to be negotiated, fourteen areas where first ministers would have to resolve further ambiguities, and twelve areas where the accord was so vague that further constitutional negotiation or extensive litigation would be needed to resolve the ambiguities.[40] The campaign effort attempted to capitalize on Canadians' desires to have the constitutional issue put behind them. Calling the accord "no final constitutional agreement at all," Reform argued that a resounding no vote would demonstrate to the political and special interest elites that Canadians would no longer tolerate the ongoing constitutional debate dominating the public agenda at the expense of economic and fiscal matters. Voters agreed in as much as they rejected the "constitutional peace" option and voted against the accord by a count of 54.3 per cent opposed and 45.7 per cent in favour. Western and Quebec voters were most opposed,[41] albeit for differing reasons,[42] which seemed to further legitimize Reform's strategy of attempting to mobilize support exclusively in English Canada and concentrated in the West.

With the No victory having been achieved, and Reform the only federalist party to have campaigned on the winning side, the party appeared to be poised for a major electoral breakthrough. However, public opinion polls had been measuring a steady decline in Reform support for over a year. Environics had measured 19 per cent national support for Reform in

March 1991, but by December it had slipped to 12 per cent, and by October 1992, despite the publicity Reform received during the referendum campaign, the party had dropped to 9 per cent nationally and had fallen to 34 per cent in its Alberta heartland.

Conclusion

By the time the Reform Party contested its first national campaign during the 1992 Charlottetown referendum, it had managed to recruit over a hundred thousand members and establish functioning branch organizations in half of all the constituencies across the country. It had expanded beyond its regional base in Alberta and British Columbia into a national presence and had managed to do so after only six years in existence. It established a set of policies and principles that firmly placed the party on the right of the ideological spectrum and in opposition to the Quebec-centred constitutional agenda. Furthermore, and often with great internal acrimony, it developed an organizational structure that allowed for many populist avenues of participation for its members.

Throughout its development and expansion, the party exhibited a dynamic tension between the opinions and ambitions of the general membership and those of the leadership. At each stage of its development the members used their formal powers, or were successful in implementing new institutional controls, to hold the leadership accountable. While expanding nationally, delegates adopted mechanisms designed to prevent an influx of central Canadian members from dominating Reform assemblies. Members placed their support for a Triple-E Senate at the top of its Statement of Principles in an effort at preserving the party's founding western principles. When faced with a leadership that appeared to be straying from Reform's founding principles by refusing to take a strong position in opposition to the Charlottetown Accord, the membership used the party's internal communications apparatus to effectively bring the leadership into line with membership opinion. Despite Manning's ongoing efforts to define the party in non-ideological terms, members continued to thwart his efforts by defining themselves as right of centre and effectively using their powers within the organization to adopt right-of-centre policies. They would continue their efforts as the party met to fine-tune its election platform at the Winnipeg Assembly of 1992.

Opinion Structure of Delegates Attending Reform's 1992 Assembly

Reformers gathered in Winnipeg on the eve of the Charlottetown referendum vote for the party's 1992 Assembly, its first to include voting representatives from eastern branches and its last before the 1993 federal election.[1] Delegates represented seven provinces and the Yukon, reflecting the party's increasingly national character. The analysis presented below is designed to measure the extent to which delegates' opinions reflected the patterns observed up to this point, and to what extent they were altered by the influx of eastern, primarily Ontario delegates. Previously, we observed that delegates typically supported a right-of-centre policy agenda, defined themselves as ideologically right wing, were not supportive of making constitutional concessions to Quebec, and held opinions that were hostile towards special interests. The earliest activists also demonstrated high levels of western and system alienation and were supportive of populist mechanisms such as recall and referenda. They did not, however, envision a completely emasculated federal government.

We will also examine the extent to which Reform recruited activists from other parties or succeeded in mobilizing a previously inactive segment of the population. We would expect that the party had some of both types of activists and, if that was the case, we will want to know the ratio of novice to experienced activists and to understand if this ratio was changing over time, if it had been altered due to eastern expansion, and what effect, if any, political experience had on opinion structure. Similar questions will be addressed concerning delegates' ideological positions in an effort at determining if the activists' collective ideology changed because of eastern expansion or possibly because the leadership was succeeding in broadening the party's ideological base.[2]

Demographics

Reform's allocation of convention delegate credentials reflected its populist orientation in that all but a handful of delegates to the 1992 Assembly were elected from the branches. Non-branch delegates came from the party's executive council, and they numbered only 1.4 per cent of the total delegate contingent.[3] The data in Table 5.1 reflect the strengths and weaknesses of Reform's mobilization efforts in the various provinces.

Almost one-third of the delegates were Albertans (30.7 per cent), although Albertans constituted less than 10 per cent of Canada's total population.[4] A further 21.9 per cent came from British Columbia, although only about 13 per cent of Canadians live in that province. The Saskatchewan and Manitoba numbers demonstrate that the party continued to experience difficulties recruiting activists on the prairies east of Alberta. Conversely, the large number of Ontario delegates, almost three in ten (29.2 per cent), testified to Reform's successful recruitment efforts over the previous eighteen months in Canada's most populous province.[5] Only 1.5 per cent of the delegates came from the Atlantic Provinces where Reform was still organizationally very weak. On a regional basis, and proportionate to the population, these data indicate that in 1992, Reform was still dominated by members from Alberta and British Columbia, but that Ontario had become a major player in delegate representation.

Similar to the 1989 Assembly, the overall demographic profile of 1992 delegates reflected Reform's unwillingness to use affirmative action measures to increase representation of traditionally underrepresented groups. The data in Table 5.2 show that there was a heavy over-representation of men (71.1 per cent) compared to women (28.9 per cent) and very few youth activists. Fewer than one in twenty delegates (4.8 per cent) were less than thirty years of age and only about one in three delegates (34.3 per cent) fell

Table 5.1 · 1992 Assembly: Breakdown of Delegates by Province of Residence[6]

Province	# of Delegates	% of Delegates	# of Respon-dents	% of Respon-dents
British Columbia	291	21.9	189	21.2
Alberta	408	30.7	267	29.9
Saskatchewan	119	8.9	76	8.5
Manitoba	88	6.6	64	7.2
Ontario	388	29.2	243	27.2
Quebec	0	0.0	2	0.2
New Brunswick	4	0.3	3	0.3
Nova Scotia	11	0.8	11	1.2
Yukon	3	0.2	3	0.3
Executive Council	18	1.4	14	1.6
No Response			21	2.4
Totals	**1330**		**893**	

Note: An overall 69.2% response rate based on 893 out of 1290 questionnaires mailed.

within the traditionally large age category of thirty to forty-nine years old. By far the largest number of delegates were those aged fifty and older who accounted for 60.8 per cent of the total.

Approximately half of the delegates had either attended or completed university, a small percentage in comparison to the other parties, but consistent with Reform's age distribution. As one would expect with a party not organized in Quebec, and at a unilingual convention, almost all of the delegates (99.7 per cent) normally spoke English at home. On most other socio-demographic indicators, 1992 Reform delegates appeared similar to activists from the other parties.

Delegates' income levels were quite high, with more than one in three (34.5 per cent) having an annual total household income greater than $80,000, and more than half (51.6 per cent) having an income greater than $60,000. Reformers were employed in a wide variety of occupations, but due to the age distribution, the largest single group was retired (25.4 per cent). Business owners accounted for the largest group of working delegates (19.9

TABLE 5.2 · 1992 Assembly: Selected Socio-Demographic Characteristics[7]

Characteristics	Number	Percentage
GENDER		
Male	641	71.1
Female	249	28.9
AGE		
21 and younger	11	1.2
22–29	32	3.6
30–39	113	12.8
40–49	190	21.5
50–59	203	23.0
60 and older	333	37.8
EDUCATION		
High School or less	242	27.4
Some Post Secondary	256	29.0
College-Trade-Technical	81	9.2
University Graduate	164	18.6
Multiple University Degrees	139	15.8
Language		
English	883	99.7
French	3	0.3
HOUSEHOLD INCOME		
Under $40,000	174	22.0
$40,000–$60,000	211	26.5
$60,000–$80,000	136	17.1
Over $80,000	274	34.5
OCCUPATION		
Business Owner	166	19.9
Self-employed Professional	109	13.1
Professional Employee	113	13.5
White-collar Worker	46	5.5
Farmer	68	8.2
Blue-collar Worker	28	3.4
Homemaker	54	6.5
Unemployed	9	1.1
Student	23	2.8
Retired	212	25.4
Other	6	0.7

per cent) with professional employees (13.5 per cent) and self-employed professionals (13.1 per cent) accounting for the next two largest groups. Farmers made up only 8.2 per cent of all delegates while homemakers (6.5 per cent), white-collar workers (5.5 per cent) and blue-collar workers (3.4 per cent) rounded out the occupation categories. Students accounted for only 2.8 per cent of the delegates. Overall, the demographic profile of the 1992 Assembly indicated that Reform activists tended to come from higher status socio-economic groups and were most likely to be relatively old, English-speaking males.

Year of Initial Involvement in Reform

The party's overall growth and regional expansion can be better understood by examining the year in which delegates first joined the party. Slightly less than three in ten delegates (29.0 per cent) became members during the party's first two years. Approximately one-third joined in each of the following two-year intervals with 36.6 per cent being recruited between 1989 and 1990 and 34.4 per cent joining after that.[8] Over half of the delegates who joined in the first two years came from the province of Alberta (51.6 per cent) while about one-quarter came from BC (26.2 per cent). Of those who joined in the latest period, 1991 to 1992, half were from Ontario (49.8 per cent) reflecting the party's 1991 eastern expansion. Interestingly, one-quarter (25.3 per cent) of those who joined in the middle years of 1989 and 1990 were Ontarians who were recruited prior to the party officially organizing in their province. Provincial breakdowns in Table 5.3 demonstrate the relative maturity of the Alberta branches where delegates were the longest serving party members: half (50 per cent) joined in the first two years and close to one-third were recruited in the next two years. These patterns indicate that the party's early organizational strength in Alberta was still a factor in delegate selection for the 1992 Assembly. British Columbia delegates had the second longest tenures as party members with nearly three-quarters (74 per cent) joining in the first four years of the party's existence. Ontario delegates began joining in earnest in 1989 with about one-third (33.9 per cent) joining prior to official expansion in 1991. Most of the Saskatchewan and Manitoba delegates joined in the later four years. Nearly half (44.2 per cent) were recruited in the 1989 to 1990 period while 30 per cent joined in the most recent two years, an indication of the party's initial weakness but growing strength on the prairies east of Alberta.

TABLE 5.3 · 1992 Assembly: Year Delegates Joined Party by Province

Year of Recruitment	BC	Alberta	Sask/ Man	Ontario	Total
1987–1988	35.4	50.0	25.8	3.3	29.0
1989–1990	38.6	32.2	44.2	33.9	36.6
1991–1992	25.9	17.8	30.0	62.8	34.4
% of Total Delegates	21.2	29.9	15.7	27.2	

The year in which delegates joined the party also underscores the party's populist mobilization strategy. As a mass-based populist party, Reform would garner votes primarily in areas where it had built a strong membership base at the branch level, something it proved much more capable at in the West than in other parts of the country.

PREVIOUS POLITICAL ACTIVITY

Reform's leadership regularly battled suggestions that the party was simply a collection of disgruntled former Progressive Conservatives. The data in Table 5.4 indicate that its arguments about a more broadly based membership were at least partially correct. Unlike in 1989, a clear majority of delegates attending the 1992 Assembly were newly mobilized activists whose involvement with Reform represented a new level of political engagement rather than an extension of previous, usually Tory activity. Although some had experience in other parties (39.1 per cent), most (60.9 per cent) were new to this level of participation, demonstrating that the party had mobilized a segment of the population into political activism for the first time in their lives.

Although 1992 activists were more likely to be political neophytes recently drawn into greater levels of activity by Reform than former activists of other parties seeking a new political home, of those who were previously active with another party, most had been associated with the federal Progressive Conservatives. Three in five (61.5 per cent) of those with some previous party activity had been Conservatives, while slightly more than one in ten (10.5 per cent) had been involved with the Liberals. Only 7.6 per cent were active with the federal Social Credit party, 4.1 per cent with the NDP and a further 3.8 per cent had been active in other federal parties or

TABLE 5.4 · 1992 Assembly: Other Party Activity[9]

Other Party Activities		**Percentage**
Have been active in other party		39.1
Have not been active in other party		60.9
Which party previously active	**All Respondents**	**Respondents with previous activity**
Federal Progressive Conservative	23.6	61.5
Federal Liberal	4.0	10.5
Federal Social Credit	2.9	7.6
Federal New Democratic Party	1.6	4.1
Federal Other Party	1.5	3.8
Provincial Parties	4.8	12.5
N/A, Don't Know	61.6	-
Vote in Previous Federal Elections	**1988**	**1984**
Reform	35.7	-
Progressive Conservative	45.8	79.3
Liberal	6.6	7.2
New Democratic Party	2.7	3.6
Other Parties	3.4	4.1
Did not vote	5.8	5.8

in some combination of several parties. Some activists had also been active in provincial political parties, but these individuals represented only 12.5 per cent of those with previous activity.

The data on previous voting patterns indicates a less eclectic partisan past. 1992 Reform delegates overwhelmingly supported the Conservatives in their previous voting preferences. Nearly eight out of ten delegates (79.3 per cent) voted for the Progressive Conservatives in the 1984 federal election. This compares to only 7.2 per cent voting Liberal and 3.6 per cent voting NDP. Over one-third (35.7 per cent) recall voting for Reform in the 1988 election, compared to 45.8 per cent Conservative, 6.6 per cent Liberal, and 2.7 per cent NDP. Thus, despite protestations from Reform officials that the party's growth had come at the expense of each of the major parties, it was still drawing its activists largely from a pool of former Conservative party supporters, and to a more limited extent, from former Conservative party activists.

But Reform was succeeding at mobilizing greater numbers of the previously uninitiated than it had in the past. In fact, the more recently a delegate joined the party, the less likely that delegate was to have been active in another party. The data in Table 5.5 show that close to half of the delegates who joined in the first two years had some previous party involvement (48.4 per cent). This rate declined to 39.3 per cent for delegates recruited during the middle two years and to less than one-third (30.6 per cent) of the most recent recruits. When broken down by province and controlling for year of recruitment, an interesting picture emerges. Initially, delegates who came from western provinces where the party was organizationally weakest, Saskatchewan and Manitoba, were most likely to have had previous party involvement (46.6 per cent). British Columbia delegates had the next highest level of previous involvement at 44.7 per cent. Alberta delegates followed at 37.7 per cent with Ontario delegates trailing at 30.6 per cent. In each province except Alberta, a consistent pattern emerges. The earlier a delegate joined the party, the more likely he or she was to have had previous party experience. For example, 59.7 per cent of the delegates from British Columbia who joined the party in 1987 or 1988 had some previous party involvement. Just over one-third of those who joined after 1988 had previous experience. Similar percentages are observed with the delegates from Saskatchewan and Manitoba with 61.2 per cent of the earliest recruits indicating previous involvement with another party. This drops to 25 per cent for the latest recruits. In Ontario, the pattern is evident if we exclude the small number (3.3 per cent) who joined in the first two-year period. Almost two in five Ontario delegates who joined between 1989 and 1990 (39.0 per cent) reported some previous involvement while only 27.0 per cent of those who joined after official expansion claimed some previous activity.

The Alberta delegates buck the trend somewhat in that 40 per cent of the earliest recruits had previous party experience, as did 42.6 per cent of the latest recruits. Only 31.8 per cent of those who were recruited during the middle years of 1989 and 1990 reported previous party experience. An explanation for the deviation from the trend can be found in the fact that most Alberta branches had completed their candidate nomination processes just prior to the 1992 Assembly delegate selection meetings. The increasing likelihood of the voters in these constituencies returning a Reform MP to

Table 5.5 · 1992 Assembly: Year Joined Party by Previous Party Involvement & Province

	Previously Active (%)	Not Previously Active (%)	Totals (%)
All Delegates	39.1	60.9	
1987-1988	48.4	51.6	29.0
1989-1990	39.9	60.1	36.6
1991-1992	30.6	69.4	34.4
British Columbia	44.7	55.3	21.2
1987-1988	59.7	40.3	35.6
1989-1990	36.1	63.9	38.3
1991-1992	36.7	63.3	26.1
Alberta	37.7	62.3	29.9
1987-1988	40.0	60.0	49.6
1989-1990	31.8	68.2	32.4
1991-1992	42.6	57.4	17.9
Saskatchewan-Manitoba	46.6	53.4	15.7
1987-1988	61.2	38.8	26.2
1989-1990	52.4	47.6	43.9
1991-1992	25.0	75.0	29.9
Ontario	30.6	69.4	27.2
1987-1988	12.5	87.5	3.3
1989-1990	39.0	61.0	33.9
1991-1992	27.0	73.0	62.8

Parliament meant that the nominations were hotly contested and recruited a large number of former party activists who now viewed Reform as the most promising vehicle for achieving their political ends. This trend also hinted at the continuing collapse of the federal Conservative organization in one of its traditional strongholds.

Overall, this analysis reveals that most 1992 Reform delegates had no previous party involvement and that the later they joined the party, the more likely this was to be the case. BC, Saskatchewan, and Manitoba delegates had the highest levels of previous involvement, while Ontario delegates had the least. This pattern was consistent across provinces with only the Alberta delegates demonstrating significant deviation. Thus, over time and as the party expanded, it was increasingly mobilizing formerly uninitiated activists.

Internal Activity, Participation and Efficacy

As a new political party, and one that enjoyed limited electoral success prior to the 1993 election, Reform was not in a position to provide its activists with the traditional opportunities for service and reward that come with having a parliamentary caucus or controlling a government. Instead, Reform promised opportunities for high levels of participation within the party organization. To test if activists believed this was indeed occurring we asked delegates about their involvement in a wide variety of party activities, to what extent they believed they were participating meaningfully in the practical governing of their party, and their levels of efficacy about their participation.

Table 5.6 demonstrates that almost half of the 1992 delegates (48.6 per cent) were members of their Reform branch executive, an avenue for participation which remains the main opportunity for ongoing party activity in all parties. A further 10.4 per cent were involved in a Reform task force while very few engaged in other national party activities. When questioned about their pre-Reform party activity, only 10.9 per cent had ever been active on the branch executive of another party, and a similar percentage (10.3 per cent) had been part of another party's provincial branch executive.

An overwhelming majority of delegates (73.2 per cent) participated in fundraising, one of the most fundamental of all party activities. These high participation rates are interesting given Reform's lacklustre Save Canada fundraising campaign and suggest that the campaign may have failed because it was based on ordinary members' willingness to engage in fundraising rather than branch activists' willingness to solicit donations. It is clear from these data that higher-level activists did not demonstrate the same aversion to fundraising as did their general membership compatriots.

Delegates participated in other traditional party activities at expected rates. Half of all delegates (49.3 per cent) had attended a previous Reform Assembly and almost one-third (29.6 per cent) previously worked for Reform in a federal election campaign. Approximately one in seven delegates (13.5 per cent) had participated at the highest level of party activity by contesting a Reform nomination. Overall, delegates were very involved in branch activities, which is not surprising given that the only route to the assembly was to be elected at the branch level. That requirement appears

Table 5.6 · 1992 Assembly: Selected Reform Party Activities[10]

Party Activity	Ever Involved in any Party (%)	Involved in Reform (%)
Member of task force	5.5	10.4
Member of provincial constituency executive	10.3	*
Member of federal constituency executive	10.9	48.6
Member of provincial executive	4.6	*
Member of national executive	2.0	1.6
Member of party youth group	3.9	2.7
Member of Parliament	0.2	0.1
Member of Provincial Legislature	0.2	*
Other Reform Party Activities		**Engaged in activity (%)**
Helped raise funds		73.2
Attended a previous Reform Assembly		49.3
Worked for Reform in campaign		29.6
Ran for a Reform nomination		13.5

* Reform had no provincial party organizations, associations or legislators

to have contributed to the recruitment of highly involved branch activists who had likely been ongoing participants in the internal governance of their branch organizations.

The data in Table 5.7 measure delegates' opinions about their efficacy within the party as well as their perceptions of Reform and its place in the larger political system. Overall, delegates supported the argument that Reform was infused by a high level of internal democracy inasmuch as activists believed they were effective in influencing policy and strategy. Over three-quarters of all delegates (77.3 per cent) felt effective in influencing policy decisions while almost all of the delegates (94.0 per cent) thought that Reform Assemblies were democratic. Delegates were also adamant about maintaining the controls placed on the leadership at the 1991 Assembly. Fully 88.8 per cent thought that resolutions passed at Assemblies should be binding on the leadership. But delegates did not think that their leadership was out of touch with the membership with only 14.5 per cent believing that the leadership was not paying sufficient attention to their opinions. Contrary to claims made about Manning's manipulation of the membership,[11] delegates supported the leadership's authority to protect the party and its image. Fully 71.1 per cent agreed with the leader's right to reject candidates who did not accept Reform policies. Furthermore, delegates did not demonstrate a strong desire to alter the funding relationships between the branches and the national party. Less than one-quarter (24.2 per cent) thought that the branches should have more control over party funds while 39.4 per cent disagreed. Delegates also demonstrated overwhelming support for Reform's policies of keeping it free of affirmative action. Fully 88.1 per cent of the delegates disagreed with the suggestion that the party institute provisions requiring gender equality on its executive council.

When asked about the Reform's image, 79.9 per cent disagreed with the statement that Reform was a protest party. They also did not think Reform was in need of an image makeover. Three-quarters (77 per cent) did not think the party should go out of its way to present Canadian voters with a more moderate image. However, a similar number (75.2 per cent) also supported the leadership's discretionary powers to protect the party's image by expelling extremist elements from within its ranks. The high level of agreement with this leadership prerogative demonstrates that while Reform had not been free from internal conflicts arising from member expulsions, the vast majority of highly involved branch activists did not view the leadership's discretionary powers in these areas as a threat to expected levels of internal democracy within the party.

A slight majority of delegates (51.3 per cent) thought that the party was well placed ideologically and that it need not move further to the right. About one-quarter (23.8 per cent) thought the party should move further to the right, approximately the same number as were uncertain (24.9 per cent). These opinions indicate that while most delegates were ideologically comfortable with their party, a significant plurality would have preferred the party to move even further right. Clearly, there existed little support for Manning's attempts to mobilize more activists from the centre or left. Considerable ambiguity existed when delegates were asked if there were significant differences between the left and the right within Reform: 43.0 per cent were uncertain as to the ideological divisions within the party. Delegates' ideological positions will be analyzed more fully below using the self-anchoring, left-right placement scales.

Results were mixed when delegates were asked about the possibility of Reform involving itself in provincial politics. Almost as many delegates

TABLE 5.7 · 1992 Assembly: Attitudes about the Reform Party

Issue	Agree (%)	Uncertain (%)	Disagree (%)
INTERNAL DEMOCRACY			
I feel effective in influencing Reform policy	77.3	12.8	9.9
Reform Assemblies are democratic	94.0	3.4	2.6
Assembly resolutions should be binding on leader	88.8	6.8	4.4
Reform leadership does not pay sufficient attention to members	14.5	15.1	70.4
Leader should have right to reject candidates who don't accept party policies	71.1	7.5	21.4
More party funds should be under control of riding associations	24.2	36.4	39.4
50% of Executive Council should be female	4.3	7.6	88.1
PARTY IMAGE			
Reform is a protest party	16.3	3.9	79.9
Reform should seek to present moderate image	13.4	9.6	77.0
Expel extremist elements from Reform	75.2	14.0	10.8
Reform should move more clearly to the right	23.8	24.9	51.3
Significant differences between left & right in Reform	23.4	43.0	33.7
STRATEGIC ISSUES			
Reform should be active in provincial politics	39.1	18.1	42.9
Cooperation with 3 traditional federal parties is not possible on any issue	9.1	12.6	78.3

wanted Reform to become more active in provincial politics (39.1 per cent) as were opposed (42.9 per cent). Delegates also demonstrated a willingness to temper their partisanship by largely agreeing (78.3 per cent) that cooperation with the other parties was possible on some issues. This suggests that although many activists were mobilized into Reform because of their anti-political-establishment sentiments, most had recently supported one of the traditional parties and still considered cooperation possible if common ground could be found.

For the most part, delegates believed that their party operated democratically and they generally agreed with its image and direction. They thought that the leadership was responsive to their opinions and, in turn, they supported the leadership and its powers to protect the party's image. Most importantly, delegates felt efficacious about their activities and believed that they had significant impact on party policy and strategy. Delegates were willing to grant the leadership the necessary authority to fulfill its roles because they believed their own participation was meaningful.

Anti-Political-Establishment Populism

Delegates' attitudes and opinions about their efficacy as citizens in the larger political system were the reverse of their opinions about their efficacy within Reform. Delegates viewed themselves as outsiders who, as voters, had little influence on government policy. To examine the degree of anti-political-establishment sentiment among delegates, including their opinions about insiders and outsiders, delegates were asked to rate the amount of influence they perceived various groups had over government policy. The scale ranged from 1 (very little influence) to 7 (a great amount of influence). The mean score for each group is presented in Table 5.8.

Like their 1989 counterparts, delegates quite correctly perceived that the most powerful group in formulating and influencing government policy was the federal cabinet, which delegates ranked 6.0 on the seven-point influence scale. Consistent with a populist view of politics, delegates ranked the average voter at the bottom of the list (1.5). Furthermore, the relatively low standard deviation on the average voter rating indicates a high level of consensus. The regional alienation sentiment of many delegates could be found in that they tended to view Quebecers (5.7) and Central Canada (5.4) as having the most influence over government policy after the federal cabinet. The other major regional groupings, westerners (2.3) and Maritimers (2.2) ranked far behind Quebec and Central Canada.

Demonstrating a decided lack of confidence in the ability of other formal institutions to influence government policy, delegates ranked the leader of the opposition (2.3), the Senate (2.2), government backbenchers (1.8) and opposition MPs (1.7) very low in the influence hierarchy. The fact that delegates ranked these formal players similarly as they did citizen

TABLE 5.8[12] · 1992 Assembly: Perceived Influence on Federal Government Policy[13]

Group/Individual	Mean	Standard Deviation
Federal cabinet	6.0	1.5
Quebecers	5.7	1.2
Central Canada	5.4	1.3
Media	5.2	1.4
Lobby groups	5.0	1.4
Banks	4.6	1.5
Trade unions	4.0	1.5
Feminists	4.0	1.7
Environmentalists	3.9	1.5
First ministers conferences	3.5	1.4
Homosexuals	3.5	1.9
Recent immigrants	2.9	1.7
Leader of the opposition	2.3	1.2
Westerners	2.3	1.0
Maritimes	2.2	1.1
Senate	2.2	1.4
Government backbenchers	1.8	1.0
Opposition MPs	1.7	0.9
The average voter	1.5	1.0

outsiders was an indication of their desires for reforming Canada's parliamentary institutions.

More evidence of delegates' anti-political-establishment attitudes was found in their rankings of the less formal, but nevertheless institutionalized power centres of the media (5.1), lobby groups (4.9), the banks (4.6) and trade unions (4.0). Following were groups Reformers most closely associated with organized special interests, such as feminists (4.0), environmentalists (3.9), homosexuals (3.5), and recent immigrants (2.9). Taken together, delegates tended to view the federal cabinet, Quebecers and central Canadians as the big winners when it came to influencing federal government policy. They perceived westerners, Maritimers and the average voter to be the biggest losers. These opinions demonstrate that delegates indeed held attitudes consistent with the themes of regional and political alienation. Delegates viewed themselves and other average citizens as having relatively little political clout when compared to other organized segments of society. But their overall system alienation must be viewed through the lenses of their regionalism given that they ranked Quebecers and other Central Canadians at the top of the influence hierarchy while westerners and Maritimers ranked near the bottom.

Ideology

Previous analysis of the underlying ideology of the Reform party indicated that although delegates were not joined by a unidimensional right-wing ideology, the party did present the Canadian electorate with a distinctly right-of-centre ideological platform on a number of salient political issues. Further, as was demonstrated above, despite Manning's reluctance to use ideological labels, Reform delegates readily accepted left-right designations and could accurately place themselves and other groups on a left-right continuum. The data in Table 5.9 indicate that almost all the 1992 delegates (93.7 per cent) made use of the battery of questions and consistently placed themselves on the right of the ideological spectrum. Delegates assigned themselves a mean score of 5.35, which indicates a right-of-centre, but not excessively right-wing collective ideology. Over two-thirds of the delegates (80.7 per cent) scored themselves on the right with 35 per cent placing themselves in the moderately right category (5), 34.6 per cent anchoring themselves solidly right (6), and 11 per cent locating themselves on the far right (7). Only 2.6 per cent located themselves in any of the left-of-centre categories while 16.7 per cent located themselves in the centre (4). Much has been made in Canadian political science of the brokerage, non-ideological character of the two mainstream parties and the limited potential of their organizations to "present the electorate with a coherent and ideologically consistent program without causing a good deal of internal disagreement."[14] It appears that Reform delegates' distinctive and consistent right-of-centre ideological self-perceptions represented an important break from this pattern.

A similar distribution was observed when delegates were asked to ideologically locate Reform. Respondents gave the party a mean score of 5.31 with 86.7 per cent placing the party on the right. Almost half (46 per cent) placed the party moderately right of centre (5), while 34.9 per cent located Reform clearly on the right (6) and 5.8 per cent placed the party on the far right (7). Only 1.3 per cent of the delegates placed the party in any of the left-of-centre categories and 12 per cent located the party at the centre.

TABLE 5.9 · 1992 Assembly: Left-Right Placement (comparison with 1989)

	1989		1992	
	MEAN	STANDARD DEVIATION	MEAN	STANDARD DEVIATION
Self	5.08	0.99	5.35	0.99
Reform Party	5.09	0.78	5.31	0.83
Most Americans	N/A	N/A	5.01	0.94
People in Province	4.41	1.08	4.41	1.04
Most Canadians	3.74	0.93	4.18	0.83
Federal PC	3.55	1.35	3.83	1.32
Current Federal Government	N/A	N/A	3.69	1.33
Federal Liberals	2.63	1.12	3.01	1.05
Federal NDP	1.84	1.03	1.66	0.93

Range = 1 (left) to 7 (right).

Those at the centre tended to view the party as more right than themselves. Delegates on the far right viewed the party to their left, but placed it closer to their own ideological position than did those at the centre. Delegates who anchored themselves in the moderate-right or strong-right categories (5 or 6) anchored the party at virtually the same position as themselves. Given that these categories account for over 80 per cent of the sample, it is not surprising that, as a group, delegates tended to view their own ideological dispositions as very similar to that of their party.

Previous analysis has also revealed that ideology played a role in much of Reform delegates' opinions on most issues and was especially important when Reformers considered fiscal policy, welfare and continentalism issues.[15] That analysis also indicated that ideology was less significant when institutional-reform questions were considered and when regional tensions within the party emerged. That is, the right-of-centre ideological positions of the delegates tended to unify them on some social and economic issues, but could not fully suppress the latent regional cleavages within the party. We shall explore these earlier findings further while undertaking the factor analysis that follows. For now, it is important to point out that like the 1989 delegates, 1992 delegates aligned the traditional federal parties in the order in which they are generally placed by analysts of Canadian parties.

TABLE 5.10 · 1992 Assembly: Left-Right Placment by Year Recruited and by Previous Party Activity

	Mean	Standard Deviation
All Delegates	5.35	0.99
Previously Active Delegates	5.36	0.86
Delegates With No Previous Party Activity	5.31	1.08
1987–1988	5.34	0.96
1989–1990	5.38	1.03
1991–1992	5.28	0.99

Note: * $p < .05$; ** $p < .01$

The New Democrats were placed farthest to the left (1.66) followed as one moves to the right by the Liberals (3.01) and the Progressive Conservatives (3.83). Similar to other party activists, Reform delegates were unusual with respect to their placement of each of the major parties. As a right-of-centre group of activists who placed themselves only moderately to the right, Reform delegates were inclined to view their competitors from other parties as ideologically distinct from themselves and to their left. In fact, 1992 Reform delegates again located even the governing Conservatives to the left of the mid-point of the scale and to the left of the Canadian electorate. Delegates, therefore, viewed themselves and Reform as the only proponents of right-of-centre political views, farther to the right than the electorate as a whole, but ideologically closer to the average Canadian voter than to the Liberals or the NDP. In most cases, delegates attending the 1992 Assembly ranked themselves and others slightly further to the right than did delegates attending the 1989 Assembly. But the patterns were consistent for both groups of activists.

Delegates demonstrated little ideological variance when year of recruitment and previous party activity were examined. As Table 5.10 demonstrates, there were no significant differences in the ideological positions of delegates depending on when they joined the party. As such, no ideological drift was measured due to differences in recruitment timing. Also, previous party activity had no significant impact on ideology except that delegates with no previous activity tended to exhibit somewhat more diversity in their ideological placements (standard deviation of 1.08 as compared to 0.86).

This analysis indicates that despite the protestation of the party's leadership, and its insistence that members not attach right-wing descriptive labels to the party, its policies, or to themselves, delegates to the 1992 Assembly were not only willing to make use of the battery of questions, but they did so consistently. They saw themselves as distinctively but moderately right of centre, viewed their party in almost identical terms, and viewed themselves as being ideologically closer to their respective electorates than to any other party or government. They tended to view all other parties and most governments as left of centre, while locating the average Canadian at the middle of the ideological spectrum. They viewed themselves as ideologically closest to most Americans, followed by the people in their provinces, and ideologically farthest away from NDP governments and parties.

As the data in Table 5.11 indicate, when broken down by province, Reform delegates continued to demonstrate ideological consistency. Delegates from all provinces anchored the average Canadian voter near the centre and showed little variation across other comparable categories. Alberta delegates distinguished themselves somewhat by anchoring themselves farthest to the right (5.50) and closest to their own provincial electorate, which they also viewed as distinctly right of centre (5.06). Some interesting differences appear where circumstances differ. For example, British Columbia and Ontario delegates correctly viewed their provincial governments at the time (both NDP) as left of centre, while Alberta delegates placed their government at the centre (4.07), almost identical to where they anchored the Alberta provincial Conservatives (4.13).

To further simplify these provincial comparisons, and for purposes of comparing differences between delegates' self-anchoring and those they assigned other groups, a measure of ideological distance was constructed by simply subtracting the mean score assigned each group from the mean score of the delegates. Most of the scores are positive because Reform delegates tended to place themselves farther to the right than any other group. Table 5.12 illustrates the ideological distance that delegates placed between themselves and other groups. In descending order, from no distance between delegates and Reform (0.0), up to the greatest distance (3.87) between Alberta delegates and the federal NDP, delegates demonstrated a consistent use of the continuum across categories where

Table 5.11 · 1992 Assembly: Ideology by Province

	British Columbia		Alberta		Saskatchewan/ Manitoba		Ontario	
	Mean	Standard Deviation	Mean	Standard Deviation	Mean	Standard Deviation	Mean	Standard Deviation
Self *	5.26	0.96	5.50	0.97	5.31	0.96	5.27	1.05
Reform Party	5.26	0.78	5.41	0.82	5.36	0.87	5.21	0.86
Most Americans	4.95	0.89	5.04	0.97	5.03	0.95	5.00	0.96
People in Province **	4.22	0.91	5.06	0.80	3.84	1.21	4.16	0.93
Most Canadians	4.21	0.69	4.17	0.92	4.15	0.86	4.18	0.83
Provincial PC[a]	4.81	1.18	4.13	1.15	4.12	1.29	4.24	1.08
Federal PC	3.81	1.37	3.68	1.25	4.06	1.52	3.87	1.21
Federal Government	3.75	1.36	3.52	1.23	3.83	1.56	3.75	1.27
Provincial Liberals **	3.66	1.10	3.44	1.12	3.29	1.09	3.17	0.92
Federal Liberal	2.99	1.05	3.00	1.10	3.21	1.16	2.92	0.90
Provincial Government **	1.81	1.04	4.07	1.11	3.38	1.51	1.76	1.09
Provincial NDP **	1.71	0.99	1.82	0.93	2.01	1.07	1.59	0.94
Federal NDP	1.71	1.04	1.63	0.87	1.68	0.84	1.65	0.95

Range = 1 (left) to 7 (right).
* $p < .05$; ** $p < .01$
[a] Indicates provincial Social Credit Party in BC.

Table 5.12 · 1989 and 1992 Assemblies: Ideological Distance

	1989 Assembly				1992 Assembly				
	All Delegates	BC	Alberta	Sask/ Manitoba	All Delegates	BC	Alberta	Sask/ Manitoba	Ontario
Reform Party	0.01	0.06	0.02	-0.16	0.04	0.00	0.09	-0.05	0.06
Most Americans	–	–	–	–	0.34	0.31	0.46	0.28	0.27
People in Province	0.67	0.97	0.49	1.19	0.94	1.04	0.44	1.47	1.11
Most Canadians	1.32	1.16	1.47	0.96	1.17	1.05	1.33	1.16	1.09
Provincial PC[a]	0.51	0.00	0.89	0.38	0.98	0.45	1.37	1.19	1.03
Federal PC	1.53	1.46	1.67	0.86	1.52	1.45	1.82	1.25	1.40
Federal Government	--	--	--	--	1.66	1.51	1.98	1.48	1.52
Provincial Liberals	1.82	1.87	1.86	1.47	1.96	1.60	2.06	2.02	2.10
Federal Liberals	2.45	2.32	2.53	2.28	2.34	2.27	2.50	2.10	2.35
Provincial Government	–	–	–	–	2.59	3.45	1.43	1.93	3.51
Provincial NDP	3.11	2.75	3.25	2.96	3.59	3.55	3.68	3.30	3.68
Federal NDP	3.24	3.03	3.33	3.12	3.69	3.55	3.87	3.63	3.62

a. Indicates provincial Social Credit Party in BC.

circumstances were similar. Delegates again revealed their anti-political-establishment tendencies by anchoring themselves closer to the various groups of citizens than to any government, including the governing Conservatives with whom many had past associations and for whom most had once voted. Where provincial differences occurred, they were slight and consistent. The Alberta delegates frequently indicated slightly greater distance between themselves and most groups with the exception of their own provincial electorate and their provincial government. Overall, it is evident that Reform delegates made consistent use of the ideological continuum, despite the party leadership's desire to have its activists describe themselves in non-ideological terms.

Factor Analysis of Issue Items

In order to better understand delegate opinion structure, a series of factor analysis procedures were performed on a range of policy items.[16] The results are presented in Table 5.13 and indicate that eleven underlying factors emerged after attitudes towards twenty-nine policy items were examined.[17] The first factor corresponded to a welfare and entitlements dimension. It contained four variables and accounted for 8.5 per cent of the variance in delegates' opinions on this range of issues.[18] The second factor measured an alienation dimension, included three variables tapping into delegates' perceived lack of efficacy within the larger political system, and accounted for 6.6 per cent of the variance. An interesting third factor emerged by combining Quebec self-determination with bilingualism and the two immigration questions. This factor represented a language and ethnicity dimension and accounted for 5.6 per cent of the variance. Two other variables that dealt with Quebec's place in the Canadian constitution formed a separate factor (the seventh) indicating that delegates made a conceptual distinction between Quebec's constitutional aspirations and other language and ethnicity issues. The fourth factor corresponded to a federalism dimension and included items such as decentralization, opting out of programs, and federal-provincial power sharing. It accounted for 5.1 per cent of the variance. The fifth factor corresponded to a neo-conservative economic agenda, included items about big government, the deficit, and government intervention, and accounted for 4.9 per cent of the variance. The sixth factor included two international trade variables and accounted for 4.3 per cent of the variance. The seventh factor corresponded to Quebec's constitutional agenda and accounted for 4.3 per cent of the variance.

The eighth factor included the abortion choice variable and the Canadian Charter of Rights and Freedoms. This factor measured a civil-liberties dimension and accounted for 3.9 per cent of the variance. Crime issues dominated the ninth factor that measured 3.9 per cent of the variance, while provincial equality issues dominated the tenth factor, accounting for 3.7 per cent of the variance. The final factor measured an immigration and multiculturalism dimension and accounted for 3.5 per cent of the variance. In total, the eleven factors that emerged accounted for 54.3 per cent of the variance explained.

The factor analysis revealed a number of interesting findings. Initially, delegates distinguished between social program issues (factor 1) and big government more generally (factor 5). They associated big government with the deficit and government intervention in the economy more than they associated it with transfers to individuals. Delegates also demonstrated a refined understanding of Quebec's place in confederation by distinguishing between Quebec's constitutional demands, to which they were adamantly opposed (factor 7), and other language and ethnicity issues, where they demonstrated considerable support for the diversity of language and ethnic groups (factor 3). For Reform delegates, it appears that their perception of the Quebec problem was not associated with language and the Québécois culture, but with Quebec's demands on the federation.

Delegates also differentiated between their strong support for provincial equality (factor 10) and other federalism issues such as decentralization (factor 4). These differences substantiate what we learned from the 1989 delegates: Reform activists were adamant in their support for equal provinces, but they did not necessarily support a massive dismantling of the federal government as the means of achieving that equality. Overall, the fact that eleven underlying factors emerged out of the twenty-nine items indicated a considerable complexity in delegates' opinion structure. More can be learned about that opinion structure by examining opinions concerning the individual items that made up the factors.

Attitudes Towards Issue Items

As indicated in Table 5.14, the first factor contains four variables that measure attitudes about the welfare state. Delegates demonstrated a high degree of consensus in their opposition to the current welfare state and its effects on Canadian society. For example, there was strong agreement that the welfare state makes people less willing to look after themselves

Table 5.13 · 1992 Assembly: Factor Analysis of Issue Items

	F1	F2	F3	F4	F5	F6	F7	F8	F9	F10	F11	Communalities
Welfare effects	**.5806**	-.0613	.0913	.0354	-.0311	.0323	.0311	-.0972	.0093	.1344	.0797	.3873
Unemployed	**.7119**	.0505	-.1154	-.0349	.0214	.0258	-.0067	.0563	-.0416	.0504	.0089	.5326
Welfare abuse	**.7060**	.0593	-.0767	.0118	-.0214	.0572	.0193	.0359	.0655	-.0961	-.0464	.5290
Welfare problems	**.6292**	.0490	-.0682	.0306	.1108	.0981	-.0802	-.1071	.1471	.0075	-.0256	.4661
No say in gov't	.0539	**.7535**	-.0032	-.0817	-.0167	.0017	.0361	-.0202	.0486	.0178	.0914	.5904
Gov't doesn't care	.0242	**.7348**	-.0911	.0573	.0774	-.0836	.0290	-.1317	.1927	-.0536	-.0258	.6239
MPs lose touch	.0128	**.6643**	.0035	.0466	.0047	-.0070	-.0594	.1563	-.1222	.1953	-.0258	.5264
Quebec self-deter.	.0555	-.0731	**.4392**	.0620	-.0049	-.0441	.1553	.1812	-.2270	.1318	.1440	.3538
Bilingualism	-.1058	-.0675	**.5613**	-.0281	-.0161	.1147	.1486	.1090	-.0302	.0169	.1054	.3913
Reduce immigration	.1564	-.0162	**-.5108**	.0154	.0039	-.2712	.1499	.2320	.0319	.0454	.2172	.4860
Take all ethnicities	-.0094	.0189	**.7216**	.0879	.0111	-.0690	-.0041	.0019	.0304	-.0485	-.0706	.5421
Decentralize	.0015	.0158	.0873	**.6982**	-.0266	.0943	.0205	-.0509	.1648	-.0404	-.1209	.5514
Opt out	-.0068	.0530	-.0686	**.5829**	.0560	.1130	.1558	.0107	-.1577	.0696	.3108	.5139
Feds yield too much	-.0439	.0416	-.0494	**-.7443**	.0211	.0729	.1231	.0035	.0303	-.0581	.0354	.5866
Big gov't problem	-.0748	.0683	-.0750	-.0283	**.7498**	.0891	.0849	-.0175	.0442	.0624	-.0076	.6003
Deficit	.0342	-.0149	-.0075	-.0258	**.7756**	-.1095	-.0045	.0542	-.0774	.0509	-.0501	.6297
Gov't ownership	.2335	-.0028	.1470	.0773	**.4476**	.1411	-.1606	-.0603	.1572	-.0088	.1153	.3699

Table 5.13 (cont.) · 1992 Assembly: Factor Analysis of Issue Items

	F1	F2	F3	F4	F5	F6	F7	F8	F9	F10	F11	Communalities
US trade	.1196	.0341	-.0293	.0329	.0785	**.7741**	.0468	.0069	-.0337	-.0120	-.0976	.6359
NAFTA	.1072	-.1261	.1421	.0561	-.0295	**.7423**	-.0062	-.0112	-.0141	.0582	.0142	.6263
Quebec veto	.0410	.0616	.0892	-.0444	.0512	-.0026	**.7471**	.0206	.0744	.0205	-.0903	.5907
Distinct society	-.0683	-.0494	.0477	.0343	-.0498	.0345	**.7843**	.0007	-.0318	-.0381	.0364	.6332
Charter	-.1457	-.0940	.2611	-.0344	.0187	.0214	.0362	**.5839**	.0265	-.1168	-.2172	.5040
Abortion	-.0186	.0572	-.0293	-.0279	-.0079	-.0360	-.0083	**.7664**	-.0138	-.0270	.1032	.6056
Capital punishment	.1246	.1408	-.1347	-.0711	.0027	.0894	.0069	.1997	**.6412**	.0814	.1021	.5347
Courts to lenient	.0629	-.0192	.0083	.0879	.0425	-.1329	.0469	-.1314	**.7692**	.0552	-.0048	.6458
3-E-Senate	.0571	.0906	-.0173	.0232	-.0597	.0587	-.0108	-.0451	.0049	**.7434**	-.0343	.5753
Provincial equality	.0231	.0348	.0229	.0360	.1861	-.0264	-.0035	-.0498	.1075	**.7225**	-.0519	.5777
Multiculturalism	.0168	.0099	-.1002	.0580	-.0038	.1238	.0925	.2865	.0192	.0891	**-.6848**	.5969
Immigrant contribute	.0307	.0523	-.0805	.0461	-.0082	.1578	.0050	.2987	.1351	-.0427	**.6231**	.5349
Eigenvalue	2.46	1.90	1.63	1.49	1.43	1.24	1.24	1.14	1.11	1.06	1.02	
% of variance	8.5%	6.6%	5.6%	5.1%	4.9%	4.3%	4.3%	3.9%	3.8%	3.7%	3.5%	54.3%

(95.6 per cent), that a great deal of abuse of welfare programs exists (89.3 per cent), and that the welfare state has created more problems than it has solved (85.8 per cent). Delegates took slightly less polar positions with respect to unemployment, but even here over three-quarters (77.5 per cent) believed that the unemployed are not trying hard enough to find jobs. Taken together, these data reflect Reform activists' considerable opposition to the current milieu of welfare programs and government entitlement programs more generally.

The alienation factor included three variables that measure Reformers' perceived lack of efficacy within the larger political system. Delegates were most united in their perception that MPs soon lose touch with the people once they are elected to Parliament (94.2 per cent). Most also thought that the government doesn't care much what people like them think (81.5 per cent). Fewer delegates (66.2 per cent) believed that people like them have no say about what the government does. Fully one-quarter (27.8 per cent) disagreed with this statement, indicating that a significant plurality of delegates had experienced higher levels of personal efficacy within the larger political system and believed that their participation had, at a minimum, given them some voice within the system. Delegate opinion was much more divergent with respect to language and ethnicity issues as indicated by their responses to the variables that made up the third factor. Delegates were most united with respect to the ethnic composition of immigrants. Fully two-thirds of the delegates (68.9 per cent) stated that immigrants should be chosen from all ethnic and racial groups. However, better than one in five (22.5 per cent) disagreed. Opinion was much more divided when delegates considered the rate of immigration, with 43.5 per cent agreeing that immigration rates should be dramatically reduced and 37.2 per cent disagreeing. Opinion was split evenly when delegates considered Quebec's right to self-determination. Fully 46.0 per cent of the delegates believed that Quebec should have the right to self-determination while an equal number (45.8 per cent) did not believe that Quebecers should have that right. Finally, delegates demonstrated considerable, but not overwhelming opposition to a bilingual federal government. While 60.3 per cent did not believe a bilingual federal government was necessary, 30.9 per cent thought that it was. Taken together, these data demonstrate considerable diversity of opinion by Reformers when thinking about language and ethnicity issues, with the greatest divergence occurring within their opinions about Quebec's right to decide its future.

The items contained in the seventh and tenth factors shed some light on how far delegates were willing to go in meeting Quebec's aspirations, should its citizens decide to remain within Canada. The seventh factor demonstrated that although delegates viewed Quebec's constitutional aspirations as being distinct from ethnicity and language issues, they held polar positions against granting Quebec any distinct constitutional status. Fully 97.5 per cent believed that Quebec should not have a constitutional veto while 89.3 per cent disagreed with Quebec being granted distinct society status within the constitution. The tenth factor, dealing with provincial equality, reinforces delegates' support of western constitutional demands and opposition to Quebec's constitutional agenda. Fully 96.3 per cent supported establishing a Triple-E Senate while 90.2 per cent believed that all provinces should have an equal say in confederation. When considered within the context of the third factor, Reform delegates appeared willing to grant the citizens of Quebec a certain amount of latitude in determining their own future, but they were by no means willing to meet Quebec's demands for special constitutional status, especially if that status conflicted with a strict notion of provincial equality.

The fourth factor measured a range of federalism issues, with delegates taking the most polar position when they considered the decentralization of services. Almost three-quarters (73.7 per cent) believed that services should be more decentralized. However, a slim majority (50.7 per cent) disagreed with provinces having the right to opt out of joint federal-provincial programs with full compensation. Slightly more than one-quarter believed that provinces should have the right to opt out while 22.9 per cent were uncertain. Thus, while delegates generally supported a further decentralization of the federation, in instances where a federal role could be justified, delegates demonstrated substantial support for provincial compliance. Opinion was most diverse with respect to federal-provincial power sharing. One-third of the delegates (33.1 per cent) believed that the federal government had already yielded too much power to the provinces, while a similar number believed the opposite (39.7 per cent). Fully 27.2 per cent of the delegates could not make up their minds on this issue. Overall, these data indicate that while Reform delegates preferred to see some programs further decentralized, they did not envision an emasculated federal government. Delegates were divided on how far the federal government should go in yielding to provincial demands for greater powers and a majority thought that provinces should either not have the right to opt-out of

Table 5.14 · 1992 Assembly: Attitudes Towards Issue Items

Issue	Agree	Uncer-tain	Disagree
Welfare & Entitlements			
Welfare state makes people less willing to look after self	95.6	2.2	2.1
Unemployed not trying hard enough to find jobs	77.5	12.4	10.0
Great deal of social security & welfare abuse	89.3	6.9	3.8
Welfare state created more problems than solved	85.8	8.8	5.4
Alienation			
People like me don't have any say about what government does	66.2	6.0	27.8
Government doesn't care what people like me think	81.5	7.1	11.3
Parliament soon lose touch with the people	94.2	3.2	2.6
Language/Ethnicity			
Quebec has right to self-determination	46.0	8.3	45.8
Bilingual federal government is necessary	30.9	8.8	60.3
Dramatically reduce the rate of immigration	43.5	19.3	37.2
Immigrants should be taken from all ethnic & racial groups	68.9	8.6	22.5
Federalism			
Government services should be decentralized	73.7	18.0	8.3
Provinces should have right to opt out with compensation	26.4	22.9	50.7
Federal government yields too much power to provinces	33.1	27.2	39.7
Government Size/Deficit			
Big government increasingly is a major problem	95.5	1.8	2.7
A Reform government should seek to reduce deficit	99.1	0.1	0.8
Too much government ownership in economy	90.1	8.8	1.1

Table 5.14 (cont) · 1992 Assembly: Attitudes Towards Issue Items

Issue	Agree	Uncer-tain	Disagree
Trade			
There should be no tariffs/duties between Canada & U.S.	68.1	17.3	14.6
NAFTA is good for Canada	57.0	26.3	16.7
Quebec/Constitution			
Quebec should have a veto in the constitution	2.1	0.3	97.5
Quebec should have distinct society status in constitution	6.1	4.6	89.3
Charter/Abortion			
Benefits of Charter outweigh disadvantages	17.6	27.2	55.2
Abortion private matter decided between woman & doctor	61.5	7.5	30.9
Crime and Punishment			
Capital punishment should be reintroduced	82.1	9.0	8.9
Courts have been too lenient with criminal penalties	96.2	2.4	1.5
Equality of Provinces			
The Senate should be reformed along 3-E model	96.3	1.8	1.9
All provinces should have equal say in confederation	90.2	3.4	6.4
Multiculturalism/Immigration			
Federal government should increase multiculturalism	1.9	1.3	96.7
Preferential treatment for immigrants who can contribute	90.6	3.9	5.5
Anti-political-establishment			
Central is struggle between elites & ordinary people	79.9	8.1	12.0

joint programs, or, if they were to opt-out, they should not be able to do so with full compensation.

Delegates were more united in their opinions about the size of government. The fifth factor measured attitudes towards the deficit, government ownership, and big government more generally. Reform activists took polar positions when considering all three variables. They were almost unanimous in their desire for deficit reduction (99.1 per cent). Similarly, 95.5 per cent thought that big government was increasingly a major problem while slightly fewer, but still an overwhelming majority (90.1 per cent) believed that there was still too much government ownership in the Canadian economy. It is clear from these data that delegates were united in their opposition to large, free-spending, interventionist governments. Opinion was more diverse when they considered trade issues. A majority of delegates approved of both the Canada-US Free Trade Agreement (68.1 per cent) and the North American Free Trade Agreement (57.0 per cent). However, over one-quarter (26.3 per cent) was undecided about NAFTA and 16.7 per cent did not believe that NAFTA was good for Canada. A similar number (14.6 per cent) did not support Canada-US free trade. Overall, delegates were trade continentalists, albeit with certain reservations.

The eighth factor measured delegate opinion concerning civil liberties and appeared to correspond to a group-versus-individual rights dimension. On the one hand, a clear majority of delegates (61.5 per cent) believed that abortion was a matter of individual choice. A significant plurality (30.9 per cent) disagreed with this statement. Contrary to many perceptions about Reform, in 1992 its delegates were pro-choice by a two-to-one margin. On the other hand, delegates were not supportive of the Canadian Charter of Rights and Freedoms. A majority (55.2 per cent) did not believe that the Charter's benefits outweighed its disadvantages. Only 17.6 per cent supported the Charter while over one-quarter (27.2 per cent) was uncertain. Opinion aligned along a civil-liberties dimension with delegates generally supportive of individual rights, but generally not supportive of the group entitlements they associated with the Charter. These data substantiate the analysis concerning delegates' perception of the increasing power and influence of Charter Canadians. Further evidence of this individualistic orientation was found in delegates' responses to the variables that made up the eleventh factor. Here delegates demonstrated overwhelming opposition to efforts at increasing collective rights by way of multiculturalism programs (96.7 per cent) and were adamant that immigrants should be chosen on their

Table 5.15 · 1992 Assembly Opinion Structure on Issue Indexes

Issue Index	Adjusted Range	Mean	Standard Deviation	Adjusted Range	Mean	Standard Deviation
Welfare & Entitlements	0–4	3.47	0.89	0–1	0.87	0.22
Alienation	0–3	2.40	0.83	0–1	0.80	0.28
Language/Ethnicity	0–4	1.69	1.13	0–1	0.42	0.28
Federalism	0–3	1.38	0.93	0–1	0.46	0.31
Government Size/ Deficit	0–3	2.83	0.44	0–1	0.94	0.15
Trade	0–2	1.23	0.79	0–1	0.62	0.40
Quebec/Constitution	0–2	1.85	0.41	0–1	0.93	0.21
Charter/Abortion	0–2	1.15	0.64	0–1	0.58	0.32
Crime	0–2	1.77	0.48	0–1	0.89	0.24
Equality of Provinces	0–2	1.85	0.40	0–1	0.93	0.20
Multiculturalism/ Immigration	0–2	1.86	0.37	0–1	0.93	0.19

ability to contribute to Canada (90.6 per cent). Taken together, these items suggest delegates placed a premium on individual choice, individual rights and merit, as opposed to collective rights and entitlements. One further factor emerged from a crime and justice dimension. Delegates took extreme polar positions with 96.2 per cent agreeing that the courts are too lenient in sentencing of criminals. Delegates were also strongly supportive of reinstating capital punishment (82.1 per cent).

Collectively, 1992 Reform delegates were very united in their opposition to the welfare state, big government, Quebec's constitutional demands and collective rights. They were also united in support of provincial equality, individual rights and a stronger stance against criminals. Opinion was more diverse when delegates considered language and ethnicity issues, federalism and trade. Delegates also demonstrated high levels of alienation from the political system. Their populist orientations were further revealed by their responses to one of the issue items not contained in the factor groupings. Fully 79.9 per cent of delegates believed that the central question in Canadian politics was the struggle between political elites and ordinary people. This variable loaded significantly on several of the factors suggesting that it may well correspond to an underlying dimension on its own. It was excluded from this round of factor analysis but will be brought back during the final round.

OPINION STRUCTURE ON ISSUE INDEXES

To further investigate the opinion structure of 1992 Reform delegates, issue indexes were created by summing the number of consistent responses to the issue items that loaded onto the various factors.[19] As was partially revealed above, delegates held polar positions with respect to six of the eleven indexes. Their most united and polar positions were found in their opposition to big governments and deficits (adjusted mean 0.94 and adjusted standard deviation 0.15). These data substantiate one of the major areas of agreement within all of the literature concerning Reform: its economic agenda was distinctively right of centre and supportive of smaller, more fiscally conservative governments. Delegates were also united in their support for Reform's constitutional agenda and in opposition to Quebec's. For example, delegates overwhelmingly supported the principle of equality of provinces (0.93) while demonstrating similar levels of opposition to Quebec's demands for recognition of its distinctiveness (0.93). The relatively low adjusted standard deviation (0.20) for both indicates little divergence of opinion when considering the various constitutional positions.

Evidence of delegates' libertarian leanings was found in their near polar position on the multiculturalism/immigration index (0.92). These opinions were consistent with Reform policy and indicated that delegates' quest for smaller government would have included dismantling Canada's state-sponsored multiculturalism and other programs that champion group over individual rights. Delegates also held near-polar opinions in opposition to the welfare state (0.87) and the functioning of the criminal justice system (0.89). Opinion was slightly less united with respect to these indexes (adjusted standard deviations of 0.22 and 0.24) but nevertheless consistent with Reform policy and distinctively right of centre. Delegates also held somewhat polar positions with respect to their levels of alienation (0.80), but here opinion was more diverse (adjusted standard deviation of 0.28).

Opinion was much more diverse with respect to the remaining indexes. For example, opinion was very disparate with respect to trade and the Charter/abortion indexes (adjusted standard deviations of 0.40 and 0.32).

Table 5.16 · 1992 Assemblies: Indexes by Previous Party Activity

	Previously Active		Not Previously Active	
	Adjusted Mean	Standard Deviation	Adjusted Mean	Standard Deviation
Welfare & Entitlements	0.87	0.22	0.87	0.23
Alienation	0.78	0.28	0.81	0.27
Language/Ethnicity	0.44	0.30	0.41	0.27
Federalism	0.47	0.31	0.45	0.31
Government Size/Deficit	0.95	0.14	0.94	0.16
Trade	0.64	0.40	0.60	0.40
Quebec/Constitution	0.93	0.20	0.92	0.21
Charter/Abortion	0.58	0.31	0.58	0.33
Crime	0.88	0.25	0.89	0.23
Equality of Provinces	0.91	0.22	0.93	0.18
Multiculturalism/ Immigration	0.93	0.19	0.93	0.18

Note: * $p < .05$; ** $p < .01$

Much of the trade opinion diversity could be accounted for in delegates' concerns about including Mexico in the North American trade alliance. Furthermore, considerable differences existed between delegates from the have provinces as compared to those from the have-not provinces. As was noted above, delegates also demonstrated substantial diversity of opinion when considering non-constitutional federalism issues. The adjusted mean of 0.46 for the Federalism index is located at about the mid-point of the index range, almost as far away from either polar position as was possible. These data demonstrate that although delegates held polar and distinct constitutional positions, there was considerably more ambiguity in their opinions about non-constitutional federal restructuring. Taken together with their opinions concerning the Quebec issues, we can see that Reform delegates tended to make clear distinctions between constitutional and non-constitutional politics.

To further understand these patterns, the index means of various groups of delegates were compared with respect to their province of residence, year of recruitment into the party (which is positively correlated with province given the party's regional mobilization and expansion strategies), and previous party activity.

OPINION STRUCTURE ON ISSUE INDEXES BY PREVIOUS PARTY ACTIVITY

As Table 5.16 illustrates, there were no statistically significant differences between delegates with previous party activity and those without. Delegates with no previous party activity registered slightly higher levels of alienation (0.81) as compared to delegates with previous experience (0.78), but even these differences were slight and not significant. In fact, these data are remarkable for their lack of significant difference between the two groups of delegates and lend further support to the proposition that few differences in opinion structure existed between delegates who were previously active in another party (mostly the Conservatives) and those who had never participated in politics at this level. Therefore, if we are interested in discovering intra-party differences in opinion, whether delegates were newly mobilized activists or were recruited away from an established party is not a good predictor of opinion. This is an important finding in itself in that it appears Reform recruited activists with similar opinions on the major issues irrespective of whether or not they had ever before participated in politics at this level.

OPINION STRUCTURE ON ISSUE INDEXES BY YEAR OF RECRUITMENT

Timing of recruitment does appear to be important. The data in Table 5.17 indicate that the year in which delegates were recruited into the party had a significant effect on opinion structure with respect to six of the eleven indexes. Delegates' opinions on federalism, government size and the deficit, Quebec's constitutional demands, the Charter and abortion, crime, and equality of provinces were each influenced by the timing of delegates' initial recruitment. Conversely, considerable unity of opinion existed with respect to all of the other indexes.

Delegates' scores on the federalism index were substantially lower for the most recently recruited delegates. Earliest recruits scored highest on the federalism index (0.53). Scores dropped to 0.46 for those recruited during the middle years of 1989 and 1990, and dropped further to 0.41 for

Table 5.17 · 1992 Assembly: Issue Index by Year Recruited into Party

	1987-1988		1989-1990		1991-1992	
	Adj. Mean	Std. Dev.	Adj. Mean	Std. Dev.	Adj. Mean	Std. Dev.
Welfare & Entitlements	0.86	0.24	0.87	0.22	0.87	0.21
Alienation	0.79	0.27	0.80	0.27	0.80	0.28
Language/Ethnicity	0.44	0.28	0.41	0.28	0.42	0.28
Federalism **	0.53	0.30	0.46	0.32	0.41	0.29
Government Size/Deficit *	0.96	0.12	0.94	0.15	0.93	0.16
Trade	0.61	0.40	0.62	0.38	0.62	0.41
Quebec/Constitution **	0.96	0.15	0.93	0.21	0.90	0.23
Charter/Abortion **	0.59	0.31	0.61	0.32	0.53	0.32
Crime *	0.90	0.22	0.86	0.26	0.90	0.23
Equality of Provinces *	0.95	0.16	0.92	0.20	0.91	0.22
Multiculturalism/Immigration	0.94	0.18	0.93	0.17	0.93	0.20

Note: * $p < .05$; ** $p < .01$

the most recent recruits. Opinion was also somewhat divided within the groups (adjusted standard deviations ranging from 0.32 to 0.29). As will be demonstrated below in the section concerning provincial differences, much of these differences can be attributed to the timing and relative success of Reform's regional mobilization and recruitment strategies. Earlier recruited western delegates were more likely to take polar positions with respect to the party's agenda for constitutional change, an agenda upon which Reform was founded and had recently strengthened within its party constitution.

A similar but weaker pattern emerged with respect to the government size and deficit index and Quebec's constitutional demands. Each group of delegates indicated strong opposition to Quebec's constitutional agenda with the earliest recruited delegates the most opposed (0.96), followed by the delegates recruited during the middle years (0.93), and the latest recruited delegates (0.90). Opinion about this index was most united within the first group (adjusted standard deviation 0.15) and became more diverse as opposition to Quebec's constitutional demands diminished (adjusted standard deviation of 0.21 for the 1989–1990 delegates and 0.23 for the

TABLE 5.18 · 1992 Assembly: Indexes by Province

	All Delegates		BC		Alberta		Sask./Manitoba		Ontario	
INDEX	MEAN	STD. DEV.	MEAN	STD. DEV.	MEAN	STD. DEV.	MEAN	STD. DEV.	MEAN	STD. DEV.
Welfare & Entitlements	0.87	0.22	0.88	0.21	0.87	0.22	0.86	0.23	0.86	0.22
Alienation	0.80	0.27	0.81	0.26	0.77	0.28	0.82	0.28	0.81	0.27
Language/Ethnicity	0.42	0.28	0.43	0.26	0.41	0.28	0.45	0.30	0.42	0.28
Federalism **	0.46	0.31	0.51	0.31	0.54	0.31	0.39	0.28	0.38	0.30
Gov't Size/Deficit **	0.94	0.15	0.98	0.08	0.95	0.14	0.92	0.18	0.93	0.17
Trade **	0.61	0.40	0.61	0.40	0.65	0.34	0.52	0.39	0.63	0.40
Quebec - Constitution	0.93	0.20	0.92	0.21	0.93	0.19	0.95	0.15	0.92	0.22
Charter/Abortion **	0.57	0.32	0.65	0.32	0.55	0.31	0.55	0.31	0.55	0.31
Crime	0.89	0.24	0.90	0.23	0.89	0.24	0.88	0.24	0.87	0.25
Equality of Provinces	0.92	0.20	0.94	0.18	0.93	0.19	0.95	0.16	0.90	0.23
Multicult/Immigration *	0.93	0.19	0.93	0.19	0.94	0.18	0.89	0.23	0.95	0.15

* $p < .05$; ** $p < .01$

1991–1992 delegates). These data indicate that, over time, Reform activists' hard line against Quebec was moderating, but only very slightly. The delegates were also very supportive of reducing the size of government and the deficit, with the earliest recruits most supportive (0.96), followed by the delegates recruited during 1989 and 1990 (0.94), and the latest recruits (0.93). Delegates in all recruitment categories were generally united in their opinions with respect to this index, although as support diminished opinion became slightly more diverse.

Opinions about the Charter and abortion were more complex. Delegates who were recruited during the middle years of 1989 and 1990 demonstrated the strongest civil-liberties position (0.61). The earliest recruits followed closely at 0.59. The latest recruited delegates distinguished themselves from the other two groups by being considerably less supportive of the civil-liberties position (0.53) than either of their earlier recruited counterparts. These data indicate that, over time, Reform was recruiting more activists who were less supportive of a civil liberties position on these matters. However, delegates in all groups demonstrated considerable diversity of opinion.

Opinions concerning the crime index and the equality of provinces index were also complex in that one group of delegates distinguished themselves in both cases. When considering crime issues, while all delegates held strong opinions in support of increased punishment, those recruited between the years of 1989 and 1990 held slightly more moderated opinions. Delegates indicated strong support for the equality of provinces, with the earliest recruited delegates slightly more supportive (0.95) than the later recruits (0.92 for the 1989–1990 recruits and 0.91 for the 1991–1992 delegates).

Overall, year of recruitment was a useful variable in measuring intra-party differences of opinion with respect to six of the eleven indexes. Definite patterns emerged with respect to the restructuring of the federation and Quebec's constitutional demands. Earliest recruited delegates were most in favour of a decentralized federation and most opposed to Quebec's constitutional demands. Later recruited delegates, although still supportive of these positions, were less intense in their support. A similar but less definite pattern emerged with respect to reducing the size of governments and their deficits. Interestingly, the latest recruited delegates were least supportive of the civil liberties position with respect to the Charter and abortion, indicating that over time, Reform was recruiting more social conservatives rather than fewer. As was to be expected given Reform's origins and founding principles, most delegates were strongly supportive of equal provinces, with the earliest recruits most supportive. Several, but not all of these patterns were replicated when we considered differences that were dependent upon delegates' province of residence.

Opinion Structure on Issue Indexes by Province

The data in Table 5.18 demonstrate that significant differences of opinion existed with respect to five of the indexes when opinions were analyzed by province of residence (federalism, government size and the deficit, trade, the Charter and abortion, and multiculturalism and immigration). However, only three (federalism, government size and the deficit, and the Charter and abortion) were the same as those where significant differences were found due to year of recruitment. This finding supports the proposition that political geography (province) is an important independent variable.

Significant provincial differences occurred with respect to the federalism index with Alberta and British Columbia delegates being most supportive of reforming the federation (0.54 and 0.51 respectively). Saskatchewan/Manitoba and Ontario delegates demonstrated markedly lower support (0.39 and 0.38 respectively) indicating a definite intra-party regional cleavage. Delegates from the two westernmost provinces, where Reform elected forty-six of its fifty-two members in 1993 and forty-nine of its sixty MPs in 1997, indicated strong support levels for decentralizing the federation that were significantly higher than the levels demonstrated by delegates from the other prairie provinces and Ontario. Therefore, it appears that where east-west cleavages occurred considering federal restructuring, in Reform they ran along the Alberta-Saskatchewan border rather than the Manitoba-Ontario border.

A similar, but less pronounced pattern emerged with respect to government size and the deficit. BC delegates led the way in being most supportive of smaller governments and deficits (0.98) followed by Albertans (0.95). Again, Saskatchewan and Manitoba delegates aligned themselves more closely with Ontario delegates in that, while still high, their support dropped to 0.92 and 0.93 respectively. These data lend evidence to the proposition that it was delegates (and by extrapolation the citizens) from the two westernmost provinces who were most likely to support neo-conservative fiscal policies and *laissez faire* economics.

Alberta delegates were most supportive of liberalized trade (0.65), followed by Ontarians (0.63), British Colombians (0.61), and delegates from Saskatchewan and Manitoba (0.52). Clearly, the most important demarcation here was between delegates from the have and have-not provinces, with have-province delegates demonstrating significantly higher levels of support for liberalized trade than that shown by delegates from the have-not provinces. A similar, although not as pronounced, pattern emerged with respect to the multiculturalism and immigration index. Here, delegates from Saskatchewan and Manitoba indicated lower levels of support for the libertarian, individualist position (0.89) than their Ontario, Alberta or BC counterparts (0.95, 0.94 and 0.93 respectively). Significant differences also occurred with respect to the Charter and abortion index with BC delegates distinguishing themselves from all other delegates by holding the highest support levels for the libertarian, individualist position (0.65 as compared to 0.55 for all the other delegates).

Overall, delegates from the different provinces and delegates recruited during different time periods demonstrated some significant differences of opinion. All delegate groups held consistent and united opinions on welfare, alienation and language issues. Differences did emerge, however, with respect to three of the indexes when compared by both province of residence and time of recruitment. Federalism issues distinguished Alberta and BC delegates from the others while have-not-province delegates distinguished themselves with respect to trade liberalization and continental economic integration. To better understand how these differences align with the overall opinion structure of Reform activists, and to further simplify the model, one final round factor analysis was performed and is presented below.

Final Factor Analysis of Indexes and Indicators

The eleven indexes were entered into the final factor equation along with ideological self-placement and the citizen-elite cleavage variable. As was indicate above, the citizen-elite variable loaded significantly on a number of the initial factors indicating that delegates' anti-political-establishment attitudes were associated with their thinking on several clusters of issues and may have constituted an underlying dimension on its own.[20] The results of the final factor procedure are presented in Table 5.19 and demonstrate that the eleven indexes and two items produced five final factors underlying the key dimensions of Reform delegate opinion structure.

The first factor corresponded to a neo-conservative policy agenda and included a considerable amount of ideological content. This factor

TABLE 5.19 · 1992 Assembly: Factor Analysis of Indexes and Items

	F1	F2	F3	F4	F5	
	Neo-con Ideology	Powerlessness	Societal Changes	Provincial Equality	Individual vs. Group	Communalities
Welfare	**.605**	.349	.075	.107	-.036	.506
Government Size	**.410**	.202	-.153	.360	-.060	.366
Trade	**.643**	-.293	-.066	.161	.127	.545
Alienation	-.058	**.659**	.034	.199	-.030	.480
Crime	.181	**.630**	-.098	-.054	.165	.469
Language-Ethnicity	.039	**.419**	**.571**	-.215	.025	.550
Quebec Const.	.096	-.147	**.715**	.083	-.144	.570
Charter/abortion	-.103	.009	**.521**	.177	**.522**	.586
Provincial Equality	.055	.025	.002	**.684**	-.028	.472
Federalism	.334	-.149	-.016	**.372**	.290	.356
Multiculturalism	.064	.113	-.134	-.122	**.806**	.699
L-R Ideology	**.654**	.076	.196	-.307	-.009	.566
Anti-establishment	.098	-.364	-.192	**-.474**	.063	.408
Eigenvalue	14.26	10.82	9.14	8.49	7.86	50.56
% of variance	12.0%	11.2%	9.6%	9.5%	8.3%	

included the welfare, government size and deficit, and the trade indexes as well as the ideological self-placement variable. This finding is significant for several reasons. Initially, one underlying neo-conservative dimension pervaded delegate opinion in relation to most of Reform's economic and social-program platform. Further, these data indicate that Reformers' neo-conservatism was ideologically charged. That is, Reform could fairly be characterized as a right-wing party with respect to its neo-conservative policy agenda. It is also significant that ideology underlay this first, and therefore most important factor (accounting for more variance than any other factor at 14.26 per cent), demonstrating that Reformers' right-of-centre ideology was most important when applied to questions about what role governments should play in managing Canadian society. The second factor linked Reformers' perceived lack of efficacy in the political system with their dissatisfaction with the functioning of the criminal justice system. This factor corresponds to Reformers sense of powerlessness in the political system, a disposition that also has implications for their thinking about language and ethnicity issues. Language and ethnicity issues, however, are even more closely related to delegates' opinions about Quebec's constitutional distinctiveness and the other rights issues, which make up the third factor. The fourth factor links Reformers' demands for provincial equality with their anti-political-establishment attitudes, and more marginally their views about the contemporary state of the federal distribution of power.[21] The final factor links Reformers' opinions about multiculturalism with their opinions about the Charter and tends to correspond with Reformers' support for individualism and individual rights over group rights and entitlements.

Interestingly, Quebec's constitutional demands were not strongly associated with the equality of provinces issue. In fact, equality of provinces stood out as a factor with its own underlying dimension most closely associated with Reformers' anti-political-establishment opinions. This linkage demonstrates the pervasive influence of Reform's western founding and its early mobilization strategy. Provincial equality and the Triple-E Senate agendas were highly charged symbols of western alienation and it is apparent that these remained a distinctive part of delegates' opinion structure, separate from their opinions on other constitutional matters.

The final factor analysis provides the most simplified portrait of Reform activists' opinion structure with ideology pervading their neo-conservatism most. In the final analysis, five major dimensions of Reform opinion structure could be identified: (1) an ideologically charged neo-conservative policy agenda; (2) a sense of powerlessness most closely associated with the functioning of the criminal justice system and to a lesser extent language and ethnicity issues; (3) a societal-change dimension that linked Quebec's constitutional demands with other changes brought about by the Charter and immigration; (4) a provincial-equality dimension that corresponded to Reform's founding as a western party; and (5) an individual versus group rights and entitlements dimension.

CONCLUSION

Analysis of delegates attending Reform's 1992 Assembly provided a demographic and opinion profile that substantiated some previous characterizations of the party while refuting others. The demographic profile demonstrated that Reform delegates came from higher socio-economic status groups, and were more likely to be relatively old, English-speaking males. This profile indicated that Reform was primarily a middle-class, urban party rather than a rural and agrarian party, as some analysis had suggested. Reform was also successful in mobilizing more than only disgruntled former Tories. In fact, it had mobilized more previously uninvolved activists than recruits from all other parties combined. Analysis did, however, reveal that most Reform delegates who had been involved with another party were likely to have been Tories and that the majority of all delegates voted for the Progressive Conservatives in past elections. Nevertheless, as the party expanded, it mobilized an even greater proportion of individuals with no previous political experience.

Contrary to claims that its leadership unduly manipulated the membership, delegates believed that their party functioned democratically, that the leadership was responsive to their opinions and, in turn, they supported the leadership and agreed that it should have powers enabling it to protect the party's image. Most importantly for a populist party, delegates felt efficacious about their power within the party, believing that their activities had significant impact on party policy and strategy. Delegates appeared to understand and accept the dynamic tension at work between the leadership and members. They were willing to support the leadership by allowing it the requisite authority to fulfill its role and did not appear to be opposed to allowing Manning considerable latitude in interpreting Reform's policy positions, so long as they continue to exercise a final plebiscitary check on all matters.

The party's anti-political-establishment populism was observed in delegates' perceptions that there was substantial inequality in the amount of influence over government policy between the average citizen and political and social elites. They demonstrated their disaffection from organized special interests and tended to view themselves as outsiders. They also conceptualized regional power imbalances in that they perceived Quebecers and Central Canadians as the most influential groups of citizens, and westerners, Maritimers and average voters least influential.

Ideologically, delegates saw themselves as distinctively right of centre. They viewed their party in almost identical terms and viewed themselves as being ideologically closer to the average Canadian citizen than to any government or other party. They viewed themselves as ideologically closest to most Americans, followed by the people in their provinces and ideologically farthest away from NDP governments and parties. Delegates tended to view all other parties and most governments as left of centre, while locating the average Canadian at the middle of the ideological spectrum. They also supported a neo-conservative policy agenda, demonstrated clear patterns of support for an anti-political-establishment, libertarian agenda, equality of provinces, and some, but not wholesale restructuring of the federation.

This analysis presents a portrait of the Reform Party that in many ways differs significantly from portraits that have focused on Manning's perspectives, goals and ideas. Throughout the remainder of Reform's history, Manning continued to attempt to position the party within what he perceived to be the contemporary currents of public opinion. Reform activists, on the other hand, continued to help keep the party's policy agenda more consistent with their right-of-centre, neo-conservative, populist, anti-political-establishment, and libertarian attitudes.

The Road to Official Opposition

Reformers entered the 1990s assured by their leadership that they were on course for a two-election climb to government. As events unfolded, the party would fall considerably short of this goal. Having failed to make an electoral breakthrough into Ontario in either the 1993 or 1997 elections, Manning would embark upon yet another expansion strategy from which Reform would not survive as a party. Paradoxically, neither would Manning. Only six months into the new millennium, both he and Reform passed into the pages of history. What follows in this chapter is an account of Reform's dramatic electoral breakthrough in the 1993 election and its rise to status as Her Majesty's Official Opposition after the 1997 election. An account of Reform's decommissioning follows in chapter seven.

Preparing the Ground – The 1992 Assembly

Reform's 1993 campaign platform was based on the party's founding principles and the resolutions emanating from the various Assemblies (primarily those from the 1991 Saskatoon gathering) that were fine-tuned into an election platform at the 1992 Winnipeg meeting. Although the party's eastern expansion necessitated a national campaign that would not be dependent alone on its western-alienation planks, because Reform was still a party in transition, both organizationally and geographically, some campaigning on the hot-button issues of regional alienation could not be avoided.

In preparation for the 1992 Assembly the executive council and its Assembly '92 Resolutions Committee established its most comprehensive policy development process up to that point. The process began one year prior to the assembly when branch executives and ordinary members were notified of the first stage of the development process. Branches submitted resolutions through January 1992 for compilation into a draft campaign platform. The resolutions committee completed the draft platform in early April. The draft was sent back to the constituencies for review and debated in over 120 branches by over five thousand members who proposed amendments and submitted nearly a hundred additional resolutions.[1] The final draft platform included nineteen planks, ten of which dealt with economic issues while only three addressed the Canadian constitution.[2]

Aided by electronic voting capabilities that allowed for quick tabulation of provincial results,[3] delegates to the 1992 Assembly debated all nineteen planks of the election platform and ten amendments to the party's constitution.[4] The platform was further synthesized into three main planks focusing on: (1) economic reform by way of deficit reduction; (2) law, order and criminal justice reform; and (3) non-constitutional parliamentary reform aimed at making Parliament more accountable.

Debate at the 1992 Assembly again demonstrated that delegates were more ideologically polarized over a number of issues than was the leadership. Delegates moved the fiscal plank further to the right than the Policy Committee had recommended. They adopted resolutions that would have forced all future federal governments to balance their budgets in each three-year period or be obliged to call an election on the issue. They also adopted policies advocating a flat income tax and a staged reduction of the GST until it was eliminated. The delegate-strengthened fiscal agenda would form the centrepiece of Reform's 1993 election campaign.

Nor did delegates shirk from dealing with sensitive social programs like health care. What emerged was a health care plank that supported revoking the Canada Health Act and allowing the provinces to establish whatever health delivery systems they desired, leaving the voters of each province to judge the efforts of their respective governments. A Reform government would be committed to ensuring only some measure of equity between the provinces by way of federal equalization payments. They also adopted policy on the Canadian constitution, language, federalism, immigration, trade, and populist reform of political institutions. For the most part, these mirrored delegate opinion structure as outlined in chapter five.

Debate broke down, however, as delegates demonstrated their divergent opinions on language policy. Many who supported a bilingual federal government objected to adopting Manning's territorial bilingualism model. Eventually the entire language plank was tabled in favour of existing policy that committed Reform only to repealing the Official Languages Act. In formally rejecting the interim policy of territorial bilingualism, delegates made the first significant use of the powers to ratify or reject interim policies that they gained at the 1991 Saskatoon Assembly. This would not completely deter the leadership from speculating about such a policy in future years, but it did force Manning and others to temper their enthusiasm for this proposal and to defer to existing Reform policy when making public pronouncements about language policy.

The debate on the final plank dealing with moral issues produced a typical reaction from delegates. After only one strongly worded anti-abortion speech from the floor that received a loud negative response from many delegates, Stephen Harper interjected from the podium. The speech from the floor argued that current Reform policy of constituency representation on moral issues could put its MPs in the position of being forced to support the "murder of babies" against their own moral convictions. Harper responded by arguing that if Reform candidates were not willing to support the principles of constituency representation then they should not be Reform candidates. After these comments received loud applause, he went on to argue that each MP had the democratic right to argue in favour of his or her position during the debate, but after a constituency consensus had been reached, an MP's duty was to vote in accordance with that consensus. Delegates responded by overwhelmingly endorsing (95 per cent support) a populist abortion plank that placed constituency representation above the personal convictions of MPs. Sensing the importance of this issue, both for the delegates and the attending media, the chairman closed the matter by stating that referenda and constituency representation constituted fundamental Reform policy and if candidates who did not support these principles were nominated, they would have done so via flawed nomination processes. Delegates overwhelmingly supported the comments and ended the policy debate by formally adopting the election platform with a vote of 99 per cent in favour.[5] In the final analysis, the resolutions that comprised the election platform accurately reflected delegate opinion on issues where opinion was united. Noticeably absent from the platform were explicit policy statements aimed at addressing regional grievances, issues where we measured greater divisions amongst delegates.

Manning provided delegates and another national audience[6] with his keynote address later that night. This speech mirrored the election platform in that it emphasized economic matters and political reform. However, given the proximity of the Charlottetown constitutional referendum, the speech was constructed around Reform's constitutional position as the only federalist party to oppose the accord. Assuming a No victory was imminent, Manning proposed a post-constitutional political agenda that included a moratorium on first ministers constitutional conferences. He argued that in voting No, Canadians would be telling their politicians to focus their energies and attentions on the economy and on making federal policies and institutions more responsive to the people.[7] The speech offered little that was new and concluded by directing voters to Reform's Blue Book and Manning's *New Canada.* The assembly closed having succeeded in providing Manning and the Reform candidates with a mandate to pursue a right-of-centre, populist agenda in the 1993 federal election campaign.

Pre-campaign Posturing

In three major speeches between March and June, Manning unveiled the party's "Zero-in-Three" economic platform. Reform's economic blueprint called for the elimination of the federal deficit in three years through a combination of spending reductions and economic growth rather than tax increases. The release of each phase was accompanied by a two-pronged strategy consisting of national media attention generated by the leader, and constituency association promotions designed to maximize publicity and raise the profile of party at the local level.

Phase I, released in a March 1993 address in Toronto, stated that in Reform's view it was "the mounting deficit and debt, and the interest payments thereon, that constitute the greatest threat to Canada's social services safety net, including Medicare."[8] Manning went further by arguing that there was "absolutely no way any federal administration could undertake to balance the federal budget, stimulate job creation, preserve essential services, or offer tax relief, without wholesale reform of federal transfers to individuals and provinces."[9] Based on the government's 1992 projections of a $34.6 billion deficit, and a predicted annual economic growth rate of 3.5 per cent over the three-year period, Reform calculated that balancing the budget would require a total of $19 billion in spending cuts. Most of that money could be found through reducing transfers to provinces and individuals. The plan would maintain federal funding at current levels in areas deemed to be of the highest priority to Canadians (health care, education, child benefits, guaranteed income supplements and veterans' pensions) but would reorganize contributory programs like the Canada Pension Plan and Unemployment Insurance along a self-sustaining model. Reform would also direct non-contributory program payments like Old Age Security to those whose incomes were below the average family income. Total savings from Phase I would equal $9 billion. Upon release of the Manning address, candidates were directed to "speak with one voice" by not deviating from the text of the plan until further details were released. While some activists and members registered their objections to again being dictated to by the leadership, the objections were few in numbers because the platform was based largely on majority opinion within the party.

Phase II, released in an address at Vancouver in early April, concentrated on job creation and the reform of federal subsidies to business and special interests. Again, spending cuts were prominent and included the elimination of regional diversification programs, reduction in grants to defence contractors, elimination of financial support for Hibernia, elimination of business tax concessions, grants and loans, and elimination of funding for special interest groups. Savings in Phase II would total $5 billion. With its release, candidates were instructed to redraft a national party news release to fit their own circumstances and spread out into their respective communities seeking media opportunities to promote the plan.[10]

Phase III was announced in the nation's capital in late April and dealt primarily with reductions in expenditures on Parliament and other federal institutions. Total savings from selected cuts in the budgets of the Prime Minister's Office, the House of Commons, Senate and Governor General's offices, and elimination of multicultural and bilingual funding, among others, were projected to save another $5 billion. This brought Reform's projected total savings to $19 billion. Although the full election platform was rounded out with planks on criminal justice and parliamentary reform, it was clear that Reform's primary focus would be economic.

The "Zero-in-Three" publicity strategy was unconventional in that it was rare for parties to release virtually their entire platform so far in advance of an election. But the strategy fit Reform's circumstances and was designed to test market its campaign organization strategy. Circumstances dictated that Reform would have to approach the election differently than would the traditional federal parties. It could not afford to finance a full-fledged leadership tour, nor a complex national media campaign. Rather, it would have to rely on its members to carry a much larger burden than would members of the traditional parties. The strategy also allowed Reform to further develop its populist structure and orientation. Establishing meaningful roles for members complimented their expectations of what their roles were supposed to be in a federal election campaign. This approach also demonstrated how much Reform differed from the traditional parties, albeit an approach that was dictated as much by circumstance as by populist design. Although all parties rely on their volunteers to some extent, for many aspects of its campaign Reform was almost completely dependent on its volunteers. Reform's campaign organization reflected its organizational structure, consisting of essentially two tiers, the national campaign team and the candidates' campaigns at the constituency level.[11]

The national campaign team consisted of a campaign committee made up of national office managers, campaign advisors, a candidate liaison network, and consultants. The campaign committee worked out of the Calgary national office and was supported by national office staff and ad hoc policy advisors and coordinators. Within that campaign committee existed a six-member campaign management committee (CMC) that included the leader and other senior members of the campaign team.[12] Communications flowed directly between the national campaign and the constituencies without further provincial or regional organization. Regional and provincial issues were addressed at the local level and by the leader in specifically tailored speeches while on tour. When local issues became national, they were managed by the national campaign team rather than by provincial sub-units, as was typically the case in other parties.

Budget constraints dictated that the party could not afford to develop or purchase a comprehensive national, in-house polling operation. Nevertheless, the party leadership believed that they had to make use of whatever polling data they could obtain and also develop some in-house polling operations for candidates who desired to make use of such campaign techniques. Similar to the overall campaign organizational structure, polling

TABLE 6.1 · Calgary South West Support Levels, Gorgias Polling – 1993

Party	1988 Election Results	May 1993	August 1993	October 1993	1993 Election Results
Reform	13.4	41.6	38.0	56.5	59.9
PC	65.2	29.7	34.3	24.1	20.1
Liberal	11.5	22.0	22.6	14.4	13.6
NDP	8.1	4.8	3.3	4.2	3.4
Other	1.8	1.9	1.8	0.8	3.0

Source for 1988 and 1993 results: Elections Canada.

operations were divided into two tiers, one national and the other designed for local campaigns. The national campaign purchased national polling data from Environics Research Group, who provided the party with its standard package of national, regional and provincial breakdowns of voter support, demographic breakdowns and daily tracking polls. While the party had previously contracted with Environics to add specific Reform-exclusive questions to their surveys, campaign organizers deemed this unnecessary (and too expensive) during the campaign period. The constituency polling operation also reflected the party's organizational structure in that the project was initiated and developed by the national office in conjunction with consultants and presented to the candidates as a standardized package that could be modified to suit local issues and interests. Gorgias Research Consultants[13] was contracted to develop a cost-effective, standardized constituency-polling package that could be implemented by volunteers at the local level. The package allowed local campaigns to use volunteer labour to collect the data with Gorgias verifying and compiling the results. Despite the low monetary costs of the local polling projects, most constituencies and candidates opted out of the project because they thought that their volunteers could be used more effectively in literature distribution and door knocking. However, the project was used extensively by Manning's Calgary South West campaign and proved effective in accurately measuring his climb in the polls.

The Reform advertising campaign had to deal with two constraints: the amount of airtime the party would be legally allowed to purchase, and the amount of airtime it could afford to purchase. Originally, the federal

Elections Act allotted Reform only eleven minutes of national advertising time.[14] After a successful challenge in the Alberta Court of Queen's Bench, Reform was awarded twenty-three minutes, later reduced to seventeen minutes. The court-imposed redistribution of airtime provided Reform with a moral and political victory but still little time when compared to the Conservatives' 116 minutes.[15] But the more pressing problem for Reform remained its inability to afford to purchase any national airtime. In stark contrast to the other major parties,[16] Reform purchased no national advertising during the 1993 campaign. Rather, the national campaign targeted a few select markets (Vancouver, Calgary, Edmonton, Toronto and Winnipeg) in conjunction with local candidates on a cost-shared, cooperative basis. Any additional advertising had to be purchased by the local campaigns.[17] The national organization sold media packages to individual candidates and local campaigns at a cost of $500 each. These included five television ads, as well as radio and newspaper ads that were produced in the second and third weeks of the campaign. Despite the party's attempts at television advertising, its major promotional efforts came by way of literature drops. Local volunteers delivered over 19 million pieces of Reform literature during the campaign.[18]

Campaign financing was also based on Reform's two-tiered organization. The national office maintained a membership list that allowed it to solicit funds directly from every member on a regular basis, allowing Reform to collect approximately $6 million in 1992, most of which was donated by individual members and was used to build up constituency war chests, fund the leader's activities, the activities of the national office, and to communicate with the membership. But the national organization was spending money almost as quickly as it was collecting contributions. At its 1993 pre-election summer meetings, the CMC reported that the national party had less than a $250,000 to spend on its part of the campaign, but was in the process of raising advertising funds through its cooperative program with key, well-funded constituency associations. Many constituency associations, on the other hand, were flush with cash. The branches had also been regularly soliciting funds from the membership, with similar success as the national party, but were spending much less on their activities. The western branches had been building their local campaign funds for three years and many in Alberta and BC started the campaign having already secured enough money to exceed their campaign spending limits. On average, the eighty-six western constituencies had each built up a $41,000 campaign war chest. Most of the recently organized Ontario constituencies, however, were not nearly as affluent, with most far short of having enough funds to spend anywhere near their expense limits.

Despite the financial successes of the western branches, the CMC deemed it necessary to attempt to finance the national campaign from funds raised during the campaign period. To that end, it sent out two fundraising letters and conducted a phone-a-thon during the campaign period. The leader's tour often charged an admission fee for its events as well as soliciting cash donations.[19] The branches and candidates continued to raise funds through membership sales, local fundraising campaigns and at local campaign events. The combined efforts succeed beyond even the most wildly optimistic predictions. During the first three weeks of the campaign the party and its members raised over $3 million, with the branches alone collecting over $2 million. The national mail campaign raised $560,000 while another $500,000 was raised through membership sales, donations to the national campaign, the leader's tour, and through contributions by businesses.[20] By mid-campaign the national letter/phone campaign surpassed the $600,000 mark while constituencies had raised an average of $11,500 each. With two weeks remaining in the campaign, the party had raised a total of $5.1 million, with the sustainer letters collecting $890,000. The national campaign collected another $800,000 and constituencies were reporting $3.5 million in contributions. By campaign's end the party had raised approximately $6 million and would finish with a surplus.[21]

The 1993 Election Campaign

As Reform entered the 1993 campaign it was on the precipice of its first significant parliamentary breakthrough. Yet it began the campaign languishing in fourth place in national public opinion polls. After an initial boost generated by the Zero-in-Three promotions, the party had settled back to 7 per cent nationally. Party strategists were privately conceding that no seat, including Manning's, was guaranteed. They nevertheless cobbled together a rather sophisticated plan. Dividing the campaign period into three distinct stages, Reform would open by introducing voters to its populism through its "let the people speak" plank. During the second stage Reform would promote its economic strategy while the third and final stage would be devoted to discussing political and social reform. For the most part, Reform was successful in sticking to its agenda.

The leader's tour succeeded in promoting Reform's platform to a national audience while at the same time allowed Manning enough flexibility to tailor his speeches to various regional subtleties. Given Reform's precarious financial position at the start of the campaign, and with few high profile candidates, none with Manning's national stature, the leader's tour would also serve as the sole vehicle used for announcing new issue positions and strategic reactions to campaign dynamics. The strategy achieved a certain measure of success in that Manning garnered substantial media attention, increasing in volume as he moved from west to east. He received as much attention from the *Globe and Mail* as did Liberal leader Jean Chrétien, although both leaders received less coverage from most major newspapers than did Prime Minister Kim Campbell.[22] The large volume of media attention generated by Manning's tour reversed the trend of the pre-campaign period when Reform received scant attention as the media focused on the new Conservative Prime Minister and her party's climb in the polls. The tour also succeeded on a national scale despite the fact that Manning had to spend a great deal more time in his riding than did the other leaders.

While national in perspective, the majority of the tour's time was spent in the western provinces and particularly in Alberta. The tour kicked off in Alberta before making four major swings through southern Ontario and four through BC. After typically not more than three or four days of campaigning outside of Alberta, the tour would return to Reform's heartland. Manning spent at least parts of twenty-one days in Alberta, fifteen of which he made appearances in Calgary including spending five of seven Saturdays there. The tour spent a total of twelve days in Ontario, including three in Ottawa for the debates. Manning made only two trips to the Maritimes The remainder of the leader's time was spent in the West; approximately nine days in BC and about four days combined in Saskatchewan and Manitoba.

Initially, the tour was a modest and unglamorous affair. Manning and the entire tour staff flew economy class, as did the media entourage. Because of budgetary constraints, the tour style complimented the anti-elite, populist image Reform was attempting to craft for itself. It also left Manning open to closer media scrutiny than any of the other leaders, a situation he handled well, reinforcing the more open, populist image. The membership also played key roles in the smooth functioning of the tour, especially in the early days when local volunteers managed to gather large crowds of supporters with often less than a few days' notice. For example, the campaign team decided to hold the first big Alberta rally in the small central city of Red Deer rather than a larger centre. With less than three days' notice the Red Deer branch activists and campaign volunteers managed to turn an expected crowd of 1,500 into over 3,000.[23] Similar organizational successes accompanied the tour across the country. As momentum and financial contributions grew, the party chartered a plane to make a cross-country final-week push, drawing over 45,000 people to the twelve scheduled events with over 6,000 gathering for the final rally in Calgary.

Manning kicked off the campaign by introducing voters to Reform's anti-political-establishment platform.[24] He was not timid in his rhetoric, attempting to establish a link between Reform and the very future of democracy in Canada.

> For six years, over 100,000 Canadians have been building a constructive alternative to the old political parties – a political movement based on democratic principles.... If Reformers are beaten down by special interests or whichever old-line party has the most money – then it won't be just Reform that fails the test, it will be democracy itself that fails.[25]

Only in populist-prone Alberta could Manning legitimately equate Reform fortunes with the future of democracy. More importantly, these early statements demonstrated the regional, sometimes parochial nature of Reform's national campaign. As he moved east, Manning adjusted the populist message to fit local circumstances. In Ontario he urged voters to break with tradition.[26] Arguing that the NDP no longer represented working Canadians and union members, Manning demonstrated his belief that Reform's brand of populism could appeal to a much broader coalition than simply disaffected right-wingers. In the Maritimes he again urged voters to break with tradition, this time by urging Maritimers to cast ballots for their children rather than for their grandfathers.[27]

With the Liberals successfully establishing their employment agenda as the early campaign theme,[28] Manning attempted to bridge his populist message with Reform's economic principles. He launched direct attacks on both the Liberals and the Conservatives without immediately spelling out his own plans, other than stating that Reform would not be advocating government intervention in the economy in an attempt at stimulating job creation. On the heels of Campbell's comments that the employment situation would not improve until the next century, Manning elaborated on the "let the people speak" theme by urging voters to "ask hard questions about the connection between debt and jobs."[29] He attacked the Conservatives' record on the deficit and declared that Campbell's new team had no new plan. He attempted to re-establish his own agenda by attacking the Liberal's economic platform for ignoring the connection between high levels of government spending, high taxes, and jobs. As the Conservatives' fortunes began to flounder,[30] Manning moved to establish Reform as the only legitimate party for right-of-centre voters.[31]

The Conservatives presented Reform with an opportunity to move more fully into the second stage of its campaign plan when the Prime Minister commented that she could not release the details of her own deficit-cutting plan because the government books were in such a mess. Manning immediately seized upon the opportunity and shifted his focus to the details of Reform's Zero-in-Three platform. Campaigning in Manitoba later that same week, he attempted to move from the negative, program cuts and deficit reduction, to the positive, what he called the light at the end of the tunnel. Upon returning to Calgary, he declared tax reform and tax relief to be the rewards for voters willing to suffer $19 billion in deficit reduction cuts.[32] He committed Reform to reducing and then eliminating the GST and replacing the current income tax system with a simplified flat tax, closing most loopholes and eliminating most tax credits and deductions.

The economic plan garnered Reform its most influential editorial support during the campaign. The *Globe and Mail* editorial of September 23 commended Manning and Reform for having "the only deficit plan we've seen." [33] The *Globe*'s endorsement was representative of the positive media coverage the party was now receiving. Reform was establishing considerable credibility on deficit reduction and, with the Conservative campaign becoming increasingly disorganized and frantic, Reform was gradually becoming the alternative for voters most concerned with the government's finances. Reform's climb in the polls attracted increased media attention and a corresponding increase in counterattacks by the other parties.[34] Up to this point in the campaign both the Conservatives and the Liberals had been content to ignore Reform, or dismiss it as a fringe player. As Reform picked up momentum, all three of the traditional parties launched attacks on its policies, keying specifically on its social policies. Campbell's comments that "this is not the time to get involved in very, very serious discussions" about important social policy reforms, strengthened Reform's message that it was the only party with a fiscally conservative plan to deal with social and governmental reform. With the Conservatives slipping in the polls, Reform and the Bloc Quebecois gaining momentum, and with both Campbell and Chrétien publicly speculating about the possibility of a minority government, Manning prepared to introduce Reform's regional representation theme as he unveiled the party's parliamentary reform plank.[35] At a rally in Red Deer attended by over three thousand supporters, Manning delivered a speech tailored specifically to Alberta voters and reminiscent of the regional rhetoric of Reform's founding. As one journalist commented, "the rhetoric, Mr. Manning's fiercest yet, appeared to shift the tone of the Reform campaign. Unlike his recent speeches in Ontario… his address purposely hit the hot buttons for the Reform Party's core membership."[36] The overriding theme emphasized the regional representation issues that Reform had been advocating for years. Manning also attempted to counter the other parties' thinly veiled suggestions about strategic voting by urging Alberta voters to stick to their convictions and not be persuaded by speculation about a minority government.

> If you want to teach those old-line parties a lesson, the ones that have failed you and the ones that have betrayed you, then elect Reformers.... No true Albertan votes out of fear... The person who says, "I'd like to vote Reform but I'm afraid I might split the vote and elect the Liberals," is voting from the wrong motivation... We should vote our conviction for what is right for our country and our province, and let the chips fall where they may.[37]

These arguments clearly demonstrated the realities of the Reform campaign. Despite attempts at gaining support in other regions, the party's electoral prospects hinged on success in the western provinces, particularly in Alberta.

As Reform came under increasing media scrutiny and further attacks from its competitors, Manning attempted to enter the mid-campaign nationally televised leaders debates on the offensive.[38] He introduced the third stage of the campaign in a speech to a meeting of the Canadian Club and Empire Club in Toronto by squarely addressing the Quebec issue and Reform's role in the next parliament. Arguing that the old federalists were losing the battle for the minds and hearts of Quebecers, he committed Reform to speaking the plain truth to Quebecers on the state of constitutional opinion outside of Quebec. "That plain truth is this: that for those Quebecers who want to separate, the choice is independence or Canada. We want to take away from the promoters of separatism that soft, mushy ground of sovereignty-association which they offer to Quebecers as intermediate ground between independence and Canada."[39] Manning concluded by introducing a theme that would become prominent in the final weeks of the campaign. For the first time in the campaign, he specifically addressed several hypothetical scenarios while speculating on the prospects of strategic voting. With the Conservative vote collapsing, he moved to exploit what he saw as the virtue of a minority government in which Reform, rather than the BQ, would hold the balance of power. "If Canadians do not trust either of the old parties enough to give either a majority, then it is absolutely imperative that the balance of power in any minority Parliament be held by federalists (we would argue by New Federalists) rather than separatists."[40] He elaborated by claiming that the parliamentary changes Reform was advocating (freer votes, fixed election dates, referenda, and recall) could also make a minority parliament more effective and representative than an un-reformed majority parliament.[41] He would repeat these arguments during the leaders debates.

There is general agreement amongst political scientists that leaders debates help shape public attitudes towards the party leaders.[42] Their impact on campaign outcomes is less dramatic. In fact, "the literature is almost unanimous in its conclusion that voting preferences are not changed."[43] Nevertheless, debates often have an impact on voters' opinions of various issues and evidence can be found of vote intention fluctuations immediately following leadership debates.[44] The normal debate dynamics were complicated in the 1993 campaign by the unique set of organizational and strategic choices that had to be made by the parties and broadcasters. The debate over who would participate in which leaders debates emphasized the changing structure of party competition that was to be the outcome of the 1993 election. That the established protocol of allowing only the three traditional party leaders to participate would no longer suffice was evident to all. But the question of what roles the leaders of the new parties would play and how much the traditional debate format would be changed in accommodating them had to be strategically negotiated amongst all the political and media players.

With Manning being the only unilingual leader, his inability to speak French left open the possibility of one regional party leader being excluded from one debate while another, Bloc Quebecois leader Lucien Bouchard, having the opportunity to participate in both the French- and English-language debates. Initially, the three traditional parties attempted to exclude both leaders from full participation in both debates. When it became evident that Bouchard would have to be allowed to participate fully in the French debate, it also became impossible to exclude Manning from full participation in the English debate. Eventually, both leaders were granted full participation in the English debate, but the problems of the French debate remained. If the unilingual Manning was to be excluded from the French debate, the traditional parties risked handing Manning a quintessential Reform issue in a reopened language debate. Not willing to risk being perceived as reducing Manning to second-class-status by excluding him, it was eventually decided that he would be allowed an opening and closing statement, in English, with limited participation in the French question-and-answer session.

Manning used his brief time in the French debate to explain to Quebecers his New Federalism vision, to invite Quebec federalists to join him, and to warn Quebec separatists that sovereignty-association was not an option. Reiterating the theme he had embarked upon the previous week, he warned Quebecers that there was no market outside of Quebec for a sovereignty-association of the type proposed by Quebec Premier Jacques Parizeau and Bouchard. While his performance in the French language debate was admirable, given his limited time and unilingual abilities, Manning's real test came a day later in the English-language debate.

The English-language debate format proved beneficial. It levelled the playing field by creating a sense of equality that no other segment of the campaign offered. As one observer commented, "the format treated all leaders equally, and thus it was easy to forget that Campbell leads a national majority government while Manning's party has only a single MP."[45] From the beginning, Manning was determined to play a non-traditional role. In attempting to demonstrate the similarities between the two old brokerage parties, and Reform's differences, he also adopted a non-traditional debating style. The strategy involved having Manning appear statesmanlike by not entering into personal attacks on the other leaders and attempting to rise above the fracas when participants interrupted each other or attempted to shout down an opponent. He urged voters to base their judgments not on the leaders' personality or debate performance, but on how each addressed the issues. The strategy initially worked well with Manning at times acting as moderator between two other excited combatants. However, as the debate progressed Manning too often used his scarce time to ask questions of the other leaders, in effect turning the podium over to his competitors and losing the opportunity to enunciate Reform's policies. With no defining moments or clear knockout-punches landed, post-debate polls indicated that the trends established in the first four weeks of the campaign were continuing. Manning had at least held his own in the English language debate and, with three weeks remaining in the campaign, had solidified Reform's position as a clear alternative for right-of-centre voters outside of Quebec.

With the Conservative vote continuing to collapse and Reform fortunes rising, especially in Alberta and BC, Reform focused its attacks on the Liberal economic plan and the rise of the Bloc in Quebec.[46] In both instances Manning argued that a large contingent of Reform MPs would keep the Liberals fiscally responsible. At the same time, he maintained that Reformers would keep the Bloc and the Liberals from negotiating any new initiatives or programs designed to appease Quebec but unacceptable to the majority of voters in the rest of Canada. Reform also continued to be on the defensive in explaining its social and healthcare politics,[47] as well as defending itself against charges of racism within its ranks.[48] Typical to how the campaign had unfolded to date, any damage done by the racism accusations was limited when the issue was moved off the front pages by the publicity surrounding the Conservatives' "Chrétien ads."[49] Manning spent the final week on a cross-country tour campaigning on the themes of trust, accountability and institutional reform, while urging voters to not give the Liberals a majority government. By this time Reform was leading the Conservatives in national opinion polls and party insiders were confident that Reform would form the official opposition, win a majority of the seats in the West, sweep BC and Alberta, pick up as many as a dozen Ontario seats, and possibly three in the Maritimes.

Once the ballots were counted, Reform placed second in popular vote with almost 19 per cent support nationally, despite not contesting seats in Quebec. In capturing 52 seats (and finishing second in 79 ridings) the party fell just short of becoming Canada's official opposition. It would take its place in Parliament with the third largest caucus, just 2 seats shy of the

Table 6.2 · 1993 Reform Party Vote and Seat Totals by Province

	Percentage of Vote	Seats Won
British Columbia	36	24
Alberta	52	22
Saskatchewan	27	4
Manitoba	22	1
Ontario	20	1
Quebec	–	–
New Brunswick	8.5	0
Nova Scotia	13	0
Prince Edward's Island	1	0
Newfoundland	1.5	0
Canada	19	52

Bloc's 54 seats. Reform winners defeated incumbent MPs in 35 ridings (19 Conservatives, 15 New Democrats and 1 independent).

Party insiders were pleased with the level of support Reform received in Ontario (20 per cent), but were disappointed that they managed to win only one seat. While not expecting a major breakthrough in the Maritimes, the party's 13 per cent support in Nova Scotia provided organizers with reason to believe that Reform had potential to grow and expand in the Atlantic region. Most disappointing were the Manitoba and Saskatchewan results. While the party was aware of its lower support levels in prairie ridings outside of Alberta, it was anticipating winning a greater number of seats in Manitoba and possibly several more in Saskatchewan. As was indicated earlier, the Reform leadership had faced considerable difficulty in expelling dissidents from the party in Manitoba and this hurt their overall organizational efforts there. The Manitoba and Saskatchewan results further emphasized how dependent Reform was on its volunteer campaigners. Where Reform was not well organized at the local level, and where it could not count on a large contingent of volunteers, it was not nearly as electorally competitive as it was in better-organized ridings.

Where members were numerous and well organized, Reform was highly competitive. Not surprisingly, the party performed best in Alberta, garnering 52 per cent of the vote and winning all but four of Alberta's twenty-six seats. The party swept rural BC and Vancouver Island, losing only one seat outside of Vancouver. It captured 36 per cent of the provincial vote in BC, and won twenty-four of that province's thirty-two seats. On the surface, the election results appeared to produce an equitable distribution of seats for Reform when compared to its percent of the national vote. Its fifty-two seats represented 17.6 per cent of the total, similar to its 18.7 per cent share of the national vote. However, when broken down by province, it is apparent that Reform both benefited from and was penalized by the distorting effects of the electoral system as it translated votes into seats. The electoral system clearly benefited the party in Alberta, where it won 84.6 per cent of the seats by capturing 52.3 per cent of the vote, and in BC, where it captured 75 per cent of the seats based on only 36.4 per cent of the vote. Reform received roughly the correct percentage of seats when compared to its popular vote in Saskatchewan (28.6 per cent of the seats on 27.2 per cent of the vote). In the other provinces the party was penalized by the electoral system and received far fewer seats than its percentage of the popular vote. The distortions were greatest in Ontario where the party won 20.1 per cent of the vote and won only 1 per cent of the seats. In Manitoba, Reform won 7.1 per cent of the seats on 22.4 per cent of the vote while in Nova Scotia it won no seats despite capturing 13.3 per cent of the vote. The results left Reform with a parliamentary caucus characterized by an even greater regional polarization than its vote distribution. Nevertheless, the long sought-after parliamentary breakthrough had arrived and Reform entered Canada's thirty-fifth parliament determined to become "Her Majesty's constructive alternative."[50]

The 1993 election campaign had been, by all accounts, a stunning success for the Reform. The party had campaigned on a platform made up of neo-conservative economic and justice policy, anti-Quebec constitutional accommodation, and anti-political-establishment populism. Its strategy of publishing and releasing its platform six months prior to the election indicated a sign of things to come. Reform had deviated from the established practices of brokerage party campaigning and forced the traditional parties to follow suit. Its strategy of building a platform based upon its members' opinions over the course of the previous six years also represented a dramatic departure from the pattern of issue brokering that had characterized Canada's party system for over thirty years. In only six years Reform had realized the first half of its two-election strategy. It had succeeded in making a breakthrough into the Canadian Parliament by displacing the Conservatives as Canada's party of the right. However, as the 1997 election results would later indicate, accomplishing the second task would prove elusive.

Into the 35th Parliament

Reform's fifty-two MPs entered Canada's thirty-fifth Parliament determined to adhere to the party's populist principles by conducting themselves differently than the traditional parties. They declared that caucus solidarity would be less important than faithful representation of constituent opinion. At the same time, the party dedicated itself to expanding its electoral base outside of the western provinces. Almost immediately, Manning was confronted with the difficult task of brokering between these two conflicting agendas. The party was often pilloried in the press for some of its MPs politically incorrect positions as MPs attempted to represent what they believed to be majority opinion in their constituencies. When Manning took action to stem the tide of media criticism, he was openly criticized by the Reform rank-and-file for allegedly ignoring grassroots opinion. This pattern characterized the party's inter-election parliamentary performance. Reform MPs would often make public statements from which Manning felt he had to distance himself. The caucus would meet to sort out their differences and would subsequently perform much better in Parliament, until the next incident became public. By mid-1994 the grassroots were becoming restless with the caucus's performance and began pointing fingers at the leadership and the large number of former Tories on the Reform payroll.[51]

As frustration with the caucus's performance grew, Manning also encountered resistance to his handling of the party's expansion strategy. The party's planned move into Quebec served as another example of the inherent contradictions within Reform's agenda. At the same time the party established a twelve-member Quebec organizing committee and opened a regional office in Montreal, the party's language critic was attempting to represent Reform's core constituents by introducing amendments to the Official Languages Act that could be perceived to be anti-French.

Further discontent erupted when it was revealed that the Quebec expansion strategy was only one part of a much larger, ambitious demographic, geographic and ideological expansion plan. The attempt at broadening the party's base confused and at times angered many of the party's core supporters.[52] On the one hand, members were generally in agreement that the party needed to broaden its base. On the other hand, most members did not support the means chosen to achieve that end as the party seemingly broke with its anti-affirmative action policies by establishing committees to plan expansion strategies for youth, women and visible minorities. Many members feared that the party was losing sight of its founding principles in its quest for acceptance in Central Canada. Their concerns would be heard and their impact felt at the party's first assembly after the 1993 election.

The 1994 Ottawa Assembly would be characterized by two significant outcomes. Delegates positioned the party's policy platform even more solidly on the right while Manning, after facing significant challenges to his management style, would again rally the delegates around his leadership. The convention opened with public opinion polls placing Reform at only 10 per cent nationally, and down to only 15 per cent in its Alberta heartland. Many delegates openly argued that Reform had lost its direction since the 1993 breakthrough. In an effort at damage control, Manning allowed policy debate to proceed largely unfettered. Unlike past assemblies where Manning or Harper chaired policy debates and intervened often, Manning did not participate in the policy debate at all. He left it up to MPs or other party officials to intervene at critical junctures when they believed delegates were about to adopt extreme or unworkable positions. However, even the MPs would not succeed in significantly altering the course of proceedings. As one observer reported, "the positions eventually adopted still reflect a party that is far more radically conservative than any other political grouping in Canada... Even if some of their MPs might appear susceptible, the delegates were determined to show they were not in danger of catching the Ottawa disease."[53] In the end, delegates strengthened Reform's core policies and ensured that the leadership would have less room to deviate from membership opinion.[54] Although the policy outcomes left many in the national media speculating about a fringe party bent on appealing to extreme elements,[55] Manning backed the delegates' agenda by stating: "I don't see anything there to apologize or back off from."[56]

In a campaign-style keynote address to the assembly, Manning acknowledged Reform's lackluster performance over the previous year and assured delegates that the situation would change as Reform attempted to take on the separatists and supplant the Tories as the voice of conservative Canadians. Manning closed his speech by dedicating Reform to achieving three objectives: (1) take on the separatists; (2) challenge the status-quo federalists; and (3) offer Canadians a constructive alternative to the traditional parties and the status quo. Manning's assembly performance helped him achieve a 92 per cent vote of support when delegates responded to the mandatory leadership review on the final day of the gathering.

Following the 1994 Assembly, the Reform caucus improved its parliamentary performance[57] as MPs generally adhered to the party's neo-conservative economic strategy by successfully challenging the government's fiscal plans.[58] Manning began to forge what he termed a working relationship with Ontario's newly elected Conservative Premier Mike Harris, and the party made Atlantic Canada the main focus of its fall recruitment drive. Manning also succeeded in re-establishing Reform as the only party to oppose the various appeasement strategies in the lead up to Quebec's 1995 sovereignty referendum. But although Manning,[59] Harper[60] and a selection of other MPs[61] participated in the referendum debate, Reform itself was not a major player. In the post-referendum parliamentary debate, Manning again created concern among party members when he appeared to be more focused on his expansion strategy than on representing Reform's founding principles. He seemingly abandoned Reform's equality-of-provinces policies by initially supporting the government's five-regional-vetoes approach to future constitutional ratification. In the face of a brewing membership revolt, he backtracked by attempting to re-establish the party's equality-of-provinces position under the guise of opposing distinct society[62] and aiding Stephen Harper's development of Reform's proposals for dealing with Quebec secession. The resulting 20/20[63] document would form the basis of Reform's national unity plank in the 1997 election.

Buoyed by its performance in two 1996 by-elections,[64] Reform again went on the attack over the government's fiscal policies. With the caucus gathering momentum and the government on the ropes over the GST,[65] Justice Minister Allan Rock introduced a series of sexual-orientation amendments to the Canadian Human Rights Act. In its worst public performance to that point, the Reform caucus imploded over the gay-rights issue.

Tension had been mounting since the fall of 1995 when Calgary Southeast MP Jan Brown quit the party's family caucus over differences with her colleagues on representing moral issues in Parliament. Brown and Calgary Centre MP Jim Silye both mused about not running for re-election unless some MPs moderated their stances on controversial social issues. When Reform whip Bob Ringma waded into the gay rights issue by stating that businesses should have the right to "move homosexuals to the back of the shop" if they were disturbing customers, and Athabasca MP Dave Chatters backed him up, Brown pronounced the Reform caucus rife with extremism and again threatened to abandon her caucus colleagues.[66] Manning was noticeably absent from Parliament when the gay rights controversy erupted, and allowed the situation to fester by delaying any action for several days. By the time he returned to Ottawa, the caucus was in chaos and Manning reacted by suspending all three MPs; Ringma and Chatters for their perceived intolerance and Brown for unfairly portraying Reform as extremist. Manning's initial delays, and then harsh reaction, satisfied few. He was criticized by the party's right-wing and populist elements for disciplining Ringma and Chatters. At the same time, many in the media chastised him for disciplining the more moderate Brown. The controversy over gay rights and Manning's handling of his caucus clearly demonstrated the party's dilemma. In attempting to adhere to its principles of representing its core constituency, Reform often found it difficult to appeal to a broader cross-section of Canadian society. In many cases it appeared it could do neither.

Many were expecting a showdown between the leadership and the party's grassroots when Reformers met in Vancouver in the spring of 1996 for their last assembly prior to the 1997 election.[67] Many members were publicly grumbling about Manning and his senior advisors. Some were openly demanding wholesale changes at the top. Anticipating the growing restlessness among delegates, Manning moved quickly to quell dissent. He began by throwing down the gauntlet in a closed-door meeting with constituency association presidents. After a series of straw polls demonstrated a lack of support on a number of fronts, Manning dug in. He told the meeting that he planned to remain leader and if delegates desired changes, they would have to seek a leadership review and risk tearing the party apart with less than a year to go before the next federal election. Furthermore, Manning declared that the already assembled campaign team would stay in place. Again, if the delegates were determined to make changes, they would have to first seek Manning's removal. He repeated the message to a similar closed-door meeting with his MPs. Faced with the ultimatum, the constituency presidents, the MPs, and most delegates fell in line, unwilling to fight a divisive leadership battle so close to an election. But they did so having reached an unspoken agreement: Manning and the campaign team must now deliver the promised breakthrough in Ontario in the next federal election or the membership would be looking to hold the entire campaign team responsible, including Manning.[68]

In presenting delegates with the party's Fresh Start election theme, the campaign team made it clear that they planned a go-for-broke strategy[69] that had as its goal a majority Reform government. Predicting it would need to win 35 per cent of the popular vote, and have that translate into 29 BC and northern seats, 43 Prairie wins, 66 Ontario seats, 6 Quebec victories, and 9 Atlantic seats, the campaign team urged delegates to do whatever it would take to produce a majority. The Fresh Start consisted of a six-point plan that was designed as a communications document rather than a formal statement of policy. It included Reform's intention to reduce the size of government as the primary vehicle for job creation, its tax reduction proposals, provisions to make families a priority, justice reform, plans to repair the social safety net, and, most importantly, Reform's plans to end the uncertainty caused by the national unity crisis.[70]

Manning then used his keynote speech to lecture delegates on the need to exercise self-discipline, a message many viewed as meant as much for the Reform caucus as for the membership.[71] He closed by articulating the twin meaning of the Fresh Start campaign theme. He told delegates about the need to offer Canadians "a party committed to governing both itself and the nation with integrity... a party able to give Canadians a fresh start, because it was capable of making a fresh start itself."[72] The speech, and the uneasy truce that had been broached earlier in the convention, had their desired effect. The following morning delegates provided Manning with an 86 per cent approval rating, his lowest yet but still large enough to put any leadership question to rest until after the 1997 election results were known.

The 1996 Vancouver Assembly represented a watershed for Reform. For the first time in the party's history, divisions between the members and leaders appeared to go beyond the natural tensions resulting from a membership determined to remain true to the party's founding principles and a leadership equally determined to expand beyond that vision in its quest for power. Although differences between Manning and the membership had been evident for several years, it was now clear that the two were heading in opposite directions. The bulk of the membership was intent on building a party that would represent their core beliefs. Manning, on the other hand, was ready to compromise in his quest for power.

Reform's candidate recruitment process commenced immediately after the 1996 Assembly. The branches again controlled the process with the national office acting in only an advisory capacity. The process proceeded as it had for the 1993 election with the exception that ridings with sitting MPs were told not to schedule nomination meetings until December 15, 1996. MPs not seeking re-election were asked to make their intentions known by October 1, 1996. A number of prominent members of the Reform caucus decided against seeking re-election. These included Stephen Harper, Jan Brown, Bob Ringma, Herb Grubel, Jim Silye, House Leader Ray Speaker, and Reform's only Ontario MP, Ed Harper. Despite Reform's new national stature, the nominations were by and large not as highly contested as they were in the lead-up to the 1993 election when the process was largely responsible for swelling Reform's membership ranks to almost 140,000. This time, membership increased to 91,500 from a low of approximately 67,000 in October 1994. The 1997 process also differed from 1993 in that the party was now seeking Quebec candidates and the leadership openly encouraged branches to seek out and recruit youth and ethnic candidates. The process produced mixed results on these fronts. The party succeeded in nominating a significant number of qualified ethnic and youth candidates and a full slate of candidates in the West. However, it failed to recruit a significant number of Quebec candidates and would contest only 23 of Atlantic Canada's 32 ridings.[73]

THE 1997 ELECTION CAMPAIGN

Reform began the 1997 campaign on a much more sure financial footing than in 1993. It opened 1997 with $1.5 million in cash reserves and secure in the knowledge that it could raise sufficient funds to host a full leader's tour and national advertising campaign. It did not fall short of its objectives. During the first quarter of 1997 the national party raised approximately $3.2 million. By the time of the June vote it had raised an additional $3.3 million, allowing it to spend almost $8 million on its national campaign without borrowing any funds, and again finish the campaign in the black. During the pre-writ period, contributions collected by branches were split 80/20 with the local organization keeping the lion's share. Likewise, the national office kept 80 per cent of the contributions sent to it and refunded the remaining 20 per cent to the corresponding branch. During the campaign period, however, the national campaign kept 100 per cent of the funds it raised with the local campaigns keeping all of what they collected.

The most well financed branches did, however, voluntarily contribute $1.5 million to the national campaign. Another $500,000 was raised through membership subscriptions. A further $1.5 million was collected from businesses, Reform's most successful efforts to date. Another $3 million was raised by way of contributions from individual members and supporters. The branches and candidates raised approximately $7 million, the vast majority of this coming from individuals and small businesses. By the time the election call came in late April, it was clear that Reform would be able to run a more traditional campaign, albeit still highly dependent on its campaign volunteers.

The campaign organization consisted of four primary groups: the war room and national office organization; the leader's tour; the research office in Ottawa; and the local campaigns. The primary focus was a communications strategy built on three pillars: the Fresh Start literature distribution, television advertising, and news coverage of the leader's tour.[74] The national media campaign would focus solely on television advertising, leaving print and radio advertising to the individual constituency campaigns. The national television budget was set at $1.3 million and was broken down by region with some ads running nationally but most running in selected provinces or regional markets only.

With all parties moving into Reform's issue space on the fiscal right, organizers struggled to find a defining issue that would distinguish Reform from its traditional party competitors. They eventually decided to focus on Reform's national unity policies. Thus it was here where Reform would emphasize its campaign theme of "now you have a real alternative" and where Reform would have its biggest impact on the overall dynamics of the 1997 election campaign. The communications strategy again broke down the campaign into three phases. The first phase covered the early campaign period, focused on the Fresh Start, and included a national television blitz and literature drop. The second phase, the longest and most important, was designed to emphasize Reform's distinctiveness. A compare-and-contrast theme was promoted exclusively through twelve television commercials. Some commercials ran nationally while others varied their content by region. The third phase asked voters to make a decision during the last week of the campaign. Television ads provided a harder compare and contrast message. This phase was intended to be Reform's most aggressive and included a high penetration of television advertisements complemented by a second national literature drop. The printed piece would again dovetail with the six TV ads and focus on contrasting the Liberal/Tory record with Reform's proposals. This final promotional literature was printed locally to allow for last minute fine-tuning, quick turnaround, and to allow customizing with local campaign information. For the most part, the 1997 campaign dynamics allowed Reform to stick to its three-phase agenda. Candidates were instructed to base their local campaigns on the three phases and to not deviate from the plan. Candidates were also asked to consider local collaboration to top up TV advertising in selected markets where the national campaign believed its buy to be too thin.[75]

During the advertising blackout period at the start of the campaign, the media focused primarily on the leaders' tours. Unlike in 1993, Reform was able to finance a leader's tour that resembled those of the Liberals and Conservatives. Reform chartered its own campaign plane that crisscrossed the country, often making three or four stops in one day. Manning demonstrated his campaigning talents by running at a hectic pace, setting the national campaign agenda during the first week. He succeeded in embarrassing the Liberals by unveiling the governing party's campaign platform two days before its scheduled release[76] and garnered headlines by publicizing an obscure Elections Act clause that would have allowed the Chief Electoral Officer to postpone the vote in southern Manitoba because of the severe Red River flooding.[77] He also launched Reform's national unity campaign while in BC, the province Reform believed to be most receptive to its unity message.

Week two saw Manning step up his attacks on the Liberal and Tory leaders. He attempted to discredit Conservative leader Jean Charest by linking him with the Mulroney government's fiscal record. At the same time he revisited an unsuccessful strategy from the last election by portraying Chrétien as tired and worn out, barely muddling his way through the campaign.[78] Like the other parties, Reform also began its television advertising campaign during the second week. As per their stated intentions, Reform aired television commercials that focused on its Fresh Start platform in every region except in BC. There it ran its first, harder-hitting national unity commercial attacking distinct society for Quebec. Given Reform's early momentum, the Liberals and Conservatives stepped up their attacks. The Liberals charged that Reform's policies were excessively right wing while the Tories accused Reform of not being a truly national party. Manning largely ignored the Liberals, now believing it to be in Reform's interests to be portrayed as conservative. He did however respond to the Tory attacks by evoking a western-alienation theme aimed at solidifying Reform's base in the West. Manning's response was vintage Reform. "It's considered perfectly possible to be a national party with your roots [in Central Canada], but you can't have your roots in western Canada and be considered a national party... We think it's possible to be a national party and have your roots in western Canada... We're out to prove that."[79]

Manning headed into the leaders debates with considerable momentum. Polls suggested Reform was again challenging the Conservatives for second place nationally, but more importantly, leading in both BC and Alberta, and ahead of the Tories in Manitoba and Saskatchewan.[80] With Charest continuing to sound conciliatory to Quebec, and former Quebec premier Jacques Parizeau having firmly placed national unity on the agenda, Manning was determined to use the debates to promote Reform's unity position and further distinguish it from all of the traditional parties.[81] Manning performed admirably during the English-language debate, but often allowed Charest to outflank him on issues where Reform had built up momentum during the first two weeks of the campaign. Manning's style of posing questions to the other leaders again created problems as he regularly turned the podium over to one of the other leaders in a debate format where each of the five leaders struggled to get their message heard. Manning's best performances occurred when he challenged the Prime Minister over distinct society and Chrétien's lack of preparation for the 1995 Quebec referendum. Manning also scored blows when he revisited Charest's record in the Mulroney government. Although early analysis suggested that no leader was a clear winner or loser during the English language debate, media attention soon focused on Charest's performance and his emotional response to the unity issue.

Charest's post-debate momentum forced Reform to shift more of his attention to the Tory leader. Manning continued with his criticism of the Mulroney record and the GST, but Reform strategists believed Charest to be most vulnerable on the national unity issue. As one election observer commented, "it's the one big issue that the Liberals and Conservatives do not want to talk about. And it is the one thing that distinguishes Reform from every other party."[82] Manning used a CBC TV Town Hall on unity and a trip to Quebec to reiterate Reform's hard line against the separatists. With respect to distinct society, he told Quebecers that "it is not going to happen" because of opposition in other provinces and if Quebecers vote for sovereignty they will "find themselves in a room with a steely-eyed, hard-nosed lawyer from Toronto or Calgary, and he's going to say to you, 'we want money, we want territory, and we want the date nailed down for the revoking of passports.'"[83]

With Charest continuing to gain momentum in Quebec after the French-language debate, Manning went for broke and challenged Chrétien and Charest to a special debate on the unity issue. Manning further intensified his attacks against Charest prior to the Tory leader returning to Alberta.[84] Charest countered by having popular Alberta Premier Ralph Klein introduce him to a Calgary audience. However, Charest also took up Manning's challenge from earlier in the campaign and spoke in support of distinct society while in Alberta, a daring but doomed move that sealed the Tories' fate in that province.

Manning's unity message began to show results, both in the polls and in the level of hostility it generated from the other parties. With the other leaders accusing Manning of using hot-button politics, Reform executed its go-for-broke strategy by airing a final national unity ad. The ad argued that the two federalist party leaders from Quebec could not be trusted with the future of Canada. It continued by asking Canadians to reject distinct society status for Quebec in favour of Reform's proposal to treat all provinces and citizens equally. Visually, the ad showed grainy black-and-white photographs of Chrétien and Charest with the message "last time, these men almost lost our country." It went on to place similar pictures of Quebec Premier Lucien Bouchard and Bloc leader Gilles Duceppe on the screen and state that the federalist leaders "will do it again with distinct society when these men hold the next referendum." Up to that point, the ad was probably no more or less controversial than other Reform campaign promotions. However, when the ad called for "a voice for all Canadians, not just Quebec politicians" the on screen image stamped the universal No message (a large red circle with a slash through it) across all four leaders' faces. The last frames of the ad suggested that it was time for a prime minister from outside Quebec, a sentiment shared by many Reformers but not often publicly stated by any national party.

The ad was immediately effective in shoring up Reform's support in the West and in producing the anticipated responses from the leaders of the other parties. The Prime Minister accused Manning of running the most divisive campaign in Canadian history. Charest claimed that Reform's campaign had reached a new low and openly stated, "Preston Manning is a bigot." However, as one journalist commented, "the raging controversy underlined just how much Reform, which started a decade ago with a few dozen Albertans who supported Mr. Manning's ideas, has dominated the election campaign for the first four weeks."[85]

Reform's national unity ad and the controversy it generated dominated the final week of campaigning. Yet Manning mysteriously moved away from the unity issue, opting instead to close the campaign with Reform's accountability theme. While Reform advisors were divided over whether this was the best strategy, the move illustrated several features of the party's 1997 campaign. Reform had set the agenda throughout much of the campaign and forced the national unity message to the top despite the other federalist parties' desires for unity to not emerge as a prominent issue. Given that the campaign dynamics did not force Reform to significantly alter its original strategy, the campaign team may have been justified in believing that they could continue to set the agenda during the final week. However, the accountability message did little to help Reform make its much hoped-for breakthrough into Ontario. Accountability is often used as a code word in western Canada to encapsulate many issues related to western alienation and a deeply rooted mistrust of Ottawa. Although this message sells well in BC and Alberta, it is much less marketable in Ontario. Given that westerners had bought this message from Reform in 1993, it is somewhat curious that the party would return to this theme at the end of a campaign where it was already assured of maintaining its western base but needed to make significant inroads into Ontario.

When the ballots were counted, Reform had improved its parliamentary standing to sixty seats and would sit in the thirty-sixth Parliament as the Official Opposition. It succeeded in solidifying its western base by making significant inroads into Saskatchewan and Manitoba. However, it failed to make its much-anticipated breakthroughs into Ontario and Atlantic Canada. The 1997 Ontario results were particularly disappointing. After spending millions of dollars and thousands of volunteer hours organizing in Canada's most populous province, the party lost its only seat there and finished second in fewer ridings than in 1993.

The election results, although disappointing to party members and especially so to a leadership team that had banked its future on an Ontario breakthrough, were nonetheless remarkable in comparison to what most pundits had recently predicted for the party. When the campaign began many were dismissing Reform as a one-election phenomenon destined to be decimated and replaced as conservative standard-bearer by a resurgent

TABLE 6.3 · 1997 Reform Party Vote and Seat Totals by Province

	Percentage of Vote	Seats Won
British Columbia	43	25
Alberta	55	24
Saskatchewan	36	8
Manitoba	24	3
Ontario	19	0
Quebec	0.3	0
New Brunswick	13	0
Nova Scotia	10	0
Prince Edward's Island	1.5	0
Newfoundland	2.5	0
Canada	19	60

Progressive Conservative party under Charest. But Reform succeeded in fighting a rearguard action, bringing back to its electoral base many voters who drifted away during its disappointing first Parliament. However, the Ontario results left many party members disillusioned, including members in the party's western heartland who would now be looking for the accountability they had bargained for at the 1996 Vancouver Assembly.

CONCLUSION

When Reformers gathered for their 1992 Assembly they were on the threshold of a parliamentary breakthrough. The party was united in support of its leadership and its platform. Yet immediately after Reform sent fifty-two members to the Canadian Parliament in its dramatic 1993 breakthrough, the tensions between its populist base and its leadership's ambitions began to emerge. The Reform caucus's performance on the national stage and the party's expansion strategies left many members wondering if the party had the will to remain true to its founding vision. By the time Reformers met for their 1994 Assembly, division between the members and the leadership were evident but were pasted over when delegates seized control of the policy agenda without a fight from Manning and his senior advisors.

Manning seemed content to let the membership dictate policy so long as he could continue, relatively unfettered, with his expansion dream.

When delegates met in Vancouver for their 1996 Assembly, the divisions within the party could no longer be ignored. Manning had to use the ultimatum of a full-blown leadership crisis to keep activists in line. He and his leadership team remained in place but they knew they would have to deliver seats in Ontario if they were to stay at the helm for very long after the 1997 election. When Reform failed to win a single seat in Ontario during the 1997 contest, a final showdown between Manning and members became inevitable.

7 The Decommissioning

Throughout these pages we have had the opportunity to analyze the Reform Party of Canada by way of its members as they fulfilled their roles as activists. We observed a membership that was characterized by a right-of-centre ideology when considering welfare, government intervention and trade issues. However, the Reform membership was not unidimensionally right wing. Members demonstrated a great deal of complexity when considering federalism and language issues, minority rights, and the Quebec question. They also perceived a citizen-elite schism where they viewed themselves as outsiders looking in. Most importantly, Reform activists held opinions that remained consistent with the party's founding principles. They remained committed to provincial equality as the bedrock of their primarily western, anti-political-establishment ethos. The leadership, on the other hand, often appeared to stray from the founding principles in its continuing efforts at expanding the party into a national, governing coalition. After the leadership failed to deliver on its promises of an eastern breakthrough in the 1997 federal election, the stage was set for the first significant showdown between the Reform members and its founder.

The United Alternative

Rather than face a protracted leadership battle within Reform following the 1997 election disappointment, Manning embarked upon a plan that would see him attempt to replace the Reform party rather than allow it to replace him as leader. Unfortunately for Manning, although he succeeded in convincing Reformers that they needed to ride a new political vehicle into the twenty-first century, he was not successful at convincing them he was the man to drive them there.[1]

Manning called his plan the United Alternative (UA) and launched it as part of an internal Reform evaluation process immediately following the 1997 election. Initially promoted as a modest effort at evaluating the vote-splitting problem in Ontario, Manning convinced the party's executive council to approve budgets to organize an Ontario United Alternative campaign. In less than a year he had expanded the idea into a national initiative but was careful to steer discussions away from talk about forming a new party. He again employed the multi-choice strategy he successfully used to create Reform in 1987, and again when he wanted to expand it nationally in 1991. When a new party was mentioned, it was couched as only one of a number of possible options. It was also again clear that Manning would attempt to structure the debate so as to eventually eliminate all but his preferred choice, the founding of a new political party. When opposition emerged, and it emerged more forcefully with respect to the United Alternative process than it had ever before, by effectively controlling all of the means of communication within the party, and also much of the broader public debate, Manning demonstrated that he could effectively quash even substantial dissent. In fact, he used the last vestige of popular control, the party-wide referendum, as an effective tool against those loyalists who wanted to maintain Reform in its existing form, albeit with a new leader. In this case we witness the true nature of the power imbalance between leaders and members of even the most participatory political parties.

By effectively controlling the multi-staged debate, and by initially declaring that a new party was not part of the package, Manning could inch closer and closer to his goal until the momentum he created became unstoppable. He also successfully primed the issue, using a peculiar but persuasive logic that argued one conservative party could capture the combined votes of both Reform and the Progressive Conservatives, if only the two parties would merge into one entity.

Manning's vote-splitting logic rested on an intentionally superficial interpretation of voting behaviour by Reform and Progressive Conservative supporters. While it is true that any time multi-party competition exists, there also exists a split in votes against the winning party. But voters cast ballots against certain parties and for others for a variety of conflicting reasons. Simply adding up the 1997 Reform and PC vote totals to predict a victory over the Liberals did not serve justice to the complexities of Canadian voting behaviour. Studies such as the 1997 Canadian National Election Study indicated that Reform was not necessarily the second choice for most Ontario Progressive Conservative voters. In fact, 44 per cent of them would have likely chose the Liberals compared to only 18 per cent choosing Reform.[2]

Nevertheless, the vote-splitting logic made for simple and therefore persuasive rhetoric. When the federal Progressive Conservative party refused to cooperate in its own demise, Manning soldiered on. Armed with post-election surveys of Reform members that indicated Ontario vote splitting was thought to be a major problem, he brought the United Alternative concept to the floor of the party's 1998 Assembly. In the face of serious misgivings by many delegates, he presented his initiative as a wild-card resolution that by-passed the branch review process. Many delegates expressed fears that the leadership was planning something much grander than they were prepared to admit and argued that the wild-card UA resolution was unconstitutional, having been sprung on an unsuspecting assembly without being properly debated at the local level. Manning supporters assured delegates that the proposed UA convention was in no way a "merger or an amalgamation with the Tories... or a proposal to change the Reform Party name or leader."[3] Rather, they seized upon the other options that were part of the discussion package and argued that mere cooperation with the federal PCs would be the most likely outcome. Understanding that there currently existed little interest in grand institutional change, Manning reiterated the multi-option approach in his keynote address to the delegates and assured them that he preferred the Reform party's principles, its name, and its current leadership to any other option. His assurances, combined with the still deep reservoir of trust he held with many delegates, sooth most fears. Delegates later granted him 91.3 per cent support to hold his United Alternative convention. Delegates also gave him an 80.9 per cent vote of confidence in the mandatory leadership review balloting, his lowest approval yet and down from 86 per cent two years prior, but sufficient enough to forego any serious leadership challenges for the time being.

Manning outlined his vision of what the United Alternative would become when he and Reform pollster Andre Turcotte published an article arguing that Canada had moved beyond the old left-right ideological labels and was therefore in need of a new vision capable of representing these new realities. In place of the old left-right dichotomy they posited a new three-dimensional decision-making axis.[4] The content of their argument represented more than Manning's latest attempt to shed the "unite-the-right" label that had already been attached to the UA. His attempt to articulate a new ideological paradigm was the latest manifestation of his desire to produce a fundamental realignment of Canadian federal politics and further evidence that Manning did not view his contribution to Canadian political life as limited to merely representing western, right-wing sentiments in a regionalized new party system. Manning's goal was to create a permanent realignment of partisanship in Canada, with him leading one of only two major parties. Knowing the opinion structure of the members he had recruited into his party, and understanding the practical power members had built up over the years within the party's organization, he now viewed Reform, the vehicle used to begin his quest, as one of the greatest obstacles to his grand plans.[5]

After attracting a number of prominent provincial Progressive Conservatives from Alberta and Ontario, and editorial support from Canada's new national daily newspaper, momentum appeared to be on Manning's side.[6] It was, however, a delicate balancing act. Manning had to keep the concept abstract enough to both attract potential PC recruits and at the same time not offend Reformers who were suspicious of excessive compromise. Part of Manning's strategy was in keeping with his leadership style: keep the details of the plan a carefully guarded secret amongst only his most trusted senior advisors. However, the lack of details combined with the populist ethos within the party and led to wild speculation by members, senior officials, MPs, pundits and the media over each new proposal and counter-proposal.[7] The increasingly frantic and disorganized optics being created by the situation led the leadership to order Reform MPs to avoid public debate over the issue. This edict only furthered speculation that the leadership indeed held a hidden agenda and had already decided to abandon Reform for a new party.

Table 7.1 · Political Action Preferences – 1999 UA Convention

	First Choice	Second Choice	Third Choice	Fourth Choice
New Party	665	296	106	27
Local Initiatives	273	409	206	42
Existing Party	252	252	222	96
Merge Several Parties	33	122	171	166
Total Votes Cast	1,223	1,079	705	331

Source: 1999 United Alternative Convention.

Manning's UA convention was held February 19–21, 1999 in Ottawa. Alberta Premier Ralph Klein opened the conference by admonishing delegates to build a fiscally conservative but socially moderate party.[8] Alberta Finance Minister Stockwell Day addressed the conference the following afternoon and provided delegates with a "blitzkrieg against the federal government that had delegates swarming him for an hour after the fifteen-minute address."[9] Day had also spoken to Reform delegates at their 1998 London Assembly and was clearly testing the waters for a possible leadership bid should Manning succeed in convincing Reformers to form a new party. Manning was the last to speak. Despite the fact that most of the delegates were Reformers (officials estimated that only 300 of the 1,500 delegates were active Progressive Conservatives), Manning's speech was addressed to the potential new recruits rather than the Reform members. In typical fashion he invoked historical images of previous bold new initiatives but added a new element to his UA address. He attempted to "speak from the heart" by invoking the image of a softer, gentler, more caring party than was Reform. He called for a "union of the heart" and "one big family meeting" of Canadians to begin the new millennium. In a similar manner as had Day only hours before, Manning unofficially launched his leadership campaign by recognizing that he would have to improve his abilities and work harder "on expressing [his] affection for Canada and Canadians in a way that connects with the heart as well as the head."[10]

The UA convention adopted three unremarkable "motherhood" themes prior to declaring their preferences for starting a new party.[11] Using a preferential ballot, delegates voted on four possible political action plans: (1) to create a new party; (2) to support local cooperation initiatives; (3) to unite behind an existing party; or (4) to merge two or more parties. They overwhelmingly chose the first option but the structure of the ballot and the ordering of preferences provided the UA leadership with ample room to manoeuvre.

With the convention results in hand, the leadership could now begin working on the new party in earnest. They nevertheless proceeded cautiously, manoeuvring mostly behind the scenes while assuaging Reformers' abandonment concerns. They continued to claim that a new party was not necessarily a foregone conclusion. Organizers were always careful to point out that members would be given not one, but two chances to reject the initiative through party-wide referenda prior to any formal changes being implemented.

The 1999 Reform Party Referendum

The first Reform Party membership referendum was scheduled for May 1999. The campaign leading up to the mail-in ballot sparked considerable debate, much of which centred on the continuing ambiguity of the concept, something opponents argued was intentionally structured into the ballot question so as to minimize dissent. Reformers were being asked if they wanted to continue with the United Alternative process. Yes or No. There was no direct vote on starting a new party or on local cooperation initiatives. Given that the resolution would not yet change the Reform constitution, party officials considered it to be a policy measure thereby requiring only a 50 per cent margin of victory overall, and a simple majority in a majority of provinces.[12] Had the ballot question included the creation of a new party, something that would have required a formal change to the party constitution, a two-thirds majority vote overall and majority support in a majority of provinces would have been required. Opponents argued that the vague question allowed for unlimited interpretation, a wholesale compromising of Reform's principles, and the eventual end of the party. Supporters countered by arguing that members were protected by their ability to reject the finished project in a second referendum down the road. Most opponents, however, correctly viewed the first referendum as their most legitimate chance to stop the initiative. If Reformers formally sanctioned the still-fluid process, it was likely that the leadership would be able to create enough momentum to move the project past the point of no return.

The referenda process demonstrated the limits of Reform's internal democratic participation mechanisms. Although Reform members enjoyed many participatory avenues at the branch level similar to those of other party members, Reform members' plebiscitary check on their leadership in the form of assembly votes or party-wide sanctioning of major strategic decisions was often held out as that which distinguished Reform's populist approach from those of the other parties.[13] In practice, however, with the leadership controlling all of the means of internal communication, including the centralized membership lists, its "Reformer" newsletter, and a near monopoly on public communication, opponents had few formal resources at their disposal and little ability to structure debate outside of the leadership's preferred paradigm.

The three-month lag between the time of the UA convention and the referendum did, however, provide opponents with a small window of opportunity to marshal what forces they could. Opponents were energized when a symbolic leader emerged in the form of Alberta MP and Reform folk hero Myron Thompson. His ability to simply articulate opponents' grassroots logic became the dissidents' unofficial slogan. "If the proposed new party is going to keep Reform policies and principles, why do we need it?" mused the rustic MP. "And if they are not going to keep our principles," he concluded, "why would we want it?"[14] But formally organizing the opposition proved difficult. UA supporters controlled the party's budgeted resources and its army of paid staff. Furthermore, while Reform's executive council took an officially neutral position, it encouraged the leader and members of caucus, most of whom where supportive, to "make their views on the wisdom of the UA widely known."[15] Nevertheless, a small but determined group of dissidents managed to piece together a rudimentary network of web pages, e-mail groups and subscriber lists. They named their organization Grassroots United Against Reform's Demise (GUARD) and quickly became the media's focal point for dissenting opinion.[16]

Opponents made gains by portraying the UA as a sell-out of Reform's principles in a misguided effort at achieving power. This message appealed to a large segment of the membership who had joined Reform out of support for its principles above the pursuit of power.[17] They also argued, with some success, that the Ontario problems lie not with Reform but with its leader.[18] Dissent continued to build as the party conducted ten regional conferences leading up to the May vote.[19] When the results were announced by Manning in Calgary on June 10, 1999, they at first appeared somewhat ambiguous.[20] Less than half of the members cast ballots, satisfying the 25 per cent minimum threshold requirement but demonstrating the limits to plebiscitarian democracy even within Reform. Only 60.5 per cent voted to proceed, more than enough to allow Manning to continue with the process but less than would be required to dismantle Reform.[21]

Opponents took some comfort in knowing that they kept support under the two-thirds threshold. But they also knew that Manning now had party-wide approval to proceed. Manning quickly let it be known that he interpreted no ambiguity in the results. Using his harshest rhetoric yet he wrote an open letter to the membership admonishing them to unite behind the process and implying that further open dissent ran counter to the practice of democracy, and would not be tolerated.

> If there are any members of our party, whether in the Caucus or on the Executive Council, or on a Constituency Executive, or at the grassroots level who repeatedly engage in undisciplined behaviour – attacking fellow Reformers, particularly on a personal level; misrepresenting the positions of others, whether deliberately or thoughtlessly; discrediting the Party's commitment to democracy by failing to respect democratically made decisions; diverting public attention away from the Party's main objectives by being repeatedly "off message" – both you and I should mark them well, and leave them behind as we make the great transition from an opposition to a governing party.[22]

The party's Vice Chairman, Ken Kalopsis, went further in an attached memorandum that was sent to all constituency associations.

> Thus, Executive Council strongly requests that members of the Party refrain from formal internal Party debates until following the receipt of presentations of Action Committee reports, and that all members of the Party and Caucus unite behind Executive Council in pursuing and supporting the United Alternative process.[23]

It was clear that the leadership intended to use all the resources at its disposal, including the referendum process itself, to stifle debate until after it had spent the summer organizing its committees. These committees, in turn, would not release their reports until early November. But towards the end of a relatively quiet summer, opponents again began to make waves. After the Progressive Conservatives voted 95 per cent against any involvement in the process, dissidents believed they might have one last chance to kill the UA initiative. This time they took dead aim at Manning. Dissidents believed that if they could force a leadership review at the upcoming Reform assembly, it might be possible to sufficiently damage Manning's credibility and eventually defeat the UA.

The Last Battle

As the UA opposition appeared to be intensifying on the eve of back-to-back Reform and UA conventions,[24] Manning decided to confront the leadership question head-on. In another open letter to Reformers he issued a warning that one observer compared to a suicide bomb threat.[25] For the first time, Manning clearly stated that he no longer had any interest in Reform and if the UA initiative failed he would not remain as Reform leader.

> It is conceivable that Reformers might reject the UA for a number of reasons. For my part, however, if I believe that Reformers had rejected the UA initiative because of a reluctance to make a special effort to reach out and include others across the country and a desire to simply consolidate our current base in the West, I would not be interested in or able to lead such a retreat. Under such circumstances, I would therefore not want to seek a renewed mandate to lead the Reform Party.[26]

With the leadership issue cracked wide open many Reformers feared the worst as they headed to Ottawa for the Reform convention in late January of 2000. When party chairman Gee Tsang resigned amidst allegations that UA supporters were undermining his authority, and caucus member Dick Harris stepped forward as a leadership contender to challenge Manning, it appeared as though UA opponents may be able to mount one last effort at derailing the project. Their last-stand strategy depended on a large number of UA opponents showing up in Ottawa and voting for a leadership review. Once the assembly began, dissidents discovered that they were severely out-gunned and would be quickly overwhelmed by the new UA organization. By the time the assembly ended, dissent had collapsed, Manning had received 74.6 per cent support for his leadership, and opponents conceded that the last battle had been lost. From this point on, opposition dissipated, with dissidents putting up only token resistance prior to the final Reform referendum.[27]

With their opponents seemingly down for the count, the UA leadership was not willing to risk a repeat of the first referendum process where the three-month delay allowed dissidents an opportunity to organize resistance. The final Reform membership referendum ballots were printed immediately following the convention with members required to return them by March 17, 2000. During the brief promotional campaign that followed, Manning and other UA supporters spoke to increasingly large and enthusiastic rallies and on March 24 it was announced that members had overwhelmingly endorsed (91.9 per cent) folding their party into the new Canadian Alliance.[28] Manning had accomplished his first task, delivering Reform's members, its organization and its finances to the new party. He immediately set his sights on the second task, obtaining the Alliance leadership.

The Alliance Leadership Campaign

Although Manning and the other leadership contenders waited until after the Reform referendum before officially launching their campaigns, the January UA convention served as the showcase for prospective candidates. Manning clearly had a head start and substantial residual support within the old Reform base. He had, however, alienated significant segments of the Reform membership and many of the new Alliance recruits were also looking for a leadership change. Stockwell Day announced his candidacy the week following the referendum by emphasizing his fourteen years as a member of the Alberta government. Experienced as Day was, most observers agreed that his greatest asset could be found in the simple fact that he was not Preston Manning. Day's "next step" leadership campaign indicated both his personal political journey and the "logic of the new party." His supporters argued that the logic of starting a new party was based on discarding the Reform image and electing a new leader was the only way to accomplish the task. The paradox lied in that although Day was a fresh face, like Manning he was an Albertan and a social conservative. In fact, in comparison to Day, Manning appeared to be a moderate. This left some Alliance members looking for a leader that could help shed both Reform's western and social-conservative baggage.

Several prominent Ontario provincial Conservatives had been participating in the UA process from the start. Prior to the second UA convention, Ontario cabinet minister Tony Clements had been the most visible, but he expressed no desire to seek the leadership. Neither did long-time Conservative strategist Tom Long, one of the most warmly received speakers at the second UA convention.[29] Eventually junior Ontario cabinet minister Frank Klees became the unofficial Ontario candidate. Hoping to be backed by a strong provincial organization, the Klees campaign speculated about delivering half of Ontario's Progressive Conservative MPPs to the new party. But when Klees withdrew his candidacy at an event many mistakenly believed would be his official campaign launch it appeared that Ontario would not be capable of fielding a candidate at all. Eventually Long entered the race and although his campaign would not live up to many of its grand expectations, he helped in recruiting a number of Ontario provincial Conservatives and lent the race a certain credibility that it would not have had without an Ontario candidate. Two-term Reform MP Keith Martin and John Stachow, an unknown Ontario Hydro nuclear worker, rounded out the field.

As with Reform, every party member would be allowed to cast an Alliance leadership ballot. Most would vote at polling stations in their ridings on June 24, 2000. Members residing in constituencies where the party was not yet well organized would be allowed to vote by telephone up to three days in advance, as would members in some rural constituencies. Membership sales would be allowed up to one week prior to voting day. This presented organizers with a number of significant administrative challenges, not least of which were verifying and processing the flood of memberships, producing voter registration lists, and ensuring PIN numbers reached televoting members. All of these had to be accomplished in less than one week after membership sales were cut off.[30]

For the first half of the campaign Manning kept a low profile, preferring small private meetings that allowed him to showcase his most effective skills, one-on-one dialogue with individual members. Day, and to a lesser extent Long, ran much more high-profile, media-driven campaigns. Regularly speaking to large rallies where organizers claimed to be signing up as many as four hundred potential supporters, Day was the most active in making fresh policy pronouncements. He also continued his practice of directly answering questions about his social-conservative views. The contenders squared off in a series of debates during late May and early June.

TABLE 7.2 · Alliance Leadership Contest Vote Totals

	First Ballot (120,557 votes cast)[31]			Second Ballot (118,487 votes cast)		
	TELEVOTING (%)	POLLS WON (%)	TOTAL (%)	TELEVOTING (%)	POLLS WON (%)	TOTAL (%)
Day	46.5	42.8	44.2	62.5	64.3	63.6
Manning	38.6	34.6	36.1	37.5	35.7	36.4
Long	13.4	21.0	18.2	--	--	--
Martin	1.4	1.3	1.4	--	--	--
Stachow	0.1	0.3	0.2	--	--	--

Having begun as a polite race that did little to distinguish the candidates, by mid-June the campaign appeared ready to turn on two key dimensions. Initially, there was the need to choose a leader who was electable in Ontario. Day, not Long, appeared to be leading on this score. But a second major cleavage emerged over social conservatism. Long occupied the most solid libertarian ground among the three main contenders and attempted to use his position as a wedge to separate himself from Day, and to a lesser extent Manning. He bluntly warned that if the party allowed social conservatism to pervade its image, it would lose the next election.

With the membership sales cut-off date approaching it became clear that the Alliance had signed up well over 100,000 new members. Before the party could celebrate its remarkable recruitment efforts, problems began to surface with some of the candidates' tactics. Especially problematic were some of Long's Quebec organization's tactics. The most publicized problems were centred in Quebec's Gaspé region where membership went from zero to 2,800 in a few short months. Similar problems were cropping up in Alberta where the Calgary North East membership exploded to 7,200 from a mere 452 prior to the leadership campaign. The membership irregularities led to calls for postponement of the vote but Alliance officials assured anxious members that all was well and the first ballot vote proceeded as planned. The results surprised many observers, including a number of the candidates. Not only had Day bested Manning by over 8 per cent, almost 60 per cent of the more than 200,000 members participated, thereby legitimizing the recruitment process and the new party's organizational capabilities.

Day's first ballot lead was substantial, but not large enough to ensure that Manning would not force a second ballot.[32] Manning immediately ended speculation that he might concede and began what amounted to the most acrimonious two weeks of the campaign. Manning and his advisors unleashed a full assault on Day's social conservatism, some predicting disaster if he became leader. To overcome Day's nine-thousand-vote lead, Manning attempted to recruit Long's supporters and the large number of members who did not participate in the first ballot. Both would prove ineffective strategies. Most of Long's support was in Ontario and Day's first ballot victory demonstrated he was capable of beating Manning there.[33] By the time Long eventually endorsed Manning much of his organization had already joined the Day camp. Entering the final week, as Manning steadfastly refused to make himself available to the media and was speaking to smaller and smaller crowds, it became evident that his campaign, and his career as leader, had run its course.

Day handily defeated Manning on the second ballot[34] and quickly announced that he would contest a soon-to-be-vacated BC seat.[35] He then embarked on an effort at making himself better known in Ontario and Quebec. Riding higher polling numbers than the Reform party had ever achieved,[36] Day spent most of the summer touring Central and Eastern Canada, brushing up on his French and recruiting former Progressive Conservative and Bloc Quebecois supporters to his cause.[37] After winning the Okanagan-Coquihalla by-election, Day prepared for a media campaign designed to introduce him to voters across the country.

Despite the transformation into a new party, and campaigning with a new leader, the Canadian Alliance made only modest gains in the 2000 election from where Reform finished in 1997. The Alliance broadened its vote base to 24 per cent (compared to Reform's 19 per cent in 1997), and it managed to elect six additional MPs (66 as compared to Reform's 60 in 1997). But it failed to achieve any of the more lofty goals it had set for itself. The Alliance failed to reduce the Liberals to at least a minority government. It failed to reduce the Progressive Conservatives to unofficial party status in its ongoing effort to finish off its rival, once and for all. Most importantly, it failed to make a significant breakthrough in Ontario and therefore failed to actualize its reasons for coming into being.

Conclusion

In attempting to shed its image as a western vehicle dedicated to seemingly radical policy positions, the Alliance project represented a shift away from the anti-political establishment characteristics that Reform exploited while entering the system. Despite protestations by party officials to the contrary, the Alliance represented a return to the national brokerage politics of the pre-1993 period. It also moved away from what many would argue was potentially Reform's most enduring legacy, the further democratization of party politics and the political system more generally. Although western voters continued to support the Alliance through the 2000 election, and although the Alliance continued to pay considerable rhetorical attention to democratic participation and marginally distinct policy positions, the evidence from the 2000 campaign and the events that followed suggest that the magnitude of change within the party was much greater than a cursory glance at its electoral results would suggest.

When the Alliance descended into a leadership crisis immediately following the 2000 general election and emerged with a new leader, former Reform MP Stephen Harper, it attempted to reassert itself as the only party capable of offering Canadian voters a legitimate alternative to the Liberals. However, as the party continued to flirt with single-digit support in national public opinion polls, pressure built for a merger with the Progressive Conservatives. When PC leader Joe Clark was replaced by Nova Scotia MP Peter MacKay, Harper successfully seized the opportunity and determinedly pursued merging the two rival parties into the new Conservative Party of Canada. In the 2004 federal election, the Harper-led Conservatives provided Canadians with the most competitive federal election in decades, limiting the Liberals under new leader Paul Martin to a minority government. However, as predicted, the new Conservative party did not capture all of the previous Reform-Alliance and PC support, and in fact polled less support than did Reform-Alliance in its former British Columbia stronghold.[38] Despite meaningful gains in securing an Ontario beachhead, the party's primary electoral objective, the new Conservatives faced some old realities by failing dismally in Quebec. Immediately following the 2004 federal election, Harper made Quebec the party's most important recruitment and organizational priority, something most Reformers would have likely found unthinkable only a few years earlier.

Quite clearly, the new Conservative party represents the formal end of the Reform project. And although it will take analysis from the new party's first few policy conventions, and another round of electoral competition, to fully understand the transformation away from the old Reform agenda, it is clear that the goal of expanding into a national party, and the consequent softening of Reform's harder-edged policy and issue positioning has superseded the strategy of pursuing votes by way of ideological or regional purity. It appears as though the process has come full circle. Alienated, right-of-centre western voters will again witness a national party they solidly support expend most of its efforts chasing votes in Central Canada. Given the history of western Canadian federal party politics, it also seems likely that as the process plays itself out, at some point in the future, some westerners will again be agitating for a new party to represent their dissenting opinions.

Appendix A

Reform Party Membership by Province: 1987–2000 (thousands)

Province	BC	AB	SK	MB	ON	PQ	Atlantic	Other[a]	Total
October 1987	-	-	-	-	-	-	-	-	3.0
November 1988[e]	-	-	-	-	-	-	-	-	15.0
October 1989[b]	10	17	1.7	1.3	-	-	-	-	30.0
October 1990[b]	17	24.5	3.3	2.7	-	-	-	2.5	50.0
April 1991[c]	20.3	28.4	5.1	4.0	-	-	-	7.6[d]	65.4
October 1991	24.7	32.0	5.3	5.2	25.8	0.1	1.1	0.5	94.7
October 1992	29.8	50.8	8.8	6.1	34.6	0.1	1.7	0.3	132.2
October 1993[e]	27.6	28.8	5.8	4.8	28.0	0.1	1.2	0.3	96.6
October 1994	18.6	19.6	3.6	3.1	20.5	0.2	1.1	0.2	66.9
October 1995	19.4	20.1	3.7	3.1	21.2	0.3	1.4	0.2	69.4
October 1996	17.9	19.7	4.2	3.2	20.8	0.5	1.8	1.1[f]	69.2
June 1997[e]	23.5	26.7	7.6	4.3	25.7	0.4	3.0	0.3	91.5
October 1997	22.4	25.7	7.2	3.9	23.1	0.4	2.8	0.3	85.8
October 1998	17.3	20.4	4.0	3.2	18.1	0.7	1.9	0.2	65.8
October 1999	16.4	19.3	4.3	3.2	16.8	0.5	2.1	0.2	62.8
March 2000[g]	19.6	25.3	5.0	3.3	18.6	0.4	2.4	0.2	74.8

Source: Reform Party of Canada.

a Includes residents of the territories and individuals not categorized by province.
b Provincial breakdowns based on estimates provided by the Reform Party.
c Date of decision to expand Reform into Central and Atlantic Canada.
d Primarily Ontario members recruited prior to official expansion.
e Indicates month and year of federal election.
f Includes 929 individuals not categorized because of boundary redistribution.
g Final membership numbers prior to folding Reform into the Canadian Alliance.

Appendix B

Index Item Direction

Welfare and Entitlements

The welfare state makes people nowadays less willing to look after themselves. (AGREE)
Too many of the unemployed are not trying hard enough to find jobs. (AGREE)
There is a great deal of abuse of social security and welfare programs in Canada. (AGREE)
The welfare state has created more problems than it has solved. (AGREE)

Alienation

People like me don't have any say about what the government does. (AGREE)
I don't think that the government cares much what people like me think. (AGREE)
Generally those elected to Parliament soon lose touch with the people. (AGREE)

Language/Ethnicity

Quebec has a right to self-determination. (DISAGREE)
A bilingual federal government is necessary. (DISAGREE)
We should dramatically reduce the rate of immigration into Canada. (AGREE)
When Canada admits immigrants, it should take them from all ethnic and racial groups. (DISAGREE)

Federalism

Government services should be decentralized more. (AGREE)

Provinces should have the right to opt out of joint federal provincial programs with full compensation. (AGREE)
The federal government has yielded too much power to the provinces. (DISAGREE)

Government Size/Deficit

Big government increasingly is a major problem. (AGREE)
A Reform Party government should seek to reduce the government deficit as much as possible. (AGREE)
There is too much government ownership in the Canadian economy. (AGREE)

Trade

There should be no tariffs or duties between Canada and the US. (AGREE)
The North American Free Trade Agreement is good for Canada. (AGREE)

Quebec – Constitution

Quebec should have a veto in the constitution. (DISAGREE)
Quebec should be granted distinct society status in the constitution. (DISAGREE)

Charter/Abortion

On the whole, the benefits of the new Canadian Charter of Rights outweigh the disadvantages. (DISAGREE)
Abortion is a private matter which should be decided between the pregnant woman and her doctor. (AGREE)

Crime

Capital punishment should be reintroduced. (AGREE)
The courts have been too lenient in handing out penalties to criminals. (AGREE)

Equality of Provinces

The Senate should be reformed along 3-E model. (AGREE)
All provinces should have equal say in confederation. (AGREE)

Multiculturalism/Immigration

The federal government should increase its efforts to further multiculturalism. (DISAGREE)
When Canada admits immigrants, preferential treatment should be given to those who can contribute to our society. (AGREE)

Bibliography

Newspapers & Magazines

Alberta Report
Calgary Herald
Calgary Sun
Le Devoir
National Post
Ottawa Citizen
The Financial Post
Globe and Mail

Unpublished Works

Ellis, Faron. "The Ideological Structure of the Canadian Reform Party." Paper presented to the 51st Annual Meeting of the Midwest Political Science Association, Chicago, March 1994.

———. "A Genealogy of Dissent: Activism and Participation in Canada's Reform Party." Ph.D. dissertation, University of Calgary, 1997.

Flanagan, Tom, and Faron Ellis. "A Comparative Profile of the Reform Party of Canada." Paper presented to the Canadian Political Science Association Annual Meeting, Charlottetown, June 1992.

Harper, Stephen. "A Reform Vision of Canada." Speech delivered to the Reform Party of Canada Assembly, Saskatoon, 5 April 1991.

———. Letter to delegates attending the 1991 Reform Party Assembly, 12 March 1991.

Manning, Preston. "A Fresh Start." Keynote address to the Reform Party of Canada Assembly, Vancouver, 8 June 1996.

———. "A New and Better Home for Canadians." Keynote address to the

Reform Party Of Canada Assembly, Ottawa, 15 October 1994.
———. "Personal Message to Canadians from Preston Manning." Open letter, 10 October 1993.
———. "The Case for a New Federalism." Address by Preston Manning, Leader, Reform Party of Canada to a joint meeting of the Canadian Club and Empire Club, Toronto, 1 October 1993.
———. "Send Reformers to Ottawa." Address to a Public Rally at Red Deer, Alberta, 26 September 1993.
———. "Stop Digging: A Presentation of the Reform Party's Plan to Reduce the Federal Deficit to Zero in Three Years." Peterborough, Ontario, 20 September 1993.
———. "Let The People Speak." Remarks by Preston Manning, Leader Reform Party of Canada to Reform Meetings/News Conferences, opening week of 1993 federal election campaign, Draft 7, 8 September 1993.
———. "Stop Digging! A plan to Reduce the Federal Deficit to Zero in Three Years (Phase II)." Address to a Reform Party Business Breakfast, Vancouver, 13 April 1993.
———. "Stop Digging! A plan to Reduce the Federal Deficit to Zero in Three Years (Phase I)." Address to a joint luncheon of the Canadian Club and the Prospectors and Developers' Association, Toronto, 29 March 1993.
———. "A New National Agenda for October 27: Keynote Address to the 1992 Reform Party Assembly." Winnipeg, 24 October 1992.
———. "Letter to Reform Party Members." 8 September 1992.
———. "The Road to New Canada." Keynote Address to the 1991 Assembly of the Reform Party of Canada, Saskatoon, 6 April 1991.
———. Letter and information sheet to Calgary Southwest Constituency Association, 18 March 1991.
———. "Preparing for the 21st Century." March 1990.
———. "Leadership For Changing Times: Keynote Address to the 1989 Assembly of the Reform Party of Canada." Edmonton, 28 October 1989.
———. "Leader's Message." Reform Association of Canada, 15 December 1987.
———. "A Western Reform Movement: The Responsible Alternative to Western Separatism." Briefs prepared for A Western Assembly On Canada's Economic and Political Future, Vancouver, November 1987.
———. "Laying the Foundations for a New Western Political Party." Address to a public information meeting sponsored by The Reform Association of Canada, Calgary, 10 August 1987.
———. "Choosing a Political Vehicle to Represent the West." Presentation to the Western Assembly on Canada's Economic and Political Future, Vancouver, 29–31 May 1987.
Reform Association of Canada. "Guidelines for the Selection of Delegates to the founding Convention at Winnipeg." 2 September 1987.
———. Newsletter. May 1987.
———. "A conference on Canada's Economic and Political Future." Reform Association of Canada Draft, 9 March 1987.
Reform Party of Canada, *Principles and Policies: The Blue Book 1995.*
———. *Final Draft Election Platform.* October 1992.

———. *Broadsheet on The Charlottetown Constitutional Accord.* 1992.
———. *Candidate Recruitment and Selection Manual.* August 1991.
———. *Constitution of Reform Party of Canada.* As amended at the Assembly of the Party in Saskatoon, 4–7 April 1991.
———. *Platform and Statement of Principles.* 1991.
———. *Platform and Statement of Principles.* 1989.
———. *Platform and Statement of Principles.* 1988.

Published Works

Ablonczy, Diane. "Reform's United Alternative looks beyond the labels." *Calgary Herald*, 11 July 1998.
Archer, Keith. "The New Democrats, Organized Labour and the Prospects of Electoral Reform." In *Canadian Political Parties: Leaders, Candidates and Organization.* Vol. 13, Research Studies of the Royal Commission on Electoral Reform and Party Financing, edited by Herman Bakvis, 313–45. Toronto: Dundurn Press, 1991.
———. "Leadership Selection in the New Democratic Party." In *Canadian Political Parties: Leaders, Candidates and Organization.* Vol. 13, Research Studies of the Royal Commission on Electoral Reform and Party Financing, edited by Herman Bakvis, 3–56. Toronto: Dundurn Press, 1991.
———. *Political Choices and Electoral Consequences: A Study of Organized Labour and the New Democratic Party.* Kingston: McGill-Queen's University Press, 1990.
———. "The Meaning and Demeaning of the National Election Studies." *Journal of Canadian Studies* (Winter 1989–90): 122–40.
———. "On the Study of Political Parties in Canada." *Canadian Journal of Political Science* 22 (1989): 389–98.
Archer, Keith, and Faron Ellis. "Activists in the Reform Party of Canada." In *Party Politics in Canada*, 7th ed., edited by Hugh G Thorburn, 336–51. Scarborough: Prentice-Hall, 1996.
———. "Opinion Structure of Party Activists: The Reform Party of Canada." *Canadian Journal of Political Science* 27 (1994): 277–308.
Archer, Keith, and Alan Whitehorn. *Political Activists: The NDP in Convention.* Toronto: Oxford University Press, 1997.
———. "Opinion Structure Among Party Activists: A Comparison of New Democrats, Liberals and Conservatives." In *Party Politics in Canada*, 7th ed., edited by Hugh G. Thorburn, 163–77. Scarborough: Prentice-Hall Canada, 1996.
———. "Opinion Structure Among New Democratic Party Activists: A Comparison of New Democrats, Liberals and Conservatives." In *Party Politics in Canada*, 6th ed., edited by Hugh G. Thorburn, 144–59. Scarborough: Prentice-Hall Canada, 1991.
———. "Opinion Structure Among New Democratic Party Activists." *Canadian Journal of Political Science* 23 (1990): 101–14.

Archer, Keith, Rainer Knopff, Roger Gibbins, and Leslie Pal. *Parameters of Power: Canada's Political Institutions.* Toronto: Nelson Canada, 1995.

Asher, Arian, and Michal Shamir. "The Primarily Political Functions of the Left-Right Continuum." *Comparative Politics* 15 (1983): 122–139.

Bakvis, Herman, ed. *Canadian Political Parties: Leaders, Candidates and Organization.* Vol. 13, Research Studies of the Royal Commission on Electoral Reform and Party Financing. Toronto: Dundurn Press, 1991.

Bell, David. *Roots of Disunity: A Study of Canadian Political Culture.* Toronto: Oxford University Press, 1992.

Bercuson, David Jay, ed. *Canada and the Burden of Unity.* Toronto: Macmillan, 1977.

Blais, André. "Third Parties in Canadian Provincial Politics." *Canadian Journal of Political Science* 6 (1973): 399–438.

Blais, Andre, Elisabeth Gidengil, Richard Nadeau and Neil Nevitte. "Do Party Supporters Differ?" In *Citizen Politics: Research and Theory in Canadian Political Behavior*, edited by Joanna Everitt and Brenda O'Neill. Toronto: Oxford University Press, 2002.

Blake, Donald. "Division and Cohesion: The Major Parties." In *Party Democracy in Canada: The Politics of National Party Conventions,* edited by George Perlin, 32–53. Scarborough: Prentice-Hall Canada, 1988.

Brimelow, Peter. *The Patriot Game.* Toronto: Key Porter Books, 1986.

Brodie, Janine, "Tensions from Within: Regionalism and Party Politics in Canada." In *Party Politics in Canada*, 6th ed., edited by Hugh G Thorburn, 221–33. Scarborough: Prentice-Hall Canada, 1991.

———. "The Gender Factor and National Leadership Conventions in Canada." In *Party Democracy in Canada: The Politics of National Party Conventions,* edited by George Perlin, 172–87. Scarborough: Prentice-Hall Canada, 1988.

Brodie, Janine, and Jane Jenson. "Piercing the Smokescreen: Stability and Change in Brokerage Politics." In *Canadian Parties in Transition*, 2nd ed., edited by A. Brian Tanguay and Alain-G. Gagnon, 52–72. Toronto: Nelson Canada, 1996.

———. *Crisis, Challenge and Change: Party and Class in Canada.* Toronto: Methuen Publications, 1980.

———. *Crisis, Challenge and Change: Party and Class in Canada.* 2nd ed. Ottawa: Carleton University Press, 1989.

Bunner, Paul, ed. *Lougheed and the War with Ottawa, 1971–1984.* Vol. 11, Alberta in the 20th Century. Edmonton: History Book Publications, 2003.

———. *Alberta Takes the Lead.* Vol. 12, Alberta in the 20th Century. Edmonton: History Book Publications, 2003.

Cairns, Alan C. *Constitution, Government and Society in Canada.* Toronto: McClelland and Stewart, 1988.

———. "The Electoral System and the Party System in Canada, 1930–1965." *Canadian Journal of Political Science* 1 (1968): 55–80.

Caldarola, Carlo, ed. *Society and Politics in Alberta: Research Papers.* Toronto: Methuen, 1979.

Campbell, Robert M., and Leslie A. Pal. *The Real Worlds of Canadian Politics: Cases in Process and Policy.* Peterborough: Broadview Press, 1989.

Carty, R. K., ed. *Canadian Political Party Systems: A Reader.* Toronto: Broadview Press, 1992.

———. *Canadian Political Parties in the Constituencies.* Vol. 23, Research Studies of the Royal Commission on Electoral Reform and Party Financing. Toronto: Dundurn Press, 1991.

———. "Three Canadian Party Systems: An Interpretation of the Development of National Politics." In *Party Democracy in Canada: The Politics of National Party Conventions*, edited by George Perlin. 15–30. Scarborough: Prentice-Hall Canada, 1988.

———. "Campaigning in the Trenches: the Transformation of Constituency Politics." In *Party Democracy in Canada: The Politics of National Party Conventions*, edited by George Perlin, 84–96. Scarborough: Prentice-Hall Canada, 1988.

Carty, R. K., William Cross, and Lisa Young. *Rebuilding Canadian Party Politics.* Vancouver: UBC Press, 2000.

Carty, R. K., Linda Erickson, and Donald E. Blake, eds. *Leaders and Parties in Canadian Politics: Experiences of the Provinces.* Toronto: Harcourt Brace Jovanovich Canada, 1992.

Cassinelli, C. W. "The Law of Oligarchy." *American Political Science Review* 47 (1953): 773–84.

Clarke, Harold D. "The Ideological Self-Perceptions of Provincial Legislators." *Canadian Journal of Political Science* 11 (1978): 617–33.

Clarke, Harold D., Allan Kornberg, Faron Ellis, and Jonathan Rapkin. "Not for Fame or Fortune: Membership and Activity Patterns in Canada's New Reform Party." *Party Politics* 6 (2000): 75–93.

Clarke, Harold D., Jane Jenson, Lawrence LeDuc, and Jon H. Pammett. *Absent Mandate: Canadian Electoral Politics In an Era of Restructuring.* 3rd ed. Toronto: Gage Educational Publishing, 1996.

———. *Absent Mandate: The Politics of Discontent in Canada.* Toronto: Gage Publishing, 1984.

Clarkson, Steven. "Yesterday's Man and His Blue Grits: Backward Into the Future." In *The Canadian General Election of 1993*, edited by Alan Frizzell, Jon H. Pammett, and Anthony Westell. Ottawa: Carleton University Press, 1994, 27–41.

Converse, Philip E., and Roy Pierce. "Comment on Fleury and Lewis-Beck: 'Anchoring the French Voter: Ideology Versus Party'." *The Journal of Politics* 55 (1993): 1110–1117.

Cook, E. J. "Roberto Michels: Political Parties in Perspective." *The Journal of Politics* 13 (1971): 773–96.

Courtney, John C. *Do Conventions Matter? Choosing National Party Leaders in Canada.* Montreal and Kingston: McGill-Queen's University Press, 1995.

Creighton, D. C. *Canada's First Century.* Toronto: Macmillan, 1970.

Dabbs, Frank. *Preston Manning: The Roots of Reform.* Vancouver: Greystone Books, 1997.

Dahl, Robert A. *A Preface to Democratic Theory.* Chicago: University of Chicago Press, 1956.

Dalton, Russell J., Scott C. Flanagan, and Paul Allen Beck. *Electoral Change in Advanced Industrial Democracies: Realignment or Dealignment?* Princeton: Princeton University Press, 1984.

Dawson, R. M. *The Civil Service of Canada.* London: Oxford University Press, 1929.

Dobbin, Murray. *Preston Manning and the Reform Party.* Toronto: James Lorimer, 1991.

Dornan, Christopher, and Jon H. Pammett, eds. *The Canadian General Election of 2004.* Toronto: Dundurn Press, 2004.

Downs, Anthony. *An Economic Theory of Democracy.* New York: Harper, 1957.

Duverger, Maurice. *Political Parties: Their Organization and Activity in the Modern State.* New York: Wiley, 1963.

———. *Political Parties.* London: Methuen 1954.

———. *Political Parties: Their Organization and Activity in the Modern State,* 3rd ed., translated by Barbara and Robert Northe with a foreword by D.W. Brogan. Cambridge: Cambridge University Press, 1964.

Dyck, Rand. *Provincial Politics in Canada: Towards the Turn of the Century.* 3rd ed. Toronto: Prentice-Hall Canada, 1996.

Ellis, Faron. "The More Things Change… The Alliance Campaign." In *The Canadian General Election of 2000,* edited by Jon H. Pammett and Christopher Dornan, 59–89. Toronto: Dundurn Press, 2001.

———. "Reformers Yet To Be Sold On '3-D' Politics." *Calgary Herald,* 27 June 1998.

———. "The Last Worst Tory Leadership Convention." In *Lougheed and the War with Ottawa, 1971–1984.* Vol. 11, Alberta in the 20th Century, edited by Paul Bunner, 274–75. Edmonton: History Book Publications, 2003.

———. "Reform's Unrepentant Warrior." In *Alberta Takes the Lead.* Vol. 12, Alberta in the 20th Century, edited by Paul Bunner, 251. Edmonton: History Book Publications, 2003.

———. "A Storied Name From the Past Leads a Modern Populist Uprising." In *Alberta Takes the Lead.* Vol. 12, Alberta in the 20th Century, edited by Paul Bunner, 240–57. Edmonton: History Book Publications, 2003.

———. "The Manning Family Business." In *Alberta Takes the Lead.* Vol. 12, Alberta in the 20th Century, edited by Paul Bunner, 244–47. Edmonton: History Book Publications, 2003.

———. "Reform Conquers the West then Invades the Wary East." In *Alberta Takes the Lead.* Vol. 12, Alberta in the 20th Century, edited by Paul Bunner, 278–91. Edmonton: History Book Publications, 2003.

Ellis, Faron, and Keith Archer. "Ideology and Opinion Within the Reform Party." In *Party Politics in Canada.* 8th ed., edited by Hugh G. Thorburn and Alan Whitehorn, 122–34. Toronto: Prentice-Hall Canada, 2001.

———. "Reform at the Crossroads." In *The Canadian General Election of 1997,* edited by Alan Frizzell and Jon H. Pammett, 111–33. Toronto: Dundurn Press, 1997.

———. "Reform: *Electoral* Breakthrough." In *The Canadian General Election of 1993,* edited by Alan Frizzell, Jon H. Pammett, and Anthony Westell, 59–77. Ottawa: Carleton University Press, 1994.

Ellis, Faron, and Peter Woolstencroft. "New Conservatives, Old Realities." In *The Canadian General Election of 2004,* edited by Jon H. Pammett and Christopher Dornan, 66–105. Toronto: Dundurn Press, 2005.

Elton, David, and Roger Gibbins. "Western Alienation and Political Culture." In *The Canadian Political Process*, edited by Richard Schultz, Orest M. Kruhlak and John C. Terry, 82–97. Toronto: Holt, Rinehart and Winston of Canada, 1979.

Everitt, Joanna, and Brenda O'Neill, eds. *Citizen Politics: Research and Theory in Canadian Political Behavior*. Toronto: Oxford University Press, 2002.

Finkel, Alvin. *The Social Credit Phenomenon in Alberta*. Toronto: University of Toronto Press, 1989.

Flanagan, Tom. *Waiting for the Wave: The Reform Party and Preston Manning*. Toronto: Stoddart, 1995.

Fleury, Christopher J., and Michael S. Lewis-Beck. "Anchoring the French Voter: Ideology Versus Party." *The Journal of Politics* 55 (1993): 1100–1109.

———. "Déjà Vu All Over Again: A Comment on the Comments of Converse and Pierce." *The Journal of Politics* 55 (1993): 1118–1126.

Fowke, V. C. *The National Policy and the Wheat Economy*. Toronto: University of Toronto Press, 1957.

———. "National Policy – Old and New." *Canadian Journal of Economics and Political Science* (1952): 217–39.

Fraser, Graham. *Playing for Keeps: The Making of the Prime Minister*. Toronto: McClelland and Stewart, 1988.

Frizzell, Alan, and Jon H. Pammett, eds. *The Canadian General Election of 1997*. Toronto: Dundurn Press, 1997.

Frizzell, Alan, Jon H. Pammett, and Anthony Westell, eds. *The Canadian General Election of 1993*. Ottawa: Carleton University Press, 1994.

Gagnon, Alain-G., and A. Brian Tanguay, eds. *Canadian Parties in Transition: Discourse, Organization and Representation*. Scarborough: Nelson Canada, 1989.

Gairdener, William C. *The Trouble With Canada: A Citizen Speaks Out*. Toronto: Stoddart, 1994.

Gibbins, Roger, "Western Alienation and the Alberta Political Culture." In *Society and Politics in Alberta: Research Papers*, 143–67. Toronto: Methuen, 1979.

Gibbins, Roger, Howard Palmer, Brian Rusted, and David Taras, eds. *Meech Lake and Canada: Perspectives from the West*. Edmonton: Academic Printing and Publishing, 1989.

Gidengil, Elisabeth, Andre Blais, Neil Nevitte, and Richard Nadeau. "The Correlates and Consequences of Anti-Partyism in the 1997 Canadian Election." *Party Politics* 7 (2001): 491–513.

Hans, G. "Roberto Michels and the Study of Political Parties." *British Journal of Political Science* 1 (1971): 55–172.

Harrison, Trevor. *Of Passionate Intensity: Right-Wing Populism and the Reform Party of Canada*. Toronto: University of Toronto Press, 1995.

Hartz, Louis. *The Founding of New Societies*. New York: Harcourt, Brace and World, 1964.

Innis, Hugh R., ed. *Bilingualism and Biculturalism: An Abridged Version of the Royal Commission Report*. Toronto: McClelland and Stewart, 1973.

Irving, John A. *The Social Credit Movement in Alberta*. Toronto: University of Toronto Press, 1959.

Johnston-Conover, Pamela, and Stanley Feldman. "The Origins and Meaning of Liberal/Conservative Self-Identifications." *American Journal of Political Science* 25 (1981): 617–45.

Johnston, Richard, André Blais, Elisabeth Gidengil, and Neil Nevitte. "The People and the Charlottetown Accord." In *Canada: The State of the Federation 1993*, edited by Ronald L. Watts and Douglas M. Brown, 19–43. Kingston: Institute of Intergovernmental Relations, 1993.

Johnston, Richard, André Blais, Henry E. Brady, and Jean Crête. *Letting the People Decide: Dynamic of a Canadian Election.* Kingston: McGill-Queen's University Press, 1992.

Katz, Richard S., and Peter Mair. "Changing Models of Party Organization and Party Democracy." *Party Politics* 1 (1995): 5–28.

———. "Cadre, Catch-All or Cartel: A Rejoinder." *Party Politics* 2 (1996): 525–34.

Key, V.O. Jr. *Public Opinion and American Democracy.* New York: Knopf, 1961.

Kitschelt, Herbert. *The Transformation of European Social Democracy.* Cambridge: Cambridge University Press, 1994.

———. *The Logics of Party Formation: Ecological Politics in Belgium and West Germany.* Ithaca: Cornell University Press, 1989.

Knopff, Rainer. "Language and Culture in the Canadian Debate: the Battle of the White Papers." *Canadian Review of Studies in Nationalism* 6 (1979): 36–65.

Koelble, Thomas A. "Party Structures and Democracy: Michels, McKenzie, and Duverger Revisited via the Examples of the West German Green Party and the British Social Democratic Party." *Comparative Political Studies* 22 (1989): 199–216.

Kornberg, Allan, Joel Smith, and Harold D. Clarke. *Citizen Politicians Canada: Party Officials in a Democratic Society*. Durham: Carolina Academic Press, 1979.

Kornberg, Allan, William Mishler, and Joel Smith. "Political Elite and Mass Perceptions of Party Locations in Issue Space: Some Tests of Two Propositions." *British Journal of Political Science* 5 (1975): 161–85.

Koole, Ruud. "Cadre, Catch-All or Cartel? A Comment on the Notion of the Cartel Party." *Party Politics* 2 (1996): 507–23.

Lambert, Ronald D. "Question Design, Response Set and Measurement of Left/Right Thinking in Survey Research." *Canadian Journal of Political Science* 16 (1983): 135–44.

Lambert, Ronald D., James E. Curtis, Steven D. Brown, and Barry J. Kay. "In Search of Left/Right Beliefs in the Canadian Electorate." *Canadian Journal of Political Science* 19 (1986): 541–63.

Laycock, David. "Reforming the Canadian Democracy? Institutions and Ideology in the Reform Party Project." *Canadian Journal of Political Science* 27 (1994): 213–47.

———. *Populism and Democratic Thought in the Canadian Prairies, 1910 to 1945.* Toronto: University of Toronto Press, 1990.

Lee, Robert Mason. *One Hundred Monkeys: The Triumph of Popular Wisdom in Canadian Politics.* Toronto: Macfarlane, Walter and Ross, 1989.

LeDuc, Lawrence, "The Leaders' Debates: Critical Event or Non-Event." In *The Canadian General Election of 1993*, edited by Alan Frizzell, Jon H. Pammett and Anthony Westell, 127–42. Ottawa: Carleton University Press, 1994.

———. "Canada: The Politics of Stable Dealignment." In *Electoral Change in Advanced Industrial Democracies: Realignment of Dealignment?*, by Russell J. Dalton, Scott C. Flanagan, and Paul Allen Beck, 402–24. Princeton: Princeton University Press, 1984.

LeDuc, Lawrence, and Richard Price. "Great Debates: The Televised Leadership Debates in Canada." *Canadian Journal of Political Science* 18 (1985): 135–53.

Lewis, David. *The Good Fight: Political Memoirs 1909–1958*. Toronto: Macmillan, 1981.

Lijphart, A. *Democracies: Patterns of Majoritarian and Consensus Government in Twenty-one Countries*. New Haven, CT: Yale University Press, 1984.

Lipset, Seymour M. *Revolution and Counterrevolution: Change and Persistence in Social Structures*. New York: Basic Books, 1968.

Lipset, Seymour M., and Sein Rokkan. "Cleavage Structures, Party Systems and Voter Alignments: An Introduction." In *Party Systems and Voter Alignments: Crossnational Perspectives*, by Seymour M. Lipset and Sein Rokkan, 1–93. New York: Free Press, 1967.

MacIvor, Heather. "Do Canadian Political Parties Form a Cartel?" *Canadian Journal of Political Science* 29 (1996): 317–34.

Macpherson, C. B. *Democracy in Alberta: Social Credit and the Party System*. Toronto: University of Toronto Press, 1962.

Manning, Preston. *The New Canada*. Toronto: Macmillan Canada, 1992.

Manning, Preston, and Andre Turcotte. "New Dimensions Shape Politics of the 21st Century." *Calgary Herald*, 19 June 1998.

Martin, Patrick, Alan Gregg, and George Perlin. *Contenders: The Tory Quest for Power*. Scarborough: Prentice-Hall Canada, 1983.

McKenzie, Robert. *British Political Parties*. London: Heinemann, 1963.

———. *British Political Parties*. London: William Heinemann, 1955.

Medding, D. W. "A Framework for the Analysis of Power in Political Parties." *Political Studies* 18 (1970): 1–17.

Michels, Robert. *Political Parties: A Sociological Study of the Oligarchic Tendencies of Modern Democracy*. New York: Free Press, 1962.

Morton, Desmond. *The New Democrats, 1961–1986: The Politics of Change*. Toronto: Copp Clark Pitman, 1986.

Morton, W. L. *The Kingdom of Canada*. Toronto: University of Toronto Press, 1970.

———. *The Progressive Party in Canada*. Toronto: University of Toronto Press, 1950.

Mudde, Cas. "The Paradox of the Anti-Party Party: Insights from the Extreme Right." *Party Politics* 2 (1996): 265–76.

Nevitte, Neil, André Blais, Elizabeth Gidengil, and Richard Nadeau. *Unsteady State: The 1997 Canadian Federal Election*. Don Mills: Oxford University Press, 2000.

Obler, J. "Intraparty Democracy and a Selection of Parliamentary Candidates: The Belgian Case." *British Journal of Political Science* 4 (1974): 163–85.

Ogmundson, R. L. "A Note on the Ambiguous Meanings of Survey Research Measures Which Use the Words 'Left' and Right'." *Canadian Journal of Political Science* 12 (1979): 799–805.

O'Neil, Terry, ed. *Act of Faith: a collection of articles originally published in Alberta Report, Western Report, and British Columbia Report.* Vancouver: BC Report Magazine, 1991.

Ostrogorski, M. *Democracy and the Organization of Political Parties*, translated by F. Clarke. New York: Macmillan, 1902.

Pal, Leslie A., and Robert M. Campbell. *The Real Worlds of Canadian Politics: Cases in Process and Policy.* 2nd ed. Peterborough: Broadview Press, 1991.

Pammett, Jon H., and Christopher Dornan, eds. *The Canadian General Election of 2000.* Toronto: Dundurn Press, 2001.

Panebianco, Angelo. *Political Parties: Organization and Power.* New York: Cambridge University Press, 1988.

Penniman, Howard, ed. *Canada at the Polls, 1984: A Study of the Federal General Elections.* Durham: Duke University Press, 1988.

Perlin, George. "Attitudes of Liberal Convention Delegates Toward Proposals for Reform of the Process of Leadership Selection." In *Canadian Political Parties: Leaders, Candidates and Organization*, Vol. 13, Research Studies of the Royal Commission on Electoral Reform and Party Financing, edited by Herman Bakvis, 57–96. Toronto: Dundurn Press, 1991.

———. "The Progressive Conservative Party: An Assessment of the Significance of Its Victories in the Elections of 1984 and 1988." In *Party Politics in Canada*, 6th ed., edited by Hugh G. Thorburn, 298–316. Scarborough: Prentice-Hall Canada, 1991.

———. *Party Democracy in Canada: The Politics of National Party Conventions.* Scarborough: Prentice-Hall Canada, 1988.

———. "Opportunity Regained: the Tory Victory in 1984." In *Canada at the Polls, 1984: A Study of the Federal General Elections*, edited by Howard Penniman, 79–96. Durham: Duke University Press, 1988.

———. *The Tory Syndrome: Leadership Politics in the Progressive Conservative Party.* Montreal: McGill-Queen's University Press, 1980.

Pinard, Maurice. "Third Parties in Canada Revisited: A Rejoinder and Elaboration of the Theory of One-Party Dominance." *Canadian Journal of Political Science* 6 (1973): 439–60.

———. *The Rise of a Third Party: A Study in Crisis Politics.* Englewood Cliffs, NJ: Prentice Hall, 1971.

———. "One Party Dominance and Third Parties." *Canadian Journal of Economics and Political Science* 23 (1967): 356–88.

Porter, John. *The Vertical Mosaic.* Toronto: University of Toronto Press, 1965.

Powell, G. Bingham Jr. *Contemporary Democracies.* Cambridge: Harvard University Press, 1982.

Presthus, Robert. *Elite Accommodation in Canadian Politics.* Toronto: Macmillan, 1973.

Rae, Douglas. *The Political Consequences of Electoral Laws.* New Haven: Yale University Press, 1968.

Riker, William H. *Liberalism Against Populism: A Confrontation Between the*

Theory of Democracy and the Theory of Social Choice. Prospect Heights, Illinois: Waveland Press, 1982.

Regenstreif, Peter. *The Diefenbaker Interlude: Parties and Voting in Canada.* Toronto: Longmans Canada, 1965.

Richards, John. "Populism: A Qualified Defence." *Studies in Political Economy* 5 (1981): 5–27.

Sartori, Giovanni. *Parties and Party Systems: A Framework for Analysis.* Cambridge: Cambridge University Press, 1976.

Schedler, Andreas. "Anti-Political-Establishment Parties." *Party Politics* 2 (1996): 291–312.

Sharp, Sydney, and Don Braid. *Storming Babylon: Preston Manning and the Rise of the Reform Party.* Toronto: Key Porter, 1992.

Sigurdson, Richard. "Preston Manning and the Politics of Postmodernism in Canada." *Canadian Journal of Political Science* 27 (1994): 249–76.

Simeon, Richard. "Regionalism and Canadian Political Institutions." In *Canadian Federalism: Myth or Reality.* 3rd ed., edited by J. Peter Meekison, 292–304. Toronto: Methuen Publications, 1977.

Simeon, Richard, and David J. Elkins. "Regional Political Cultures in Canada." *Canadian Journal of Political Science* 7 (1974): 397–437.

Smith, David E. *The Regional Decline of a National Party: Liberals on the Prairies.* Toronto: University of Toronto Press, 1981.

Stevenson, H. Michael. "Ideology and Unstable Party Identification in Canada: Limited Rationality in a Brokerage Party System." *Canadian Journal of Political Science* 20 (1987): 813–50.

Tanguay, A. Brian, and Alain-G. Gagnon, eds. *Canadian Parties in Transition.* 2nd ed. Toronto: Nelson Canada, 1996.

Thorburn, Hugh G., ed. *Party Politics in Canada.* 7th ed. Scarborough: Prentice-Hall Canada, 1996.

———, ed. *Party Politics in Canada.* 6th ed. Scarborough: Prentice-Hall Canada, 1991.

———, ed. *Party Politics in Canada.* 5th ed. Scarborough: Prentice-Hall Canada, 1985.

———, ed. *Party Politics.* 3rd ed. Scarborough: Prentice-Hall Canada, 1974.

———, ed. *Party Politics in Canada.* Scarborough: Prentice-Hall Canada, 1963.

———, ed. *Party Politics.* Scarborough: Prentice-Hall Canada, 1962.

Thorburn, Hugh G., and Alan Whitehorn, eds. *Party Politics in Canada.* 8th ed. Toronto: Prentice Hall/Pearson Education Canada, 2000.

Tossutti, Livianna S. "From Communitarian Protest Towards Institutionalization: The Evolution of 'Hybrid' Parties in Canada and Italy." *Party Politics* 2 (1996): 435–54.

Trudeau, P. E. *Federalism and the French Canadians.* Toronto: Gage, 1982.

Waite, P. W. *The Life and Times of Confederation.* Toronto: University of Toronto Press, 1962.

Ward, Norman. "The Redistribution of 1952." *Canadian Journal of Economics and Political Science* 19 (1953): 341–60.

Wearing, Joseph. *Strained Relations: Canadian Parties and Voters.* Toronto: McClelland and Stewart, 1988.

Whitaker, Reginald. *The Government Party.* Toronto: University of Toronto Press, 1977.

White, Graham. "One-Party Dominance and Third Parties: The Pinard Theory Reconsidered." *Canadian Journal of Political Science* 6 (1973): 399–421.

Whitehorn, Alan. "Ideologies and Parties in Canada." In *Mapping Canadian Federalism for India*, edited by Rekha Saxena 318–51. Delhi: Konark Publishers PVT, 2002.

———. *Canadian Socialism: Essays on the CCF-NDP.* Toronto: Oxford University Press, 1992.

———. "The New Democratic Party in Convention." In *Party Democracy in Canada: The Politics of National Party Conventions*, edited by George Perlin 272–87. Scarborough: Prentice-Hall Canada, 1988.

Whitehorn, Alan, and Keith Archer. "Party Activists and Political Leadership: A Case Study of the NDP." In *Leaders and Leadership in Canadian Politics*, edited by Richard Price and Ron Wagenberg, 28–52. Toronto: Oxford University Press, 1993.

Winn, Conrad, and John McMenemy, eds. *Political Parties in Canada.* Toronto: McGraw-Hill Ryerson, 1976.

Wiseman, Nelson. "The West as a Political Region." In *Canadian Politics: An Introduction to the Discipline*, edited by Alain G. Gagnon and James P. Bickerton, 308–24. Peterborough: Broadview Press, 1990.

Zipp, John F. "Left-Right Dimensions of Canadian Federal Party Identification: A Discriminate Analysis." *Canadian Journal of Political Science* 11 (1978): 251–77.

Notes

Prologue

1 Panebianco, *Political Parties*, xi.

2 Ibid., xii.

3 See Edmund Burke's assessment of the development of parties as analyzed by Giovanni Sartori, *Parties and Party Systems*, 9.

4 Ibid., 15.

5 Sartori, *Parties and Party Systems*, 16–23 and Duverger, *Political Parties*, xxv–xxix; see also Ostrogorski, *Democracy and the Organization of Political Parties* and Key, *Public Opinion and American Democracy*, 433.

6 The terms "mass" and "cadre" parties were introduced by Duverger. See *Political Parties.*

7 Michels, *Political Parties*, 70.

8 Ibid., 72; see also Sartori, *Parties and Party Systems*, 23.

9 Michels, *Political Parties*, 62.

10 Seymour Martin Lipset, "Introduction," in Michels, *Political Parties*, 15.

11 See Duverger, *Political Parties*; Robert McKenzie, *British Political Parties*; Lipset, "Introduction, in Michels, *Political Parties*, 27–31; and Thomas A. Koelble, "Party Structures and Democracy."

12 See Lipset, "Introduction," in Michels, *Political Parties*, 34–35.

13 See McKenzie, *British Political Parties*, and Koelble, "Party Structures and Democracy," 201.

14 Panebianco, *Political Parties*, 21–22. See also Cassinelli, "The Law of Oligarchy"; G. Hans, "Roberto Michels and the Study of Political Parties"; Medding, "A Framework for the Analysis of Power in Political Parties"; Cook, "Roberto Michels: Political Parties in Perspective"; and Obler, "Intra-party Democracy and a Selection of Parliamentary Candidates: The Belgian Case." For similar criticisms of Manning with respect to his perceived manipulation of the Reform membership

see Dobbin, *Manning and Reform*, 139–185; and Flanagan, *Waiting for the Wave*, 27–32.

15 It is likely that the evidence presented here will provide support to both adherents and detractors of the "iron law of oligarchy" thesis.

16 Duverger, *Political Parties*, xxiii.

17 Koelble, "Party Structures and Democracy," 213.

18 Panebianco, *Political Parties*, xiii–xiv.

19 Ibid., 22–23.

20 See Duverger, *Political Parties.* For an examination of the organizational structure of the NDP, which includes union affiliation and individual membership, see Keith Archer, "The New Democrats, Organized Labour and the Prospects of Electoral Reform," in Bakvis *Canadian Political Parties.* Also see Carty, "Campaigning in the Trenches: the Transformation of Constituency Politics," in Perlin, *Party Democracy in Canada*, 84–96. For a more detailed analysis of Duverger's theories as applied to Reform see Ellis, "Genealogy of Dissent."

21 See Katz and Mair, "Changing Models of Party Organization"; Koole, "Cadre, Catch-All or Cartel? A Comment on the Notion of the Cartel Party"; Katz and Mair, "Cadre, Catch-All or Cartel: A Rejoinder." Katz and Mair base their analysis on the following criteria: the degree of social-political inclusion, level of distribution of politically relevant resources, the principal goals of the parties' politics, the basis of party competition, patterns of electoral competition, the nature of party work and party campaigning, the principal source of a party's resources, the relations between ordinary members and the party elite, the character of membership, party channels of communication, the position of the party between civil society and the state, and parties' representation styles. Katz and Mair, "Changing Models of Party Organization," 18.

22 Ibid., 18.

23 See Heather MacIvor, "Do Canadian Political Parties Form a Cartel?".

24 Andreas Schedler, "Anti-Political-Establishment Parties," 292–93.

1 · INTRODUCTION

1 R. K. Carty, "Three Canadian Party Systems," in Carty, *Canadian Political Party Systems*; and Carty, Cross and Young, *Rebuilding Canadian Party Politics.* Although the later authors contend that the contemporary period under study represents more of a transition into a fourth party system, it will be argued throughout this book that the election of 1993 indeed demarcated the beginning of a new, fourth party system.

2 The formal titles for each of these sections and the corresponding dates are borrowed directly from Carty.

3 See Dawson, *The Civil Service of Canada*; Gordon T. Stewart, "Political Patronage Under Macdonald and Laurier 1878–1911," in Carty, *Canadian Political Party Systems*, 45–76.

4 J. C. Courtney, "Leadership Selection in the New Dominion," in Carty, *Canadian Political Party Systems*, 100–121.

5 Ibid. See also Paul Rutherford, "The Politician's Dominion: Party Media Relationships in Early Canada," in Carty, *Canadian Political Party Systems*, 128–46.

6 See Fowke, *The National Policy and the Wheat Economy*; and Fowke, "National Policy – Old and New."

7 John McMenemy, "Fragment and Movement Parties," in Winn and McMenemy, *Political Parties in Canada*, 29–48. The Progressives represented the federal arm of the agrarian movement that was sweeping much of the country between the Rockies and the Ottawa River. Agrarian parties would succeed in capturing three provincial governments in the early 1920s. The United Farmers of Ontario won a majority of seats at Queen's Park in 1919, the United Farmers of Alberta formed a majority government in 1921 and would govern uninterrupted until being displaced by Social Credit in 1935, and the United Farmers of Manitoba won a majority government in that province in 1922. See Morton, *The Progressive Party in Canada*, 210–35.

8 W. L. Morton, "The Progressive Tradition in Canadian Politics," in Thorburn, *Party Politics in Canada*, 79.

9 Ibid., 83.

10 McMenemy, "Fragment and Movement Parties," 41; and Morton, "The Progressive Tradition," 81.

11 Morton, "The Progressive Tradition," 81.

12 McMenemy, "Fragment and Movement Parties," 43.

13 See Roger Gibbins, "Western Alienation and the Alberta Political Culture," in Caldarola, *Society and Politics in Alberta*, 143–67. Gibbins argues that western alienation meets certain conditions of a full-fledged political ideology. At its core, western alienation is an estrangement from the central Canadian domination of political events and institutions by a "vigorous, prosperous and dynamic" region that often leads to greater participation in the political system rather than a withdrawal from it.

14 The two exceptions were Diefenbaker's 1958 landslide and the 1962 election where the Créditistes denied the Liberals a majority of seats.

15 However, the Liberal's domination of electoral competition in Quebec and its large number of seats allowed that party to control the national parliament during most of this system.

16 John English, "The End of the Great Party Era," in Carty, *Canadian Political Party Systems*, 147–54.

17 However, see Ward, "The Redistribution of 1952."

18 See Whitaker, *The Government Party.*

19 Social Credit won 15 of 17 seats with 48 per cent of the vote in Alberta in the 1935 federal election. In the provincial election of the same year Social Credit formed the Alberta government winning 56 of 63 seats on 54 per cent of the vote. See Dyck, *Provincial Politics in Canada.*

20 See Finkel, *The Social Credit Phenomenon in Alberta.*

21 For a full elaboration of Social Credit in Alberta see Macpherson, *Democracy in Alberta*; Irving, *The Social Credit Movement in Alberta.*

22 See Leo Zakuta, "The CCF-NDP: Membership in a Becalmed Protest Movement," in Thorburn, *Party Politics in Canada*, 96.

23 See Regenstreif, *The Diefenbaker Interlude.*

24 In the 1968 election the Tories would place second to the Liberals in Manitoba, while in 1988 they would place second to the NDP in Saskatchewan.

25 Social Credit would continue to receive between 22 and 29 per cent until 1968 but never again elect more than two Alberta MPs.

26 During the 1970s and early 1980s the Tory grip on Alberta would strengthen over time, increasing to 57 per cent support in 1972, 61 per cent in 1974, 66 per cent in the 1979 and 1980 elections and reaching a peak of 69 per cent in 1984.

27 See Morton, *The New Democrats*; and Archer, *Political Choices and Electoral Consequences.*

28 See Perlin, *The Tory Syndrome*; and Martin, Gregg and Perlin, *Contenders: The Tory Quest for Power.*

29 See Smith, *The Regional Decline of a National Party*; David Smith, "Grits and Tories on the Prairies" in Thorburn, *Party Politics in Canada*, 4th ed., 273–89; David Smith, "Party Struggles to Win the Prairies" in Thorburn, *Party Politics in Canada*, 7th ed., 446–61.

30 Johnston et al., *Letting the People Decide*, 67.

31 Wiseman, "The West as a Political Region," 318.

32 John C. Courtney, "Reinventing the Brokerage Wheel: The Tory Success in 1984," in Penniman, *Canada at the Polls, 1984*, 190–210.

33 George Perlin, "Opportunity Regained: the Tory Victory in 1984," in Penniman, *Canada at the Polls, 1984*, 79–96.

34 For an insightful collection of essays analyzing the Meech Lake agreement from a western perspective see Gibbins et al., *Meech Lake and Canada.* For a full account of the political and policy process that led to the Meech Lake constitutional accord see Pal and Campbell, *The Real Worlds of Canadian Politics.*

35 Mulroney was slow in dismantling many of the tax provisions contained in the NEP, including the hated Petroleum and Gas Revenue Tax.

36 See Pal and Campbell, *The Real Worlds of Canadian Politics*: 19–52; and O'Neill, *Act of Faith*, 32–36, 46–47.

37 See "A Western Reform Movement: The Responsible Alternative to Western Separatism," briefs prepared for *A Western Assembly On Canada's Economic and Political Future*, Vancouver, 1987; and Preston Manning, "Laying the Foundations for a New Western Political Party," an address to a public information meeting sponsored by the Reform Association of Canada, Calgary, 10 August 1987.

38 See Lipset and Rokkan, "Cleavage Structures, Party Systems and Voter Alignments"; Rae, *The Political Consequences of Electoral Laws*; Cairns, "The Electoral System and the Party System in Canada, 1930–1965"; Royal Commission on Electoral Reform and Party Financing, *Reforming Electoral Democracy.*

39 Alan Cairns, "The Electoral System and the Party System in Canada, 1921–1965," in Cairns, *Constitution, Government and Society in Canada*, 119–21. For more recent analysis of electoral system effects in Canada see Leslie Seidle, "The Canadian Electoral System and Proposals for Reform," in Tanguay and Gagnon, *Canadian Parties in Transition*, 282–306.

40 See Pinard, "One Party Dominance and Third Parties"; Pinard, *The Rise of a Third Party*; Pinard, "Third Parties in Canada Revisited." See also White, "One-Party Dominance and Third Parties" and Blais, "Third Parties in Canadian Provincial Politics."

41 White, "One-Party Dominance and Third Parties."

42 Pinard, "Third Parties Revisited," 441.

43 White, "One-Party Dominance and Third Parties," 420.

44 See Jon H. Pammett, "Tracking the Votes" and Faron Ellis and Keith Archer, "Reform: Electoral Breakthrough" in Frizzell, Pammett and Westell, *The Canadian General Election of 1993.*

45 See Dabbs, *Preston Manning: The Roots of Reform*; Dobbin, *Preston Manning and the Reform Party*; Flanagan, *Waiting for the Wave*; Manning, *The New Canada*; and Sharp and Braid, *Storming Babylon*.

2 · The Founding

1 The "Western Assembly on Canada's Economic and Political Future" was held 29–31 May 1987 in the Hyatt Regency Hotel in Vancouver, BC.

2 Stan Roberts was a former Manitoba MLA, former vice-president of Simon Fraser University, former president of the Canadian Chamber of Commerce and the Canada West Foundation.

3 Robert Muir was past president of the Canadian Petroleum Law Foundation and former general counsel for Dome Petroleum.

4 Francis Winspear was an Edmonton financier now retired and living in Vancouver.

5 The Canada West Foundation is a non-partisan research institute that advocates for western concerns.

6 Alberta Report founder and publisher Ted Byfield was an early proponent of a new western-based political party and could be counted upon for strong editorial support throughout Reform's existence. *Alberta Report*, 13 April, 1 June and 8 June 1987.

7 The subjects to be discussed included constitutional policy, social policy, economic policy, political reform, institutional reform and the best vehicle for achieving the West's demands within the Canadian party system.

8 Reform Association advertisements, *Alberta Report*, 4 May and 25 May 1987; Reform Association of Canada Newsletter – May 1987; and "A conference on Canada's Economic and Political Future," Reform Association of Canada, 9 March 1987.

9 Kenneth Whyte, "Assembling a solution: Organizing the initial gathering," in O'Neil, *Act of Faith*, 18.

10 Ibid.

11 Philip Day, Mike Byfield and Kenneth Whyte, "All eyes west: Setting the scene for the first Assembly," in O'Neil, *Act of Faith*, 20.
12 Ibid., 20.
13 Ibid., 20.
14 About 100 of the 200 voting delegates were Albertans. Fifty-eight came from BC while 38 came from Manitoba and Saskatchewan. There were 23 observers and resource people, about 350 delegates at large, and 100 outside observers. Most resolutions that were put to votes had about 150 to 170 delegates returning ballots. Manning, *The New Canada*, 135.
15 Flanagan, *Waiting for the Wave*, 52.
16 Preston Manning, "Choosing a Political Vehicle to Represent the West," a presentation to the "Western Assembly on Canada's Economic and Political Future," Vancouver, 29–31 May 1987.
17 Ibid.
18 It will be demonstrated below that Manning was indeed less right wing than many members of his party, which often made him look less ideologically pure. However, it must also be remembered that Manning himself authored many of Reform's early policy proposals. See the *Reform Party Blue Book*, 1989. For a more complete understanding of Manning's populism, conception of regional alienation, and his views on ideology, see Manning, *The New Canada*, 5–27 and 118–24; and Flanagan, *Waiting for the Wave*, 5–37.
19 Both Manning and Roberts were nominated to the steering committee.
20 See Steve Weatherbe, "Proposing Policy Alternatives," in O'Neil, *Act of Faith*, 24–27.
21 See Appendix A for a complete summary of the Reform Party of Canada's membership numbers.
22 New members could join the Association and vote at selection meetings in their ridings up to and including the time of the meeting, a practice that would change to some predetermined point prior to meetings and become a highly symbolic, practical application of both Reform's populism and its determination to demonstrate it would not participate in the crass recruitment politics being displayed by the traditional parties of the time. For an illustration of the public relations problems associated with membership recruitment in the Progressive Conservative Party's 1983 leadership contest see Faron Ellis, "The Last Worst Tory Leadership Convention," in Bunner, *Lougheed and the War with Ottawa.*
23 Reform Association of Canada, "Guidelines for the Selection of Delegates to the founding Convention at Winnipeg," 2 September 1987.
24 Flanagan, *Waiting for the Wave*, 56–57.
25 See Faron Ellis, "A Storied Name From the Past Leads a Modern Populist Uprising," in Bunner, *Alberta Takes the Lead;* and Manning, *The New Canada*, 151.
26 See Manning, *The New Canada*, 151–153; Flanagan, *Waiting for the Wave*, 54; and Kenneth Whyte and Mike Byfield, "Born with a bang:

A controversial leadership race marks the first convention," in O'Neil, *Act of Faith*, 35–42.

27 Manning reportedly spent less than $2,000, most of it on travel prior to the assembly, while Roberts reportedly spent $25,000. See Whyte and Byfield, "Born with a bang," 39–42; and Manning, *The New Canada*, 152–53.

28 See Manning, "Leader's Forward: 'The Next Canada,'" in *Reform Party of Canada: Platform and Statement of Principles, 1988*, 4; and Appendix I, especially principles 7, 8, 15 and 17.

29 See Duverger, *Political Parties.*

30 Constitution of the Reform Party of Canada, Section 11 (a), 1987. For a complete overview of the organizational structures of all three traditional federal parties see Wearing, *Strained Relations: Canadian Parties and Voters*; and Rand Dyck, "Relations Between Federal and Provincial Parties," in Gagnon and Tanguay, *Canadian Parties in Transition*, 186–219.

31 Constitution of the Reform Party of Canada, Section 2 (a), 1994. Persons aged 14 through 17 were eligible to be associate members. The age threshold for associate membership was lowered from 16 to 14 at the 1994 Assembly.

32 Constitution of the Reform Party of Canada, Section 2 (d), 1987.

33 The party experimented briefly with regional councils but these represented a direct challenge to the centralized direction of the executive council. They also represented a potential threat to the autonomy of the branches and were quickly disbanded with little resistance from the branches.

34 See Duverger, *Political Parties: Their Organization and Activity in the Modern State*; and Duverger, *Political Parties.* See also Michels, *Political Parties*; and Panebianco, *Political Parties.*

35 Constitution of the Reform Party of Canada, Section 8 (b), 1991. This minimum requirement was lowered to 5 per cent by a decision made at the 1991 Assembly.

36 Constitution of the Reform Party of Canada, Section 7 (a), 1991. Assemblies were required to be held at least every two years, 7 (b).

37 Réjean Pelletier, with the collaboration of Francois Bundock and Michel Sara-Bournet, "The Structures of Canadian Political Parties: How they Operate" in Bakvis, *Canadian Political Parties*, 272–78.

38 Constitution of the Reform Party of Canada, Articles 1 (c), 7 (g) and 8.

39 Constitution of the Reform Party of Canada, Section 1 (d), 1991. This clause was added at the 1991 Assembly.

40 Constitution of the Reform Party of Canada, Articles 5 and 6, 1991.

41 "If more than 50 per cent of the votes cast are in the affirmative, the Executive Council shall, within 15 days of the Assembly Vote, announce when a Leadership Vote will be held and notice shall be given to all members of the Party by the Executive Council within a further 21 days. The Leadership Vote must be held not sooner than 3 months and not later than 6 months from the date of the vote held at the Assembly." Constitution of the Reform Party of Canada Article 6 (c), 1991.

This procedure was changed at the party's 1991 Assembly from the original requirement that a review be held after each general election in which the party did not form some part of the government.

42 The party constitution also stated that Members of Parliament, Senators, employees of Members of Parliament or Senators, and full-time employees of Reform Fund Canada or the party may not be members of the executive council. Constitution of the Reform Party of Canada, Article 5 (l), 1997.

43 Constitution of the Reform Party of Canada, Section 4, 1991.

44 See the Constitution of the Reform Party of Canada, Schedule B, Article IX: Candidate Selection, 1991 and the party's two 1991 publications, "Constituency Organizational Procedures Handbook" and "Candidate Recruitment and Selection Manual." One of the distinguishing features of the constituency constitution was the provision that persons voting at annual general meetings and candidate nomination meetings must be members of the party for at least 30 days prior to the meeting (down from the original 45 days). Schedule B, Article VI, 6.2 and Article IX (e).

45 Constitution of the Reform Party of Canada, Section 5, 1991.

46 Preston Manning, "Leaders Message," Reform Association of Canada, 15 December 1987.

47 The six-city tour included stops in Winnipeg, Saskatoon, Edmonton, Calgary, Vancouver and Victoria. See "Summary of Results of Senate Reform Workshops – May 9–17, 1988," Reform Party of Canada, 1988.

48 Reform Party of Canada, "Constituency Organization Handbook and Draft Constituency Constitutions," 1988.

49 Only parties that had officially registered fifty candidates could have their party's name included on the ballot with the candidate's name. Candidates whose parties did not meet these requirements were considered independents.

50 Greg Heaton, "The battle for Yellowhead: Leader Preston Manning becomes the first RPC Candidate," *Alberta Report*, 6 June 1988. Stan Roberts lost his bid to secure the nomination in the Victoria constituency of Sannich and the Islands, Steve Weatherbe, "Two-time loser: The party rejects Stan Roberts," *Alberta Report*, 4 July 1988.

51 Reform supported the Canada-US Free Trade Agreement.

52 Reform Party of Canada, *Platform and Statement of Principles*, August 1988.

53 For a discussion of how the CCF spent considerable time in its later years attempting to ensure that it would not be infiltrated by communists see Lewis, *The Good Fight.*

54 See Stephen Lequire and Paul Bunner, "The Collins Affair: The party kills the candidacy of a BC columnist," in O'Neil, *Act of Faith*, 61–62.

55 Manning, *The New Canada*, 155–83.

56 Ibid., 161.

57 See Johnston et al., *Letting the People Decide*, 141–67.

58 The Alberta Senate election was not a constitutionally sanctioned election but more of an attempt by the Alberta government to promote its Senate reform agenda.

59 See Faron Ellis, "Reform's Unrepentant Warrior," in *Alberta Takes the Lead*, 251; and Manning, *The New Canada*, 200–202.

3 · The Maturing Membership

1 For a discussion of the theoretical and practical implications of populism see Harrison, *Of Passionate Intensity*, 5–16, 251–60.

2 Courtney and Perlin, "The Role of Conventions in Representation and Accommodation of Regional Cleavages" in Perlin, *Party Democracy in Canada*, 128–31.

3 Courtney, *Do Conventions Matter*, 330.

4 Archer, "Leadership Selection in the New Democratic Party," in Bakvis, *Canadian Political Parties*, 6.

5 Whitehorn and Archer, "Party Activists and Political Leadership."

6 Archer, "Leadership Selection in the New Democratic Party," 8.

7 Ibid., 6; and Whitehorn and Archer, "Party Activists and Political Leadership."

8 In most instances delegates were elected but some appointments were made to fill vacancies in weakly organized branches.

9 The Constitution of the Reform Party of Canada, Section 7 (d). Only Deborah Grey qualified under the "sitting member" category. Stan Waters had not yet been appointed to the Senate by the Prime Minister. Even if Waters had been a Senator the party constitution would not yet have entitled him to automatic voting delegate status. A provision that created a minimum threshold of three delegates per constituency was added at the 1991 Saskatoon Assembly. Changes to the constitutional proposed by the executive council at the 1989 Assembly would have set a minimum threshold of five voting delegates per constituency association. The proposals would have also changed the length delegates had to be party members from 45 to 15 days prior to notice of the Assembly.

10 Porter, *The Vertical Mosaic*; Kornberg, Smith and Clarke, *Citizen Politicians Canada*.

11 George Perlin, "Attitudes of Liberal Convention Delegates Toward Proposals for Reform of the Process of Leadership Selection," in Bakvis, *Canadian Political Parties*, 61; and Courtney, *Do Conventions Matter*, 336.

12 Whitehorn, *Canadian Socialism*.

13 See Whitehorn and Archer, "Party Activists and Political Leadership."

14 Ibid.

15 Kornberg, Smith and Clark, *Citizen Politicians-Canada*.

16 Perlin, "Attitudes of Liberal Convention Delegates," 62.

17 The 1989 Assembly Study was conducted by distributing a questionnaire to all 636 delegates attending the 1989 Edmonton Assembly, of which 481 returned completed questionnaires for a completion rate of

75 per cent. Principal investigators were Faron Ellis and David Robb. The 1991 Membership Study was commissioned by the Reform Party and conducted via telephone interview during the summer of 1991. It consisted of a provincially stratified random sample of 1,786 Reform Party members. Principal investigator was Faron Ellis. The 1992 Assembly Study was sponsored by the University of Calgary Research Grants Committee and by the Social Science and Humanities Research Council (410-93-0400) and was conducted by mailing a questionnaire to all of the 1,290 delegates whose names appeared on party mailing lists, of which 893 returned completed questionnaires for a completion rate of 69 per cent. Principal investigators were Keith Archer and Faron Ellis. The 1993 Membership study was funded through a National Science Foundation research grant (SES-931135) and consisted of a questionnaire mailed to a provincially stratified random sample of 4,000 party members in 1993, of which 2,574 returned completed questionnaires for a completion rate of 64.4 per cent. Principle investigators were Harold D. Clarke and Allan Kornberg. For a more extensive demographic profile of the 1991 membership see Tom Flanagan and Faron Ellis, "A Comparative Profile of the Reform Party of Canada," paper presented to the Canadian Political Science Association Annual Meeting, Charlottetown, June 1992. See also Archer and Ellis, "Opinion Structure of Party Activists"; and Clarke et al., "Not For Fame or Fortune."

18 Any member or associate member of the party could attend an assembly as a delegate-at-large and was entitled to speak to motions and amendments but was not entitled to vote. Constitution of the Reform Party of Canada, Article 7 (f), 1996.

19 Reform Party of Canada, "Memorandum – To all Registered Participants at the October 27–29 Assembly of the Reform Party of Canada," from Wayne Smith, Assembly Chairman, 15 December 1989.

20 Includes delegates-at-large, voting delegates and other delegates but excludes observers who may not have been party members.

21 As the party expanded it began to recruit many more activists with no previous political activity. Also, activists who attend assemblies tend to be the most highly engaged partisans and would therefore be more likely to have been involved in other parties than would ordinary members. The 1991 membership study indicated that only 37.4 per cent of the general membership had previously belonged to another federal party. See Flanagan and Ellis, "A Comparative Profile of the Reform Party of Canada;" and Chapter 4, below.

22 See George Koch, "War on two fronts," *Alberta Report*, 5 February 1990.

23 A score of one on the scale indicated the farthest left position, a four was considered to be at the centre, while a seven indicated the farthest left position.

24 Considerable debate exists about the use of ideological self-placement scales and the ability of political scientists to accurately use them in measuring ideology in the electorates. See Lambert et al., "In Search of Left/Right Beliefs in the Canadian Electorate"; Stevenson, "Ideology

and Unstable Party Identification in Canada"; Ogmundson, "A Note on the Ambiguous Meanings of Survey Research Measures"; Zipp, "Left-Right Dimensions of Canadian Federal Party Identification"; Conover and Feldman, "The Origins and Meaning of Liberal/Conservative Self-Identifications"; Asher and Shamir, "The Primarily Political Functions of the Left-Right continuum"; Lambert, "Question Design, Response Set and Measurement"; Fleury and Lewis-Beck, "Anchoring the French Voter"; Converse and Pierce, "Comment on Fleury and Lewis-Beck"; and Fleury and Lewis-Beck, "Déjà Vu All Over Again." Some attention has also been devoted to the party activists. See Richard Johnston, "The Ideological Structure of Opinion on Policy," in Perlin, *Party Democracy in Canada*, 54–70; Whitehorn and Archer, "Party Activists and Political Leadership"; Carty, Erickson and Blake, *Leaders and Parties in Canadian Politics*; also see Clarke, "The Ideological Self-Perceptions of Provincial Legislators". For analysis of elites see Kornberg, Mishler and Smith, "Political Elite and Mass Perceptions of Party Locations in Issue Space." Also see Andre Blais et al., "Do Party Supporters Differ?" in Everitt and O'Neill, *Citizen Politics*; and Whitehorn, "Ideologies and Parties in Canada."

25 See Ellis, "The Ideological Structure of the Canadian Reform Party," paper presented to the 51st Annual Meeting of the Midwest Political Science Association, Chicago, March 1994; and Faron Ellis and Keith Archer, "Ideology and Opinion Within the Reform Party," in Thorburn and Whitehorn, *Party Politics in Canada*, 8th ed., 122–34.

26 See "Statement of Principles" 12 through 15.

27 The governing Conservatives later reduced the rate and implemented a 7 per cent GST.

28 See Gairdener, *The Trouble With Canada*, 389–420, and Brimelow, *The Patriot Game*, 142, for examples of arguments that were influencing many Reform supporters concerning the language debate. Also see Innis, *Bilingualism and Biculturalism.*

29 By 1989 the Meech Lake constitutional accord and its provision to grant Quebec distinct-society status was receiving substantial critical evaluation in the west. See Gibbins et al., *Meech Lake and Canada*; and Campbell and Pal, *Real Worlds of Canadian Politics.*

30 Reform Party of Canada, Platform and Statement of Principles, 1989.

31 Peter Macdonald and Paul Bunner, "Expanding the vision: The RPC ponders a provincial role," *Alberta Report*, 21 August 1989.

32 Wayne Smith, Reform Party of Canada Memorandum, "Summary of Assembly Results," 15 December 1989.

33 See Flanagan, *Waiting for the Wave*, 28–29, 76–78 and 92–94.

34 Reform Party of Canada, proposed amendments to the Constitution of the Reform Party of Canada, 1989, Section 3 (e).

35 Ibid.

36 The Abortion Resolution represented the formal adoption of the strategy taken by Deborah Grey in attempting to best represent her constituents' interests with respect to the Conservative government's abortion bill of 1989. The Quebec Resolution had been drafted by

Harper, Manning and Tam Deachman of British Columbia. See Manning, *The New Canada*, 216 and 224–25.

37 Reform Party of Canada, "Abortion Resolution," 1989 Edmonton Assembly.

38 The party never adopted a formal mechanism to be used in determining what constituted a constituency consensus, however, referenda were suggested in the Abortion Resolution.

39 "Abortion Resolution."

40 Preston Manning, "Leadership For Changing Times: An Address to the October 27–29 Assembly of the Reform Party of Canada," 28 October 1989.

41 Ibid., and Reform Party of Canada, "Quebec Resolution," 1989 Edmonton Assembly.

42 See Flanagan, *Waiting for the Wave*, 37–50.

4 · Expanding Beyond the West

1 The Meech Lake period refers to the three years between April 1987 and June 1990 when Canada's First Ministers negotiated and debated alterations to the failed Meech Lake Constitutional Accord. The Charlottetown period refers to the two years of extensive constitutional negotiations that led to the Charlottetown Constitutional Accord and its defeat in the 1992 Charlottetown referendum.

2 Because of the differing political situations in each of the western provinces, the Reform executive council established separate task forces in each province. The Alberta task force solicited input from all provincial Progressive Conservative constituency associations, federal Reform Party constituency associations and other interested individuals and groups.

3 Reform Party of Canada, "News Release: Reform Task Force to examine provincial politics," 26 January 1990. See also Preston Manning, "Preparing for the 21st Century," March 1990.

4 Paul Bunner, "Into Ontario: Manning's first official tour east of Manitoba," *Alberta Report*, 2 April 1990.

5 Waters was not appointed to the Senate until June 1990, on the eve of the ratification deadline for the Meech Lake Accord. While there was no requirement for the Prime Minister to make the appointment, the delay served Reform well in that it provided the party with another high profile spokesman and salient regional issue. See Paul Bunner, "Senator Waters: Alberta's RPC champion is appointed to the upper chamber," *Alberta Report*, 25 June 1990; and Paul Bunner, "Capitalizing on disillusionment: After the Meech Lake fiasco, the RPC's growth skyrockets," *Alberta Report*, 9 July 1990.

6 *CBC News/Globe and Mail* survey as reported by Kenneth Whyte "Filling a vacuum: The RPC is short of organizational expertise," in O'Neil, *Act of Faith*, 117.

7 By the time the 1991 Assembly took place, the party had organized fifty interim constituency associations in Ontario and was preparing to organize in the Atlantic provinces. See Kenneth Whyte, "The East

wants in: The RPC establishes its first constituency associations in Ontario," *Alberta Report*, 3 September 1990.

8 Steven Harper, "A Reform Vision of Canada," Reform Party of Canada Assembly, Saskatoon, 5 April 1991.

9 Stephen Harper, letter to delegates attending the 1991 Reform Party Assembly, 12 March 1991.

10 Manning, *The New Canada*, 273–74.

11 The Resolution formally read: "Resolved that, having had a full opportunity to express their views and vote freely in caucus, with such caucus votes always made public, Reform MPs shall vote with the Reform Party majority in the House, unless a Member is instructed to abstain or vote otherwise by his/her constituents. The Reform Party of Canada shall provide criteria for proper processes to elicit the will of the constituency and such processes shall be initiated by constituents or by the member."

12 Manning's resolution included the following. Upon receipt of an application for the formation of a provincial party, the executive council would arrange to have that proposal distributed to members, along with a mail ballot asking members for approval. The application would need the support of a majority of members in the province in question and majority support of the total membership. Further, the application would need to be supported by the names and addresses of one thousand members in the province, names and addresses of sponsors of the application, a cheque to cover all costs. Reform Party of Canada, "Memorandum on Provincial Involvement," 1 March 1991; Manning, *The New Canada*, 277–82.

13 The formal resolution read: "Resolved that the following resolution be submitted to the membership of the Party residing west of the Manitoba/Ontario border, through a Special Party Referendum to be held immediately after this Assembly, and that the Party adopt that resolution as a course of action, provided that it receives the affirmative support of a majority of the members casting ballots in the Special Referendum: Resolved that the Reform Party of Canada should authorize the establishment of constituency associations and the nomination of Reform candidates in federal electoral districts east of the Manitoba-Ontario border with the regional safeguards as proposed by the expansion and constitutional committees."

14 The territories together count as one province. Constitution of the Reform Party of Canada as amended at the 1991 Saskatoon Assembly, Section 7 (g).

15 Ibid., Section 1 (d).

16 Further technical amendments included a change to 14 from 30 days needed to notify the constituency membership of meetings, and a change to 30 from 45 days that a member had to be registered with the party prior to voting at a constituency meeting. Constitution of the Reform Party of Canada, Section 3 (b), (c), (d), (e), 1991.

17 Constitution of the Reform Party of Canada, Section 3 (c) and Section 4 (a), (b), (c), 1991.

18 Preston Manning, "The Road to New Canada," an address to the 1991 Assembly of the Reform Party of Canada, Saskatoon, 6 April 1991; see also Manning, *The New Canada*, 281–84.
19 Manning, "The Road to New Canada."
20 Ibid.
21 Ibid.
22 See Flanagan, *Waiting for the Wave*, chapters 1 and 5.
23 The 1993 membership survey revealed that 52 per cent of members made financial contributions to the party but only 14 per cent were willing to ask others to contribute. See Clarke et al., "Not for Fame or Fortune."
24 Area councils were an experiment in regional organization where several geographically close ridings would hold joint meetings to discuss policy and strategy.
25 The Brockville flag-stomping incident became a national symbol of constitutional and language tensions after several pro-English-language activists unsuccessfully attempted to burn a Quebec flag and began stomping on it as it lay on the ground. See George Koch, "Heading off a certain smear: The RPC moves against its Manitoba executive and stomps a flag-stomper," *Alberta Report*, 3 February 1992.
26 University of Alberta political scientist Allan Tupper as quoted by George Koch in "Frustration on the first plateau," *Alberta Report*, 16 December 1991.
27 University of Calgary political scientist Barry Cooper as quoted by George Koch, ibid.
28 *Candidate Recruitment and Selection Manual*, Reform Party of Canada, August 1991.
29 Jim Johnston, "Protesting too much: The Tory anti-Reform ad campaign is imported from Ontario," *Alberta Report*, 20 April 1992; Ralph Hedlin, "Why name-calling won't stop the Reform party," *Alberta Report*, 4 May 1992; Lorne Gunter, "Joe Clark and Reform fatigue: As the unity minister ponders retirement, the panicky Tories bash the RPC harder than ever," *Alberta Report*, 4 May 1992; Jim Johnston, "The charge of the light-weight brigade: An anti-Reform publicity stunt that backfires leaves Calgary Tories looking ridiculous," *Alberta Report*, 1 June 1992; Jim Johnston, "The Tories swing left to hit Reform: Money pours into billboards, radio ads and flyers to halt the RPC's march," *Alberta Report*, 8 June 1992.
30 Rick Anderson was an Ottawa political consultant who had organized for Paul Martin's unsuccessful 1990 Liberal leadership bid and had recently taken up with Manning and his close circle of advisors.
31 Scott Reid, "Let's call the whole thing off: Manning, Wells and others demand a moratorium on constitutional talks," *Alberta Report*, 6 July 1992; Jim Johnston, "No more Mr. Nice Guy: Reform's Manning pledges war on youth thuggery and the YOA," *Alberta Report*, 22 June 1992; Reform Party news release, "No Constitutional Deal Better Than a Bad Deal, Says Manning," 22 June 1993; see also Flanagan, *Waiting for the Wave*, 99–122.

32 Reform Party News Release, "Reform Party Encouraged by Premiers' Agreement," 8 July 1992; Reform Party News Release, "Manning Says Mulroney Must Act on Constitutional Deal and Support Senate Reform," 22 July 1992.

33 Flanagan, *Waiting for the Wave*, 103.

34 The official choices listed on the return ballot read as follows: (1) Oppose the package, because we feel it is a bad deal for Canada and worse than the status quo; (2) Hold our noses and reluctantly support the package, only because the public wants this whole constitutional discussion brought to an end; (3) Provide the public with a balanced assessment of the package and then "let the people decide" in the national referendum, with the Reform Party indicating its willingness to go along with the final result. Preston Manning, "Letter to Reform Party Members," 8 September 1992.

35 Shortly after the deal was announced, Harper, speaking on behalf of the party, declared the deal "entirely unacceptable" and a "tragic mistake." See Jim Johnston, "A moderate 'No' campaign: The Reform party takes the high road in its referendum strategy," *Alberta Report*, 14 September 1992; and Flanagan, *Waiting for the Wave*, 104.

36 Gordon Shaw, "Reform Party memorandum to constituency presidents and candidates," 30 October 1992.

37 Manning's initial hesitation, and the party's resulting return to its traditional approach of consulting its membership on the issue, demonstrated the structural populism that the party's organization allowed. Manning was free to interpret the populist sentiments as he saw fit, but when serious disagreements between the leadership and members occurred, the party organizational structure, particularly the centralized membership list, allowed quick and easy access to membership opinion that, in this case, revealed overwhelming opposition to Manning's position.

38 The fallout was documented by Flanagan: "As a result [of the referendum strategy] the party's roster of strategic advisers was temporarily wiped out. Alan Wiggan was long gone, Frank Luntz was marginalized, Rick Anderson had rendered himself suspect in the eyes of party members, Stephen Harper didn't want to be involved, and [Flanagan] was returning to the university. Important operational staff became casualties, too, as communications manager Laurie Watson and speech writer George Koch were fired the day after the referendum." Flanagan, *Waiting for the Wave*, 112.

39 "Statement by Preston Manning for the Official Launch of the Reform Party of Canada's Referendum Campaign," Reform Party of Canada, 18 September 18 1992.

40 Reform Party Broadsheet on The Charlottetown Constitutional Accord, 1992.

41 British Colombians voted most strongly against the Charlottetown Accord (68.3%), followed by Manitobans (61.6%), Albertans (60.2%), Quebecers (56.7%), Saskatchewan voters (55.3%) and Nova Scotians (51.2%). Ontario voters narrowly supported the accord (50.1%) while

New Brunswick (61.8%), Newfoundland (63.2%) and PEI (73.9%) voters all approved the accord by substantial majorities.

42 See Johnston et al., "The People and the Charlottetown Accord."

5 · Opinion Structure of Delegates Attending Reform's 1992 Assembly

1 Ontario constituency associations would be entitled to approximately one-third of the Assembly delegates and would outnumber delegates from BC.

2 Each of the 1,290 delegates whose names appeared on the party's 1992 Assembly registration list were mailed a sixteen-page questionnaire designed to measure their attitudes and opinions on a wide variety of issues. Over two-thirds of the delegates (893) returned completed questionnaires resulting in a response rate of 69.2 per cent. The analysis examines opinions about various avenues for participation within the Reform party, opinions about leadership-membership relations and about previous associations with other parties. It continues by examining opinions about perceptions of the influence of various groups within the Canadian political system. The ideological content of Reform activists and the ideological differences between delegates from the various provinces, between those with more or less previous political participation, and between the earliest and later recruits are examined. Province of residence was re-coded into the categories of British Columbia, Alberta, Ontario and Saskatchewan/Manitoba. Because only fourteen respondents came from the Atlantic region (1.5 per cent of the sample) no statistically significant analysis could be conducted on these delegates and they were excluded, as were the two delegates from Quebec and the three from the Yukon. The Saskatchewan and Manitoba delegates were placed in a single category to represent provinces where the party had been officially organized since its founding, but where the party was organizationally weakest at the time of the survey. This categorization also represents the only group of respondents who resided in have-not provinces. Year of joining the party was re-coded into three categories to represent the two-year intervals that demarcate the three stages of Reform's extra-parliamentary development. The 1987 to 1988 period represents the formative, founding years up until the 1988 election. The 1989 to 1990 period represents the western consolidation stage prior to eastern expansion in the spring of 1991. The last period represents the post-expansion years of 1991 through 1992.

Delegate opinion structure is then analyzed with respect to a variety of issue items by employing factor analysis at several stages. Initial exploratory factor analysis identified the underlying dimensions of delegate opinion structure. On the basis of that analysis, eleven additive indexes were constructed to measure delegate opinion on the various policy dimensions. Opinion structure was then analyzed to measure differences in opinion based on the same measures used when analyzing ideological differences. A final round of factor analysis was conducted to further simplify the model and identify a smaller number of policy dimensions. At this stage, the eleven additive indexes were entered into the factor equation along with the participation and recruitment variables. Also included at this stage were the ideological self-placement variable and a citizen-elite cleavage variable. Ideology was included to determine in which policy areas ideological thinking underlies delegate opinion most. The citizen-elite variable was included as an indicator of delegates' anti-political-establishment populism. This round of analysis further simplified the policy space into six underlying factors and demonstrated how the later two variables converged with these policy dimensions.

3 The remaining 98.6% of delegates received their credentials at the branch level. The only exception was the party's lone Member of Parliament. In order to protect her confidentiality no independent analysis was conducted using this category.

4 Alberta accounted for about 12 per cent of the population in the parts of Canada where Reform was officially organized at the time of the 1992 Assembly. British Columbia accounted for approximately 17 per cent.

5 Ontario accounted for almost half of the total population in the parts of Canada where Reform was officially organized in 1992.

6 See Archer and Ellis, "Opinion Structure of Party Activists," 284.

7 Ibid, 286.

8 This pattern mirrors the growth in membership. See Flanagan and Ellis, "A Comparative Profile of the Reform Party."

9 See Archer and Ellis, "Opinion Structure of Party Activists," 290.

10 Ibid.

11 See Dobbin, *Preston Manning and the Reform Party*; and Flanagan, *Waiting for the Wave*. For a critique of Dobbin's charges of resolution manipulation, see Ellis, "A Genealogy of Dissent."

12 Question: Some people say that some groups or individuals have more influence over government policy than other groups or individuals. What do you think? On a scale of 1 (very little influence) to 7 (a great amount of influence) please indicate how much influence you think these groups or individuals have on federal government policy.

13 See Archer and Ellis, "Opinion Structure of Party Activists," 292.

14 Donald Blake, "Division and Cohesion: The Major Parties," in Perlin, *Party Democracy in Canada*, 48.

15 See Ellis and Archer, "Ideology and Opinion Within the Reform Party."

16 Thirty-eight items were included in the original round of factor analysis. Upon rotation, eight of the items did not load significantly on any factors. These items typically involved hypothetical policy proposals dealing with new or expanded social programs such as government subsidized housing, a guaranteed annual income and child care. These were excluded from the analysis at this stage. One variable loaded significantly on more than one factor (the citizen-elite cleavage variable).

This variable was temporarily excluded from the analysis but was brought back in during the final round of factor analysis.

17 Index construction can, at times, be somewhat arbitrary, at least in that it is often dependent on a researcher's reading of the structure of policy debates and sense of the logical relations between ideas. But survey respondents may conceptualize the dimensions underlying any given policy item differently than the researcher. Factor analysis attempts to simplify and clarify the policy space empirically by producing a number of factors that promote the structure underlying a number of specific policy positions. By focusing on the attitudes of delegates, factor analysis rests ultimately on the empirical evidence, rather than the researcher's assumptions. That is, factor analysis allows us to construct indexes that are statistically significant, as well as intuitively meaningful. A factor was considered significant if it received an eigenvalue equal to or greater than one. An item was treated as having loaded significantly on an individual factor if it received an absolute value of 0.40 or greater. See Johnston, "The Ideological Structure of Opinion," 68.

18 Question wording can be seen in Appendix B.

19 Additive indexes were created by summing the number of consistent reposes to each item after first determining the direction in which each index would be scored (such as support for or opposition to the current welfare state). The direction in which items were scored on each index can be seen in Appendix B. Where delegates responded in the direction in which the index was scored, they would score one point. Each response that was consistent with the index direction would count towards the respondent's total score for that index. A delegate's score was partially dependent upon the number of items used in index construction. For example, the welfare and entitlements index contained four variables. Any individual delegate could score as high as four (if all responses were consistent with the direction in which the index was scored) to a low of zero (if no responses were consistent with the direction in which the index was scored). The results in this case produced an additive index with a range of 0 to 4. Indexes with smaller number of variables would produce results within a smaller range.

Delegates' opinions are represented by the mean scores and accompanying standard deviations presented in Table 5.15. Because the indexes derived from the factor analysis were constructed using different numbers of issue items, the means can be understood only in relation to their ranges. For example, the mean for the language/ethnicity index (1.69) would appear to be greater than the mean for the federalism index (1.38). However, because the range of the language/ethnicity index is 0 to 4 and the range for the federalism index is 0 to 3, each mean must be adjusted prior to making any comparisons. Each mean and standard deviation was adjusted by simply dividing it by the index range. After adjusting for the ranges we observe that the mean for the federalism index is slightly greater (0.46) than is the mean for the language/ethnicity index (0.42). Similarly, the un-adjusted standard deviations would indicate that there exists a greater diversity of opinion concerning the language/ethnicity index (1.13) than the federalism index (0.93). However, the adjusted standard deviations demonstrate that there is slightly greater diversity of opinion concerning the federalism index (0.31) than for the language/ethnicity index (0.28).

A large adjusted standard deviation indicates a lack of consensus in opinion. A smaller adjusted standard deviation indicates a greater level of consensus amongst delegates in relation to the mean score

20 Province of residence was omitted because factor analysis requires interval-level variables and province is usually thought of as nominal.

21 Interestingly, the federalism index does not formally load on any single factor (a score of 0.40 or greater) but receives its strongest loading (0.372) on the fourth factor.

6 · The Road to Official Opposition

1 Vic Burstall, "Reform Party of Canada Memorandum: Assembly '92 Resolutions Committee Report," 22 September 1992.

2 The nineteen planks of the draft election platform presented to assembly delegates were as follows: (1) deficit reduction; (2) balanced budget; (3) tax reform; (4) economy and international trade; (5) inter-provincial trade; (6) agriculture; (7) fisheries; (8) medicare; (9) environment; (10) immigration; (11) constitutional reform; (12) Triple-E Senate; (13) popular ratification of constitutional changes; (14) better representation in parliament; (15) referendum, initiative and recall; (16) official languages; (17) multiculturalism; (18) criminal justice; (19) moral issues. Three additional planks were proposed that had substantial support in a number of constituencies but did not constitute official election platform planks. These were electoral reform, native affairs and property rights.

3 Seven provinces qualified for provincial status in the formal vote counts at the 1992 Assembly: BC, Alberta, Saskatchewan, Manitoba, Ontario, New Brunswick and Nova Scotia. Similar systems were subsequently used at every Assembly after 1992 allowing delegates to debate and vote on a large number of issues while at the same time actualizing the party's double majority constitutional provisions.

4 All but one of the constitutional amendments was of a minor or housekeeping nature. The only substantive amendment included a provision where the party would establish an executive council-party caucuses liaison committee in an effort at ensuring a close and harmonious working relationship between the Reform Party grassroots membership and the caucus of Reformers elected to the House of Commons. *Constitution of the Reform Party of Canada*, Article 5A.

5 Delegates adopted two additional planks, one calling for fixed election dates and another calling for a constitutional amendment to protect property rights. Delegates tabled a plank dealing with native affairs and another from the floor dealing with firearms.

6 Manning's live national audience was undoubtedly more sparse than may have been the case if he had not been competing with the Toronto Blue Jays as they won their first World Series Championship.

7 Preston Manning, "A New National Agenda for October 27: Keynote Address to the 1992 Reform Party Assembly," 24 October 1992.

8 "Stop Digging! A plan to Reduce the Federal Deficit to Zero in Three Years (Phase I)," an address to the Canadian Club and the Prospectors and Developers' Association, Toronto, by Preston Manning, 29 March 1993.

9 Ibid.

10 Reform Party of Canada Memorandum, 6 April 1993.

11 An adjunct advisory group called NERN (National Election Advisory Network) existed at the fringes of the campaign and consisted of approximately fifty regional advisors across the country.

12 For a list of key personnel and their duties see Ellis and Archer, "Breakthrough."

13 Gorgias Research Consultants was owned and operated by University of Calgary graduate student Faron Ellis.

14 The formula for allocating advertising time was based on a party's performance in the last election.

15 See David Taras, "Political Parties as Media Organizations: The Art of Getting Elected," in Tanguay and Gagnon, *Canadian Parties in Transition*, 423–37.

16 See Lionel Lumb, "The Television of Inclusion," in Tanguay and Gagnon, *Canadian Parties in Transition*, 121–23; and Khayyam Zev Paltiel, "Political Marketing, Party Finance, and the Decline of Canadian Parties," in Tanguay and Gagnon, *Canadian Parties in Transition*, 410–18.

17 The party also made used of its free-time allocations of nine minutes on national television and radio. Reform Party Memorandum, 7 September 1993.

18 National office produced and printed these brochures, and initially sold but later gave them to the local campaigns. See Ellis and Archer, "Breakthrough," 68.

19 The national campaign split what it collected fifty-fifty with the local campaigns. Branches kept 100 per cent of the funds they collected. Reform Party Memorandum, 15 September 1993.

20 Reform Party Memorandum, 26–27 September, 1993.

21 Ellis and Archer, "Breakthrough," 66; and Reform Party memoranda, 3, 9, and 14 October 1993.

22 Alan Frizzell and Anthony Westell, "The Press and the Prime Minister," in Frizzell, Pammet and Westell, *The Canadian General Election of 1993*, 93.

23 Reform Party Memorandum, 26 September 1993.

24 "Let The People Speak," remarks by Preston Manning, Leader Reform Party of Canada to Reform Meetings/News Conferences, opening week of 1993 federal election campaign, Draft 7, 8 September 1993.

25 Reform Party News Release, "Let The People Speak: This election is a Test of Democracy Itself," Edmonton, 9 September 1993.

26 Reform Party News Release, "Let The People Speak: Manning Encourages Voters to Break with Tradition," Oshawa/Toronto, 10 September 1993.

27 Reform Party News Release, "Let The People Speak: Vote for Your Children" Fredericton/Halifax, 11 September 1993.

28 See Steven Clarkson, "Yesterday's Man and His Blue Grits: Backward Into the Future," in Frizzell, Pammet and Westell, *The Canadian General Election of 1993*, 27–42.

29 Reform Party New Release, "Let the People Speak: Manning Urges Canadians to Ask Hard Questions About the Connection Between Debt and Jobs" Vancouver, 13 September 1993,.

30 See Peter Woolstencroft, "Doing Politics Differently: The Conservative Party and the Campaign of 1993," in Frizzell, Pammet and Westell, *The Canadian General Election of 1993*, 9–26.

31 Reform Party News Release, "Manning Says Liberal Plan Ignores Economic Connections" Victoria, 16 September 1993.

32 Reform Party News Release, "Manning Pledges Tax Reform and Tax Relief When Deficit Eliminated," Calgary, 27 September 1993,.

33 "The only deficit plan we've seen," *Globe and Mail* editorial, 23 September 1993.

34 Reform moved from 10 per cent nationally in the 11 September 1993 Angus Reid poll to 18 per cent in their 8 October 1993 poll. See Frizzell and Westell, "The Press and the Prime Minister," 101.

35 Reform Party News Release, "Manning Says Election is a Battle For Trust," Medicine Hat, 25 September 1993,.

36 Miro Cernetig, "Old-line parties betray Alberta, Manning says: Make Ottawa change its ways, leader exhorts Reformers," *Globe and Mail*, 27 September 1993.

37 Preston Manning, "Send Reformers to Ottawa," address by the leader of Reform Party, Red Deer, Alberta, 26 September 1993.

38 Reform Party News Release, "Manning Welcomes Health Care Debate: Accuses Opponents of Fear-Mongering and Distortion," Vancouver, 30 September 1993,.

39 Preston Manning, "The Case for a New Federalism," address to a joint meeting of the Canadian Club and Empire Club, Toronto, 1 October 1993.

40 Ibid.

41 Ibid. Also see Reform Party Press Release, "Manning Says Liberals Don't Deserve a Majority Government; Minority Parliament is best for Canada," Cambridge/Sarnia, 12 October 1993.

42 Clarke et al., *Absent Mandate.*

43 Johnston et al., *Letting the People Decide*, 11. See also, Lawrence LeDuc and Richard Price, "Great Debates: The Televised Leadership Debates in Canada," Canadian Journal of Political Science, XVIII, 1985, 135–53; and Lawrence LeDuc, "The Leaders' Debates: Critical Event or Non-Event," in Frizzell et. al., *The Canadian General Election of 1993*, 127–142.

44 Johnston et al., *Letting the People Decide*,

45 Roger Gibbins, "Debate Taught Few Lessons" *Calgary Sun*, 8 October 1993.

46 Reform Party News Release "Manning Says Liberal Economic Program Dangerous," Prince George, BC, 7 October 1993.

47 See Preston Manning, "Personal Message to Canadians from Preston Manning," open letter, 10 October 1993.

48 The party asked for and received the resignation of York Centre Reform candidate John Beck after he made what the media and party declared to be inappropriate comments concerning immigration and employment. Reform Party News Release, "Resignation of Reform Candidate in York Centre," and "Reform Party Memorandum to All Candidates from the CMC RE: Resignation of Candidate John Beck – Media Response," Calgary, 13 October 1993.

49 The Conservatives aired, and then quickly pulled off the air, an advertisement that featured photos of Jean Chrétien's facial distortions and a thinly veiled attack on his personal suitability to serve as Canadian prime minister. See Woolstencroft, "Doing Politics Differently."

50 Preston Manning as quoted by Mark Miller, "Manning eyes major role," *Calgary Sun*, 27 October 1993.

51 Steve Chase, "Reform's 'new politics' look like the old: More than two dozen Mulroney backroomers are now working for the RPC," *Alberta Report*, 27 June 1994.

52 See Tossutti, "From Communitarian Protest Towards Institutionalization."

53 Hugh Winsor, "Reform's ideological purity diluted: The party's parliamentary wing argued for policies that would be more salable in mainstream politics," *Globe and Mail*, 17 October 1994.

54 See Reform Party of Canada, "Assembly 1994 Successful Policy Resolutions and Amendments to the Party Constitution," October 1994.

55 Jane Taber, "Can't put the Ottawa in Reform," *Ottawa Citizen*, 15 October 1994; Editorial, "Reform or fail: Although the Reform party has tasted political success, its Ottawa convention has only reinforced an image of intolerance," *Ottawa Citizen*, 15 October 1994.

56 Tu Thanh Ha, "Manning spoiling for a fight on unity: Reform Leader foresees crisis," *Globe and Mail*, 17 October 1994.

57 See Tom Flanagan, "Ten reasons why it's absurd to call the Reform party a 'failure'," *Alberta Report*, 22 May 1995.

58 See Reform Party of Canada, "The Taxpayers' Budget: The Reform Party's Plan to Balance the Federal Budget and Provide Social and Economic Security for the 21st Century," 21 February 1995.

59 See Preston Manning, "You Don't Have To Go. There's A New Canada Coming," open letter to Quebecers, 28 September 1995; Preston Manning and Stephen Harper, "Where Will a No Vote Lead Canadians?," *Le Devoir*, 3 October 1995 and *Globe and Mail*, 3 October 1995.

60 See Stephen Harper, "Where will a NO vote lead Canadians?... to the New Canada," Reform Party Newsletter, October 1995.

61 Reform also released the first half of what would become its 20/20 national unity policy: See Reform Party of Canada, "It is possible, A New Confederation: A 20 point plan to modernize and decentralize Canada," *Globe and Mail*, 25 October 1995.

62 Preston Manning, "Speech on the Distinct Society Motion," House of Commons, 29 November 1995.

63 Reform Party of Canada, *20 Proposals for a New Confederation, 20 Realities About Secession: A Vision For The Future Of Canada*, January 1996. See also Preston Manning, "Awakening the Sleeping Giant," speech to the Canadian Club, London, Ontario, 2 November 1995.

64 Despite not winning either of the two seats it serious contested, Reformers were encouraged by their showing and by the Tories' dismal performances. In Labrador, Reform won over 30 per cent of the vote and in Etobicoke North, Reform support nearly doubled from 20.8 per cent in 1993 to 36.1 per cent. The Tories, in contrast, performed dismally, garnering only about 10 per cent of the vote in each riding.

65 Michael Jenkinson, "The relative cost of hyperbole and honesty: Copps goes down on the GST while Reform blows up over gay rights," *Alberta Report*, 13 May 1996.

66 See Jan Brown, "I've drawn my line in the sand," *Calgary Herald*, 18 May 1996.

67 Michael Jenkinson, "Reform once again prepares for its Waterloo: Manning could face his ugliest assembly yet in Vancouver," *Alberta Report*, 3 June 1996.

68 Delegates to the 1996 Assembly debated and passed 38 policy resolutions that were, in most respect, vintage Reform. The bulk of the policy resolutions dealt with justice (10), federalism, citizenship and equality (11), and taxes and economic issues (9). Delegates passed resolutions calling for binding national referenda on capital punishment (89 per cent support) and abortion (58 per cent support). They also formally adopted the party's 20/20 proposals as official policy.

69 Michael Jenkinson, "Reform goes for broke: Manning reveals his battle plan in Vancouver – but is he the man to carry it out?" *Alberta Report*, 24 June 1996.

70 Reform Party of Canada, *A Fresh Start for Canadians: A 6 Point Plan to Build a Brighter Future Together*, 1996.

71 For a more full analysis of Manning's keynote address, see Ellis and Archer, "Crossroads."

72 Preston Manning, "A Fresh Start," keynote address to the Reform Party of Canada Assembly, Vancouver, 8 June 1996.

73 Reform fielded a total of 227 candidates in the 1997 federal election. Reform candidates ran in all western and northern ridings, 102 ran in Ontario, 11 in Quebec, 2 in P.E.I., 9 in Nova Scotia, 8 in New Brunswick and 4 in Newfoundland.

74 Brian Thomas, "Election '97: A Reform Government Right Now!", 26 April 1997; and ReformAD, "A Writ-Period Communication Plan For Reform Candidates and Campaign Teams," 1997.

75 The national campaign believed it needed 50 per cent more ad time in Calgary, 13 per cent more in Vancouver, and a further 10 per cent more in the Toronto/Hamilton region.

76 Reform Party News Release, "Good-by Red Book, Hello Cheque Book, Manning says," Ottawa, 30 April 1997.

77 Reform Party News Release, "Flood vote shows Liberal arrogance, Manning says," 4 May 1997.

78 Reform Party News Release, "Reject Liberal underachievers, Manning says," 5 May 1997.

79 Manning as quoted by Norm Ovenden, "Manning defends national standing," *Calgary Herald*, 7 May 1997.

80 The Southam/CTV/Angus Reid poll placed the Liberals at 42 per cent, the Conservatives at 19 per cent, Reform at 18 per cent, the NDP at 11 per cent and the BQ at 9 per cent. Reform led in BC and Alberta with 41 per cent and it stood at 25 per cent in Manitoba and Saskatchewan. See Lisa Dempster, "Campaign survey says we're heading for Reform Opposition – Liberal Government," *Calgary Herald*, 10 May 1997.

81 Reform Party News Release, "Do you finally agree that it's time for a real plan?" 8 May 1997; and Reform Party News Release, "Chretien and Charest: Prove you can lead on unity issue," Victoria, 8 May 1997.

82 Barry Cooper as quoted by Michael Jenkinson, "Distinct society strikes again: Though a bane to the Grits, Reform may yet force the issue forward," *Alberta Report*, 12 May 1997; and Reform Party News Release, "Manning Extends Unity Challenge," 14 May 1997.

83 Manning as quoted by Jeff Sallot, "Reform uses Quebec podium: Manning's visit a bid to woo voters outside province," *Globe and Mail*, 15 May 1997.

84 Reform Party News Release, "Liberals Have No Plan, Tories Have No Substance on Unity," 16 May 1997.

85 Jeff Sallot, Murray Campbell and Anne McIlroy, "Manning attacked over unity views: His 'Quebec' message and new Reform ad draw angry words from Liberal, NDP and Tory leaders," *Globe and Mail*, 24 May 1997.

7 · THE DECOMMISSIONING

1 See Faron Ellis, "The More Things Change… The Alliance Campaign," in Pammett and Dornan, *The Canadian General Election of 2000*, 60.

2 Nevitte et al., *Unsteady State*, 98.

3 Nancy Branscombe, a former Ontario candidate heading the UA project in Ontario, as quoted by Sheldon Alberts, "Manning plans puzzles party faithful," *Calgary Herald*, 29 May 1998.

4 See Preston Manning and Andre Turcotte, "New Dimensions Shape Politics of the 21st Century," *Calgary Herald*, 19 June 1998. For a critique see Faron Ellis, "Reformers Yet To Be Sold On '3-D' Politics," *Calgary Herald*, 27 June 1998. For a response to the critique see Diane Ablonczy, "Reform's United Alternative looks beyond the labels," *Calgary Herald*, 11 July 1998.

5 Manning had insisted that a sunset clause be put into the original 1987 Reform constitution. The party would cease to exist in the year 2000 unless the members decided that it still served a purpose in Canadian federal politics. Ironically, the members had to vote to extend the date by a few months, just long enough to ensure an orderly decommissioning.

6 Sheldon Alberts, "Klein backs unite-the-right movement," *National Post*, 27 October 1998. This story ran on the front page of the inaugural edition of the National Post, which for the next two years could be counted on to report on and often provide editorial support for the UA initiative.

7 Faron Ellis, "United Alternative evolving into anti-Reform," *Calgary Herald*, 1 February 1999.

8 Alberta Premier Ralph Klein, "Address to the United Alternative Convention," Ottawa, 19 February 1999.

9 Don Martin, "Stockwell may have his day in the sun with new party," *Calgary Herald*, 21 February 1999.

10 Preston Manning, "Uniting for the 21st Century: Address to the United Alternative Convention," Ottawa, Saturday, 20 February 1999.

11 The three themes that were to define the United Alternative were economic and fiscal, social, and democratic and governance themes. See "Report to Reformers from Preston Manning, Leader – Reform Party of Canada," 8 March 1999.

12 The Reform constitution also required that a minimum of 25 per cent of the membership cast valid votes. Reform Party of Canada Constitution, Article 8 (b). *Constitution of the Reform Party of Canada*, Article 7 (g).

13 It has been argued that this was one of Reform's major contributions to the new party system. See Carty, Cross and Young, *Rebuilding Canadian Party Politics.*

14 Sheldon Alberts, "Popular Reform MP rejects Manning plan to unite right: Myron Thompson's opposition reflects grassroots resistance," *National Post*, 29 April 1999.

15 Manning, "Report to Reformers," 20. Eventually 15 of 58 Reform MPs would oppose the initiative.

16 See "GUARD'S 10 reasons to vote not to the UA question," *Calgary Herald*, 10 April 1999. Important members of GUARD included former Reform executive council member Christine Whitaker, and Albertans Bruce Stubbs, Ron Thorton, Real Gagne and Don Reimer.

17 See Clarke et al., "Not for Fame or Fortune."

18 For an analysis of Manning's impact on Ontario vote intentions see Nevitte et al., *Unsteady State*, 101.

19 One conference was held in each of BC, Alberta, Saskatchewan and Manitoba. Four were held in Ontario, one in the Atlantic region and one in Quebec.

20 All ballots had to be postmarked by May 21.

21 Of the approximately 65,000 Reform members, 32,099 cast valid ballots, 19,417 voted Yes while 12,682 voted No (176 ballots were spoiled). Reform Party News Release, "United Alternative Referendum Results," 10 June 1999. The question also passed in all provinces except Saskatchewan, where a majority of Reform's MPs, led by Cypress-Grasslands MP Lee Morrison, had opposed the UA.

22 Preston Manning, "An Open Letter to Reformers," 19 July 1999.

23 Ken Kalopsis, "Update on United Alternative Activity," 19 July 1999.

24 Bruce Stubbs, "An idea doomed to failure: Preston Manning's United Alternative has four key flaws," *National Post*, 14 January 2000.

25 Lorne Gunter, "Taking hostages," *Calgary Herald*, 18 January 2000.

26 Preston Manning, "An Open Letter to Reformers on the Leadership of the UA and Reform," 7 January 2000.

27 See Faron Ellis and Ron Thorton, "Vote NO," and Grassroots 4UA-Yes Committee, "Think Big: Vote Yes!," the two essays that were printed with the Alliance constitution and accompanied the Reform membership referendum ballots.

28 Approximately 75,000 ballots were issued and 48,838 were cast (65 per cent of the membership).

29 See Tom Long, "So long, Tories, I hate to go," *National Post*, 18 January 2000.

30 Over the course of the campaign, the Alliance would see its membership swell from the approximately 75,000 Reformers, who were automatically made members of the new party, to over 220,000.

31 Returns indicated that Albertans were still the single largest group of participants, accounting for 33.5 per cent of those who cast ballots, Ontario followed closely at 32.4 per cent; BC 20 per cent; Saskatchewan 4.8 per cent; Manitoba 3.8 per cent; Quebec 2.5 per cent; the Atlantic provinces and the North accounted for only 3 per cent of the vote.

32 The Alliance constitution allowed for only one runoff ballot between the two top condensers. Alliance Constitution, Article 11 (e).

33 Returns indicated that Day beat Manning in seventy-seven Ontario constituencies.

34 Returns indicated that Day beat Manning in every province except Newfoundland.

35 Sitting Alliance MP Jim Hart had already announced that he would not be seeking re-election in the British Columbia riding of Okanagan-Coquihalla. It was later revealed that the party paid Hart $50,000 to hasten his departure. Hart won the riding in 1997 with 53.1 per cent of the vote compared to 26.4 per cent for the second-place Liberals.

36 The Alliance was polling up to 24 per cent nationally and enjoying a 27-point shift in leadership approval as a result of the leadership change, according to Angus Reid pollster Darrell Bricker. See Shawn McCarthy, "Alliance surges, Tories collapse: Day helping new party make gains while Liberals maintain solid national lead, poll finds," *Globe and Mail*, 29 July 2000.

37 The most high profile recruits included two former Bloc Quebecois MPs and sitting independent Markham MP Jim Jones, who was elected as a Conservative in 1997.

38 See Faron Ellis and Peter Woolstencroft, "New Conservatives, Old Realities," in Pammett and Dornan, *The Canadian General Election of 2004*.

Index